mgs

A HISTORY AT

500

YEAR NINE

SHOW 2014

mgs

A HISTORY AT

500

Nigel Watson

III

THIRD MILLENNIUM
PUBLISHING, LONDON

MGS: A History at 500

2015 © MGS and Third Millennium Publishing Limited

First published in 2015 by Third Millennium Publishing Limited,
a subsidiary of Third Millennium Information Limited.

2–5 Benjamin Street, London, EC1M 5QL, United Kingdom
www.tmiltd.com

ISBN: 978 1 908990 05 1

British Library Cataloguing in Publication Data
A CIP catalogue record for this book is available from the British Library.

Project managed by Susan Millership
Designed by Susan Pugsley
Production by Debbie Wayment
Reprographics by Studio Fasoli, Verona, Italy
Printed by 1010 International Limited, China

CONTENTS

ACKNOWLEDGEMENTS

Perhaps because of my own northern roots (albeit from the right side of the Pennines),
I felt very much at home at MGS during my time carrying out research and interviews.
Rachel Kneale, the school archivist, who has been doing a wonderful job in cataloguing
an extensive series of records, was always helpful; and I enjoyed and appreciated my
informative conversations with Jeremy Ward and John Bever, both historians who have
taught at the school, during their regular visits to the archive. Simon Jones proved an
invaluable guide to the school, and was indispensable in persuading people to allow
themselves to be interviewed for the project. I am also indebted to Simon, Jeremy, Ian
Thorpe and Joanna Badrock for their careful scrutiny of the text, which has resulted in
many improvements.

Finally, I also owe a debt of gratitude to all those who kindly agreed to be interviewed
for the history and whose recollections have helped to enliven and inform the story of
the school: Hassan Abod, Peter Ainsworth, Harry Bardsley, Gillian Batchelor, John Bever,
Martin Boulton, Adrian Dobson, Sidney Dobson, Danny Downs, Jonathan Fogerty,
Ernest Fox, Geoff Fox, Ernest and Pauline Fuller, Diane Hawkins, Sean Heathcote, John
Horsfield, Sandip Jobanputra, Stephen Jones, Christopher Kenyon, Jim Leathley, Stuart
Leeming, Jim Mangnall, Chris Ray, Ken Robbie, Paul Rose, John Shoard, Martin Stephen,
the late Geoffrey Stone, Brian Taylor, Paul Thompson, Ian Thorpe, David Walton, Jeremy
Ward, Maurice Watkins, John Whitfield and Russell Withington.

Nigel Watson
Winter 2015

FOREWORD

When Alfred Mumford wrote his history of Manchester Grammar School in 1919, his re-evaluation of the school's place in history had been delayed from its intended publication in 1915 because of the terrible events that swept through Europe at the time of the 400th anniversary.

Much has changed in the century that has passed, and as we enter our 500th year it is timely that a fresh look is taken at the entire history of the school.

Would Mumford recognise MGS today? The biggest change is surely the relocation of the school from the cramped confines of the original buildings in the centre of Manchester to the open farmland of Rusholme. That farmland has now been replaced by housing, but the school remains on a magnificent 28-acre site with wonderful playing fields that were so dearly desired in 1919.

Perhaps the biggest change in the last century is to the educational environment. Gone are the classical and modern sides and closed scholarships to Oxford and Cambridge. League tables, inspections and grade inflation are the latest challenges to schools, but MGS has adapted well to the modern world because of the foresight and leadership of a succession of skilled staff. The result is that MGS has maintained its position as a leader in the field of education.

One thing that has not changed is the ethos of the school, as set out by our founder, Hugh Oldham, that we should educate the brightest boys in the north-west of England, irrespective of their background. There have been many challenges to this ideal, though, including the loss of the Direct Grant and then the Assisted Places Scheme. However, the generosity of our alumni has ensured that over 200 bursaries are still offered each year. We have some way to go before we reach our goal of being truly needs-blind, but this will, I hope, be something that is achieved before the school reaches its 600th anniversary.

Nigel Watson has done a wonderful job of producing this comprehensive History of MGS at 500. I do hope that you enjoy reading it.

Martin Boulton
High Master

1 THE FOUNDER

Hugh Oldham, Bishop of Exeter

Hugh Oldham, the founder of Manchester Grammar School (MGS), is a sketchy figure, flitting wraith-like across some of the darkest pages in British history, leaving only the slightest traces of what he was really like. This was a man who reached a position of influence under Henry VII, a shifty, secretive and manipulative monarch, and owed much of his success to the patronage of the equally wily Margaret Beaufort, the king's mother and the most powerful woman in the kingdom. He had close ties with some of their closest advisors, including the devious Sir Reynold Bray, chancellor of the duchy of Lancaster and treasurer to the king, and the shrewd and ruthless John Morton, cardinal, archbishop of Canterbury and king's chancellor.

During the reign of a perpetually insecure monarch, who, with his mother, saw threats to his position in everyone and everything, retreating into the shadows was an act of self-preservation for men in public life like Oldham. It somehow seems appropriate that for many years Oldham's life-size statue was tucked away around the back of the school, although in advance of the 500th anniversary he has recently been moved to the school's main quadrangle from where he can cast his inscrutable gaze upon those committed to sustaining his foundation into the future. Yet this insubstantial historical presence has left a more lasting memorial than many of his more illustrious contemporaries, founding an institution that almost since its inception has been regarded as one of the country's leading schools.

His name is honoured every year on Founders' Day, and his emblem, the owl, has long been adopted by the school as its own. The owl was Oldham's rebus, a pictorial representation of his name, a play on words ('owl-dom' is the way his name would have been pronounced during his lifetime). The stone medallion of an owl that once graced the school buildings in the centre of Manchester now fixes its beady eyes on hungry boys from its place in the current school refectory. When boys still wore caps, Oldham's owl was the cap badge. The school song, written in 1888 when such things were popular, is titled 'Hugh of the Owl'. And the weekend retreat at Disley in Cheshire has been known as the Owl's Nest since it was started in 1921, although the question of where to place the apostrophe is still debated.

Hugh Oldham was born about 1452, the younger son of Roger and Margery Oldham.[1] It is claimed his birthplace was a house in Goulborn Lane in Oldham. He was one of three sons who would become clerics, the others being Bernard and William. His father was prosperous enough to dabble in property and bought land at Ancoats in 1462, which later formed part of the endowment attached to the new grammar school.[2] Details of his early life and education are meagre but by 1475 Oldham is described as a 'Clerk of Durham',[3] suggesting his career in the Church began under the influence

Right: Oldham's owl, detail from stained-glass window, St Chrysostom's, Manchester (see page 12).

Opposite: Statue of Hugh Oldham, the school's founder, recently relocated to the quad.

Stained glass from St Chrysostom's Church, Manchester, depicting Hugh Oldham with the school he founded.

of Lawrence Booth, bishop of the mighty diocese of Durham from 1457 to 1476, whose family came from Barton near Manchester. Booth, a staunch supporter of the house of Lancaster, was not alone in developing a knack for treading deftly along the narrow line between loyalty and treason during unsettled times when the throne swung from one royal house to another. His example might have rubbed off on young Hugh.

Very soon, and certainly before the battle of Bosworth in 1485, Hugh had become part of the household of another influential man of the times, as adept as Booth at appearing to be loyal to both sides of the royal divide. Thomas, Lord Stanley, was the most powerful man in the north-west of England, his authority unchallenged, the ruler of immense estates. Moreover, his wife was Lady Margaret Beaufort, mother of the exiled Henry Tudor, a woman who understandably found it more difficult to profess constant loyalty to the house of York, and whose treasonable behaviour under Richard III received lenient treatment thanks only to Stanley's protection and status as lord high constable of England.

Hugh's ambition seems clear from the close relationships he formed with the two most important members of Lady Margaret's own household, John Morton, then bishop of Ely, and Reynold Bray. (He would late act as executor for Bray's estate.) Hugh also became close to William Smith, another young Lancashire cleric in the household. Since advances in Smith's own career tended to be one step ahead of Hugh's, he was able in turn to give his friend a helping hand up the ladder of preferment. The two men also developed a shared interest in further education.

Lady Margaret's patronage would propel Hugh Oldham to prominence. The catalyst for Hugh's advancement was the battle of Bosworth and the ascendancy of Henry Tudor, Margaret's son. True to form, her husband had distinguished himself at Bosworth by taking no part in the battle, holding back his troops until a clear victor had emerged, sending them in only to harry and kill Richard's fleeing army, and ingratiating himself by placing the battered crown on the head of the new monarch.

Hugh Oldham proved himself to be an able member of the company of administrators and lawyers supplied by the Church in the service of the state. During the late 1480s the series of livings he was granted by Lady Margaret helped to fund his legal studies at Oxford and Cambridge. During the 1490s his career began to prosper in the wake of his friend William Smith's advancement. When Smith became dean of St Stephen's, Westminster, Hugh became a canon. In 1493, when Smith became bishop of Coventry and Lichfield, he placed the administration of the local hospital in Hugh's hands. After Smith moved to the diocese of Lincoln, his friend became a canon of the cathedral.[4] And the benefices Smith

Powerful patrons of Hugh Oldham: Lord Thomas Stanley and Lady Margaret Beaufort.

gave up as he took up his successive bishoprics were granted to Hugh by Lady Margaret.

Hugh was also cementing his ties with Reynold Bray. In 1492 the two men became administrators of the earl of Northumberland's estates, Bray as receiver, Hugh as deputy receiver. Soon afterwards they were appointed in the same capacity to look after Lady Margaret's estates in the south-west, for which Smith was also a trustee. It seems that even as Hugh moved further up the Church's career ladder – as well as being appointed to several cathedral canonries, he became dean of Wimborne in 1499 and archdeacon of Exeter in 1502[5] – most of his time was spent in London, handling legal and administrative matters on behalf of Lady Margaret.

In 1504, once again through Lady Margaret's influence, Hugh succeeded to the bishopric of Exeter. In this position he worked closely with another of Henry VII's key advisors, the unscrupulous Richard Fox, bishop of Winchester, whose lands adjoined those of the Exeter see. Fox himself had been bishop of Exeter some years earlier, although it was a place he had never visited.

All these relationships testify to Hugh's ability to work closely with some of the most powerful, influential and dangerous people in the kingdom while remaining determinedly in the half-light. There was self-knowledge in the motto, adapted from Horace, that he took as bishop, *Sapere Aude*, or 'Dare to be wise', later appropriated by MGS. His biographer Mumford wrote that 'it has not been possible to find records of any public discourse or similar utterances delivered by Hugh Oldham, nor even anything in the way of a personal letter which would reveal his inner mind'.[6]

Perhaps the sharpest insight into Hugh's character comes from the way he seized the opportunity to exercise his power as a bishop. He proved himself to be as ruthless as his peers in stamping his will across his domain, refusing to countenance opposition to his plans. His antipathy to the monasteries was evident in his clash with the abbot of Tavistock, whose battle to assert monastic independence from his bishop ended in 1517 with the pope's confirmation of the abbey's exemption and Hugh's excommunication, lifted only on the latter's death two years later.

Hugh's friendship with William Smith seems to have kindled a philanthropic interest in education. As master of St John's Hospital, Lichfield, in 1493–4, he was in charge of rebuilding the hospital at Smith's expense. Smith also endowed the hospital to fund the care of ten poor men and a free school to teach poor children reading and grammar. As bishop of Lincoln, Smith, for a time chancellor of the University of Oxford, also endowed a fellowship at Oriel College for scholars from Lincolnshire, and was one of the founders of Brasenose College. Hugh Oldham, with Reynold Bray and others, set up similar fellowships, and after Smith's death in 1514 anonymously donated much of the money needed to complete Brasenose and furnish its library. As he got older, like many successful men of his time, Smith also sought a lasting memorial in the place of his upbringing, and in 1507 endowed a grammar school in Farnworth, the village of his birth, south of Bolton.

Hugh was sufficiently close to Richard Fox to support the latter's foundation of Corpus Christi College, Oxford. Hugh had intended to give funds to Exeter College, Oxford, but changed his mind after the college rejected his nominee for a fellowship. Instead, he gave Corpus Christi the enormous sum of £4,000 plus land in Chelsea.[7] He is reputed to have persuaded Fox in 1517 that the college should not admit monks but should be entirely secular, advising him that 'monks were but a sort of bussing [buzzing] flies, and whose state could not long endure'.[8] Hugh's involvement with Corpus Christi would influence the later decision to give the college's president the right to appoint the High Master of Hugh's new grammar school.

Hugh's preference for secular education, clearly generated partly through his dislike of the monastic tradition, was also evident in Exeter, where he insisted that the young clerks of the cathedral choir should attend the city's high school. For Hugh, the able administrator and shrewd politician, education should be for 'such as who by their learning shall do good in the church and commonwealth'.[9] He followed this precept by example, appointing to offices in his gift a high proportion of graduates, and insisting secular priests should be better prepared for preaching.

It was therefore not surprising that when Hugh, like his friend William Smith, began to consider a suitable memorial for his own

Corpus Christi College, Oxford, endowed by Hugh Oldham. The president of Corpus appointed the High Master and Usher for 350 years, and is still an ex-officio governor of the school.

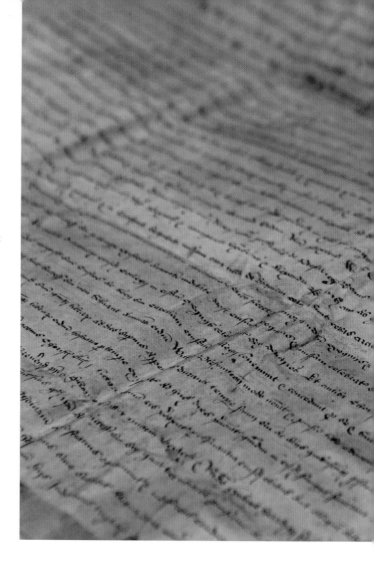

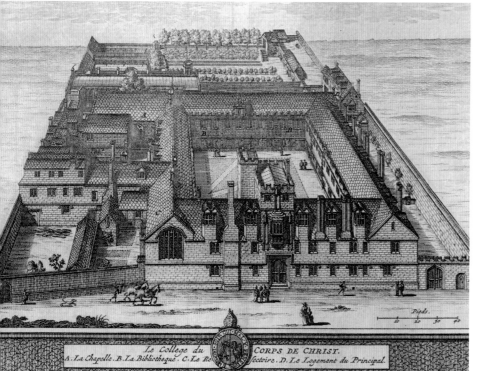

Le College du CORPS DE CHRIST.
A. La Chapelle. B. La Bibliotheque. C. Le Re... ...fectoire. D. Le Logement du Principal.

temporal achievements, his mind turned to education. In 1509 he had also visited his brother Bernard, rector of Crewkerne in Somerset, where a grammar school had been founded ten years before. In the same year John Colet founded St Paul's in London. Hugh knew Colet, taking part in a service in which Colet's sermon was devoted to the need for reform of the Church, a cause towards which Hugh was instinctively sympathetic.

Perhaps it was family ties that finally persuaded Hugh to establish a free school in Manchester. His sister Joan had married Robert Bexwyck or Beswick, whose father Richard was a wealthy cloth merchant, dealing between Manchester, Dublin and Drogheda, and had established in Manchester the Guild of St Saviour, with endowments to support two chantries attached to Manchester's collegiate church. Chantry priests were often required to act as schoolmasters and the commissioners engaged in dissolving the chantries in 1548 reported that the chantry priests in Manchester were teaching at the school Hugh founded.[10] It seems that this had not happened prior to 1515 and that Beswick's endowment was redirected to the new school.

This supplemented other endowments put in place for the new school. The first was the income from the long lease of the

water corn mills, essentially a corn-grinding monopoly, on the river Irk from Lord de la Warr, lord of the manor of Oldham, who had agreed a reduced annual rent in consideration of the educational purpose behind the purchase. The second was an annual income of £40 from the family property in Ancoats, taken on a long lease from Bernard Oldham, Hugh's brother, no doubt also on preferential terms. Both these endowments were transferred to the warden and fellows of the collegiate church. The revenue was to be allocated to paying for a master and an usher. The plot of land for the new school was next door to the church, not unusual for many grammar schools. Bought by Hugh's personal chaplain, another Hugh, also a member of the Beswick family, for £5 from George and Margaret Trafford in September 1516, it placed the school at the heart of Manchester, making it an intrinsic part of the town for more than four centuries. Building began on 28 April 1517 and was completed on 28 August 1518, with Hugh settling the final bill of £218. This generosity, however, should be placed in the context of the many thousands he had already given to Corpus Christi and Brasenose.

In the meantime the foundation deed had been signed and sealed on 15 August 1515. The warden and fellows as trustees were tasked with appointing the first master and usher in conjunction with Hugh, Thomas Langley, Hugh Beswick and Ralph Hulme, an arrangement that would expire on the deaths of the latter four, when this right reverted solely to the warden and fellows. Thomas Langley was the vicar of Prestwich, the mother church of the church at Oldham, while Ralph Hulme was the husband of Margaret Beswick. Should the warden and fellows prove negligent in making such appointments, they would be made by the abbot of Whalley, the second wealthiest abbey in Lancashire. The first post-holders, both named in the deed, were William Pleasington and Richard Wolstoncraft.

Hugh Oldham was now in his late sixties and in declining health. He made his will in December 1518, an indication that he considered himself near to death, but lived until 25 June 1519. His excommunication was lifted to allow his body to be buried in the chapel dedicated to St Saviour the bishop had built within his cathedral in Exeter.

Every year on the date of Hugh's death a party of Old Mancunians, boys and staff make a pilgrimage to his tomb to remember their founder. Hugh would no doubt be gratified but perhaps also slightly surprised that a lifetime spent scheming in the shadows should still be recalled 500 years later.

Above: Hugh Oldham's tomb in Exeter Cathedral.

Above left: Detail from the school's foundation deed, signed on 15 August 1515.

THE EARLY SCHOOL 1515–1808

'The Liberal Science or Art of Grammar'

Manchester Grammar School (MGS) was not immune from the religious and political conflict and economic change that peppered much of this period. While the school escaped the disturbances of the Reformation and the Marian revival, disputes between Protestant and Papist, Cavalier and Roundhead, Whig and Tory, mercantilist and cleric, bound up in part with Manchester's own development, all coloured its fortunes. The school's development as an institution that gave able boys a route out of Manchester, coupled conversely during the 18th century with the recruitment of the sons of wealthy families from some distance away, tended to aggravate the school's relationship with certain opinion-formers in the expanding city.

These differences became more marked in the early 19th century as the trustees, alarmed at the deteriorating local environment created by Manchester's industrialisation, became anxious to gain the support of the city's merchant and commercial classes, supporters of a more vocational education, while maintaining the classical education that would allow the most able boys to enter university.

Throughout this span of history these events helped to define the school's character, not simply in terms of its reputation for sending bright boys to university. The school's location placed it in the very heart of one of the most important towns in the kingdom. Yet that relationship was often schizophrenic. Even as the school was part of the town, it was also set apart from it. The school's links with the collegiate church, part of the establishment and generally Tory in politics, and its leadership by High Masters who were generally Tory Anglican clerics would often place it at odds with the rather more free-wheeling radical and nonconformist character of a town that lacked any institutional form of government until the late 18th century. While the school welcomed many boys from within the town, it also welcomed those from beyond the town's boundaries, something else that antagonised local opinion, and

Opposite: The second Grammar School building, constructed in 1776.

while it sent many pupils back into Manchester to take up careers in trade and commerce, underpinning its remarkable economic growth, MGS also sent many boys, born within and without the town, into the wider world, where many of them would make a distinctive contribution.

The school's early years were not uneventful. On Hugh Oldham's death, John Hulme, whose role was to ensure the master and usher were paid, tried instead to get his hands on the money from the profitable corn-grinding monopoly, precipitating a legal wrangle that lasted six years. Hulme lost the case in 1524, when he was fined in the court of the duchy of Lancaster. In the aftermath, a new deed dated 1 April 1525 was drawn up, which reformed the governance of the school, appointing 12 lay trustees in place of the warden and fellows. Among them were members of several leading local landowning families such as the Byrons, Traffords and Radcliffes. They were all practical men who helped to maintain the corn mills, secure improved rents and protect the local monopoly on corn grinding. The appointment of the master and usher fell to Joan Beswick, Hugh Oldham's surviving sister, and his nephew and former chaplain, Hugh Beswick, upon whose deaths the role

John Colet, Deane of St Pauls

The school's statutes included a ban on boys wearing daggers or taking part in cock-fights, and borrowed heavily from the work of John Colet (pictured), who founded St Paul's School in 1509.

would be filled by the president of Corpus Christi. The warden still had the power to dismiss the master in exceptional circumstances, and appoint a replacement if the president failed to do so, while the abbot's task was confined to appointing the school's receiver or treasurer.

The deed of 1525 was also important for confirming the original intentions of the founder. It was held in a specially made strong-box with four locks, the warden, High Master and two trustees each holding a key, ensuring the box could be opened only when all were present. The deed was copied but the terms were closely guarded and it was published for the first time only in 1826 as part of a printed inspection report on the school. Until the 19th century it could be altered only by an Act of Parliament.

The statutes governing the school laid down in the deed case echoed those of similar schools, borrowing, for example, from those of John Colet's St Paul's. Boys were forbidden to wear any 'dagger, hanger or other weapon invasive nor bring to the school any staff or club except meat knives' and from taking part in cock-fighting or other unlawful games.[11] More important was the stress placed on the teaching of grammar since 'the liberal science or art of grammar is the ground and fountain of all other liberal arts and science which surge and spring out of the same, without which science, the other cannot profitably be had, for Science of Grammar is the Gate by which all other be learned and

known in diversity of tongues and speeches'.[12] Important too was the stipulation that all boys should be admitted free other than paying an entrance fee of one penny. These two provisions were fundamental to the way the school developed during its first 300 years, the first hindering attempts to broaden the curriculum, the second checking efforts to raise more revenue.

When the deed referred to 'the Science of Grammar', this was Latin not English grammar. In this, Manchester's new grammar school was no different from any other grammar school of the 16th century. Latin was the lingua franca of government and the law and it was government and the law for which grammar-school boys (and they were mainly boys) were educated. It was a concept that undoubtedly appealed to Hugh Oldham. Few pupils would have gone on to the country's two universities at Oxford and Cambridge, but, in a largely illiterate society where even fewer could understand Latin, they possessed skills worth a premium. It was an education for a leadership elite. In Manchester the High Master and the usher taught Latin, later adding Greek. Boys whose skills in reading and writing required improvement were taught by a poor scholar chosen by the High Master until they were ready to join the usher's Latin class. The High Master prepared a handful of the most able for university. For these few boys, it was the beginning of a long and expensive training that would see them graduate in theology or law and take up positions in government, the Church or the law.

Mumford, in his history of the school, reckoned that there would never have been more than 100 boys at the school during its first 150 years or so. A boy was sent up to Cambridge for the first time in the 1520s and two boys went up to Oxford in the late 1530s. By then the school was sending around three or four boys to university every five years, a pattern that remained much the same until the 1630s.[13]

The school attracted little attention during the 16th century. The connection with the abbot of Whalley was severed when the last abbot was hanged in 1537 as a consequence of his failure to be sufficiently loyal to the king during the abortive Pilgrimage of Grace in the previous year. Both John Leland in the 1530s and William Camden in the 1580s ignored the school in describing Manchester for their topographical works. Leland described the town as the busiest and most populous in Lancashire. It was already an important centre for cloth manufacturing, and one of the school's mills on the Irk was a fulling mill for cleaning grey cloth.

When Edward VI dissolved collegiate churches, chantries and religious guilds in 1548, the collegiate church in Manchester was dissolved but the £8 a year previously paid to the teaching priest was channelled instead directly to the school. The collegiate

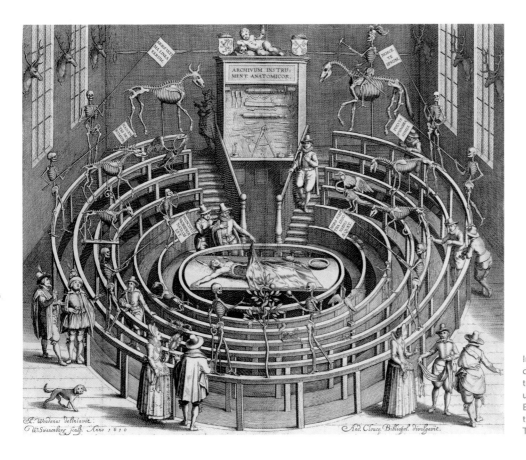

In the mid-seventeenth century the school started to send boys to the universities of Leiden and Edinburgh. Shown here is the gruesome Anatomy Theatre at Leiden.

church was revived under Edward's sister, Mary, and would become a focus for local tension over the next two centuries, beginning with discontent over an absentee warden appointed under Elizabeth I. This prepared the ground for Manchester's radical reputation, which often pitted popular opinion against the establishment represented by the Church of England. Since the warden remained a trustee, and most of the High Masters were Anglican ministers, this had repercussions for the school.

The most notable of the High Masters during Elizabeth's reign was James Bateson. Most grammar-school masters were both graduates, necessarily from either Oxford or Cambridge, and ministers, since a degree was seen as an almost essential qualification for churchmen. The masters of Manchester Grammar School were no different. Bateson was an Oxford graduate, appropriately enough from Brasenose. Appointed in 1559, he counted among his pupils Henry Bury, a major benefactor of Bury Grammar School, and John Smith, later president of Magdalene College, Cambridge, who established fellowships and scholarships linked to MGS. After Bateson's death in 1583, there was a lack of continuity. There is evidence that the remuneration for High Masters was now inadequate, which reflected the negligence of the trustees in failing to protect their corn-grinding monopoly. Edward Chetham, High Master from 1597 to 1602, and his

usher even had to sue the trustees for failing to pay their salaries. Frequent outbreaks of the plague also disrupted teaching, probably causing the deaths of several ushers and leading to the hasty appointment of poor replacements. When the warden, Dr Dee, visited the school in 1600, he spoke of 'great imperfections'.[14] John Rowlands, High Master from 1616, was often absent, leaving his brother in his place, apparently with the approval of one of the trustees, an unsatisfactory situation that took the trustees 14 years to resolve.

Manchester was claimed by the Parliamentarians at the start of the Civil War and repelled a siege by Royalists in 1642 that caused considerable distress within the town. By then the school was sending some boys to the universities of Edinburgh and Leiden in the Netherlands, reflecting the Puritan backgrounds of many local families. Able and ambitious, Ralph Brideoak, the High Master from 1638 to 1645, trimmed his sails according to the shifting political winds. A Royalist at the outset of hostilities, he encouraged his scholars to write Latin verse to commemorate the birth of Prince Henry in 1640, and became chaplain to the Royalist James Stanley, the seventh earl of Derby, who lost his head in 1651. But he strove to accommodate himself with Manchester's Parliamentarians, returning to the Royalist fold in 1660, and ending his days as bishop of Chichester in 1678.

In 1647 the people of Manchester petitioned for the appointment of new trustees. Four of the existing trustees, three with Puritan sympathies, were reappointed, and were joined by eight other loyal Parliamentarians. In 1648 they appointed a practising Presbyterian, John Wickens, as High Master. Although Wickens had been appointed to his previous post as master of Rochdale school by Archbishop Laud in 1638, his subsequent conversion to Presbyterianism was said to have been genuine.

In 1649, on the declaration of the Commonwealth, the warden of the collegiate church was forced out even though he had supported the winning side, and the church itself was seized. The warden had care of the early school registers and their fate is recorded by a later author unafraid to indicate his own prejudices in colourful language. The registers, he writes, 'were sacrilegiously carried off, along with much more substantial prey, by the strippers of the religious foundations, during the canting and hypocritical days of the Cromwellian interregnum; and the statue of the good and pious Bishop … was destroyed by the reckless iconoclasts of the same age, whose hatred to the episcopal habiliments was quite consistent with their smooth-faced

and puritanical innovations'.[15] This time the collegiate nature of the church was lost forever and the trustees of Sir Humphrey Chetham, himself a former MGS pupil, bought the old buildings as a boarding school for poor boys.

Although Manchester retained a strong radical stream of opinion, the town welcomed the coronation of Charles II in 1661. The school's Parliamentarian trustees had already been dismissed. The Stuart sympathies of the warden and the collegiate church led them to disregard the deed of 1525, which stipulated trustees should be drawn from those living in Manchester. Instead, on the grounds that the town's Parliamentarian sympathies made its people unsuitable to govern an Anglican school, the new trustees were appointed from more politically sympathetic gentry living outside the parish.

Wickens, however, survived as High Master until his death in 1676. He was saved by his academic reputation, with one noted local nonconformist minister, Adam Martindale, whose son attended the school, describing him as 'a most excellent teacher'.[16] A former pupil, William Butterworth, wrote in his support to the clerk of the privy council, Sir John Nicholas, in 1660, stating

The Battle of Preston in 1648, fought largely at Walton-le-Dale near Preston, resulted in a victory by the troops of Oliver Cromwell over the Royalists and Scots. The school suffered during the Interregnum that followed.

that he owed everything to his school master. Wickens was well respected within Manchester, and his reputation extended beyond the town. In 1663 news that he had been invited to become head of a new school established by the Haberdashers' Company in Newport, Shropshire, led to a public meeting in support of keeping him in Manchester and to prevent his departure the trustees agreed to increase his salary.

Wickens's reputation was based on the school's achievement in sending 26 boys to Oxford and 88 to Cambridge, that is, roughly four every year out of a school probably no more than 150 strong.[17] Not all of them were from families wealthy enough to finance the costs of a university education; some of the less well off were supported by exhibitions funded from the school's endowments.

William Barrow, who succeeded Wickens, was High Master from 1677 to 1721. He began recruiting boys from a much wider area. Some of them took lodgings close to the school, in property acquired by the trustees for the High Master and usher in Long Millgate. Barrow was sympathetic to the Whig cause but many of his boarders came from homes more inclined to favour the Stuarts. In 1690, at an unsettled time in English politics, just two years

after William of Orange had deposed James II, this tension resulted in 'one of the school riots which frequently sprang up between boys and masters on such questions as the length of Christmas vacations. This particular one assumed graver proportions than usual. The boys locked themselves in the school and defied the masters. The townsfolk as usual took the side of the boys, and supplied them both with food and with firearms, with which the boys shot at the legs of their opponents. The siege lasted a whole fortnight, and neither origin nor conclusion is very intelligible.'[18] The differences between Puritan and Royalist thrown up by the Civil War had become entrenched as a Whig–Tory divide.

Barrow and Richard Thompson, his long-serving usher, maintained the school's academic success. Between 1677 and

Humphrey Chetham (c.1592–98) was educated at Manchester Grammar School. In his will he left money to found Chetham's Hospital, which contains both the library and Chetham's School of Music. Chetham's Library is the oldest free public reference library in the United Kingdom.

1720, 38 boys took up places at Cambridge and 57 at Oxford.[19] Several university scholarships and exhibitions were established in the latter part of the 17th century. In 1679 the influence of the first Lord Delamere, a trustee who was married to the niece and only surviving relative of Sarah Alston, Duchess of Somerset, led the duchess to endow four exhibitions to Brasenose, where her first husband had been educated. In 1686 the duchess included poor boys from the school among those eligible for the scholarships she had endowed at Brasenose and St John's, Cambridge. In 1691 William Hulme, a successful Manchester merchant who had probably been a pupil at the school, endowed four more exhibitions to Brasenose, his own college, to support boys taking up further study beyond the degree of bachelor of arts, which Hulme considered essential for producing well-educated and able ministers of the Church. Hulme's only son, Bannister, had been a pupil at MGS when he died at the age of 17 in 1673 following a head injury received in a schoolboy fight.

Under Barrow, the school had expanded, adding another room to create the petty or lower school in 1688. This was a form of elementary school, taking in boys to teach them English for a couple of years. Later some of these boys were given the chance to begin learning Latin in preparation for joining MGS. Varying in number between 50 and 100, the lower school in this form would

From 1686 boys from the school were eligible for scholarships to Brasenose, Oxford and St John's, Cambridge, endowed by Sarah, Duchess of Somerset.

remain part of MGS for the best part of two centuries.

The first master in charge of the lower school was a man named Broxup, who eventually had to be retired by the trustees in 1724 'by reason of his insufficiency'. Broxup himself confessed to the trustees that at the age of 68 he was starting 'to feel myself in decline'. His letter continued that 'the first time I heard you had a design of displacing me, it was surprising and amazing to me and I was almost sunk down with horror and despondency, but my sorrow was soon alleviated when Mr Richards informed me you would continue me in my place until the 25th March next ensuing'. He had pleaded for an annual pension, otherwise 'I shall certainly want common necessaries of life'. This was a sentiment that would have struck a chord with staff employed at the school nearly 200 years later.[20]

Barrow and Thompson had both died in 1721 and by the time of Broxup's departure the school was in an unsettled state. Barrow's

had given up the job in the first place to return to his much more prosperous ecclesiastical living, but he did step down and Henry Brooke was appointed to succeed him in 1727.

The trustees were eager to keep Brooke once they had got him and, conscious of the problems they had had with Richards, gave him a house substantial enough to take in boarders to increase his income. They may have been anxious about a private boarding school recently opened in deliberate competition by Thomas Ryder, who had given up the headship of Bury Grammar School after scenting an opportunity arising from the unsettled state of Manchester Grammar School. Another rival came along a little later in 1735 when John Clayton opened a private school, which he called Salford Grammar School, ostensibly to attract the sons of more prosperous families who were reluctant for their sons to mix with the poorer pupils at Manchester Grammar School. In fact, MGS was never threatened by any of these local 18th-century rivals, and most of them failed to survive the death or retirement of their founders.

In appointing Henry Brooke, the trustees had overlooked the claims of William Purnell, the young usher who had loyally covered for the failings of Richards and would do so again in the case of Brooke. Purnell therefore took the opportunity to submit a claim for three years' arrears of salary as well as the cost of repairs to his house. The trustees were gracious enough to pay up, and add a further £10 a year to cover housing costs.

Judging from the admissions registers, Brooke appears to have recruited few boarders. In 1733–4, for instance, only three boys were the sons of gentlemen, coming from Middleton and

Above: Back view of the second Grammar School, built in 1776.

Left: 'Breaking-Up Day at Dr Clayton's School at Salford' by Arthur Devis, 1738. Dr Clayton, who was educated at Manchester Grammar School, stands at the far left of the picture. He set up the school to compete with MGS but it closed on his death in 1773.

immediate successors proved unsuitable. John Richards, appointed in 1726, was the second High Master to absent himself from the post in favour of his brother, and apparently for the same reason, that is, the failure of the trustees to pay him promptly. The trustees were struggling to manage the school's erratic income and for a brief period permitted the masters to admit girls, the sisters of boys already in the school, on a fee-paying basis to supplement irregularly paid and inadequate salaries. Of the 52 children admitted to the school in 1724–5, Mumford records that 16 were girls.

Richards' behaviour led some trustees to seek his dismissal and in July 1726 the trustees recorded that they had received 'many complaints against Mr Richards the High Master as to his gross negligence and absence'. Some parents had withdrawn their sons. But the trustees lacked the power to get rid of Richards, and their only sanction was to reduce his salary to £10 until he improved his performance. This can hardly have troubled Richards, who

Above: List of 'holiday' library books from the school's library, 1730.

Above right: The ill-fated Jacobite rebellion of 1745 received only limited support as Bonnie Prince Charlie passed through Manchester. The 300 volunteers who came forward were formed into the Manchester Regiment.

Whitchurch respectively. Almost all the boys admitted came from Manchester, mainly from commercial backgrounds, the sons of tailors, shearsmen (who worked in the cloth industry), reedmakers, whitesmiths (who made items out of metal, usually tin), innkeepers, hatters, slaughterers, saddlers and joiners. The balance appears to have changed little during the 1740s, although the list of fathers' now long-forgotten occupations, such as jersey-comber, white-limer, peruke maker, checkman and calendar-man, continued.[21]

Within a few years Brooke had followed his predecessor by placing his brother in charge while he returned to his parish in Gloucester. Once again Purnell stepped in. With the school short of funds, he collected donations from the town's wealthier citizens, which he used, for instance, to cover the costs of staging Christmas plays and to buy modern literature for the library, including *Robinson Crusoe*, *Don Quixote* and several works by French authors.

The trustees were hard up because they were no longer getting as much money from their corn-grinding monopoly. After losing the tenancy in 1716, Sir Oswald Mosley had built his own mill and set up in competition. The action the trustees took against him to protect their monopoly was financed by their depleted income. Despite the fact that the mills were in a state of neglect, resulting in poorly ground corn, the trustees won the case but it took several years to persuade Mosley to part with the badly needed £500 in damages. With funds running dry, the trustees even took the drastic step of closing the school for a brief period in 1739–40. The ever-faithful Purnell remained at his post, rewarded when the school re-opened with a bonus paid for through the reduction in the salary of the absent Brooke, who had also been deprived of his boarding

house. Brooke came scurrying back and stayed until 1749, when Purnell was finally appointed to take his place.

The ups and downs of the school were a reflection of the unsettled state of the town. Only four years previously, antipathetic to the Hanoverians, Manchester had initially welcomed the Young Pretender as he and his rag-tag army made their way down the country. All the clergy, with the exception of the warden and the High Master, favoured the Stuarts. Clayton took his boys to meet the Pretender as he entered the town. But, although a regiment (the Manchester Regiment) was raised in support of the prince, relatively few volunteered to march by his side and his reception as he retreated to Scotland was hostile. The Manchester Regiment lamely surrendered to Cumberland when he took the town in his pursuit of the Pretender, and many of those who had joined were hanged. Among them was the regiment's chaplain, Thomas Coppock, executed at Harrowby, near Carlisle, on 18 October 1746. Coppock, the son of a tailor, had been a pupil at MGS, which he joined in 1730, and had taken a place at Brasenose, graduating in 1742. Another pupil, Willam Brettargh, an attorney's son, who had joined the school in 1734, was also apprehended for his involvement. He avoided Coppock's fate but was transported for life.[22]

Lacking a corporation, the expanding town was ineffectively managed, but many people liked it that way. This was particularly the case with the town's nonconformist population. Where corporations did exist, legislation barred nonconformists from holding public office and they had to endure being governed by their antagonists. At least they were spared this in Manchester. This was at the cost of a congested town badly served by an

Le College du NEZ de BRONZE.
A. La Chapelle. B. La Bibliotheque. C. Le Re...fectoire. D. Le Logement du Principal.

inefficient transport system that frequently led to high prices and food shortages, sparking regular riots. High Tory clergy, such as John Clayton, were impatient with such protest, inflaming opinion further by blaming the poor for failing to help themselves.

These were years when corn was often in short supply, making the trustees' corn-grinding monopoly more and more unpopular. In any case it was becoming almost worthless. Local people could take their corn to competitors while corn ground at other mills, such as those in Salford, was sold openly in Manchester by flour merchants. In 1758 legislation abolished the wheat monopoly in return for compensating the trustees and allowing them to sell the mills. This turned out to be salvation for the trustees, whose wise investment of the proceeds yielded an annual income of £2,000. The malt monopoly remained untouched, but for the time being there was little improvement in the fortunes of the malt mill.

As an established and respected figure, Purnell's tenure as High Master proved beneficial, and admissions steadily increased. The number of boys rose from around 80 in 1745 to in excess of 170 by the time of Purnell's death in office in 1764. He was assisted by a new usher, a young man called Charles Lawson, equally as determined to restore the character of the school. In Mumford's assessment, 'William Purnell exerted a genial and

Above: Hugh Oldham's good friend, William Smith, was a co-founder of Brasenose College, Oxford. After Smith died in 1514 Oldham and others donated large sums to finish building the College and furnish its library.

Left: Charles Lawson, High Master (1764–1806).

The High Master's house on Long Millgate.

enlightening influence fed by his love of modern literature, while Lawson exerted the equally necessary exact discipline involved in the rigid study of classics and mathematics'.[23] The calibre of that maths teaching was evident in 1759 when boys from the school took the places of first, third and fifth wrangler at Cambridge.

While the admission of local boys increased, the most noticeable aspect of the rise in numbers was the growing number of boarders solicited by Purnell and Lawson, which reached a peak of 60 around 1760. The first sign of a change in the pattern of entry comes with Purnell's appointment as High Master. Although local boys continued to dominate admissions, there was a marked increase in the number of boys from better off and more

distant families, such as William Lover-Parry, a gentleman's son from Pwllheli, Peter Atkinson, a gentleman's son from Beverley in the East Riding of Yorkshire and Robert Harding, the son of a clergyman from Pottersbury in Northamptonshire. Admitted free to the school, they paid a significant sum for their board and lodgings (20 guineas a year in the 1770s), helping to supplement the incomes of the High Master and usher. The appeal of the school to the better-off was the advantageous route it offered to the ancient universities through numerous school-leaving exhibitions and closed college exhibitions and scholarships. These included a dozen leaving exhibitions worth £40 each paid for out of surplus school funds; the 32 Somerset scholarships, divided between

Brasenose and St John's, ranging in value from £18 to £26 a year; and the 15 Hulme exhibitions for post-graduates from Brasenose.[24] They all helped to sustain entries to Oxford and Cambridge but appeared to favour boys from wealthier backgrounds. Mumford calculated that between 1745 and 1765, 84 university places were awarded to boarders and just 16 to day boys. He concluded that few of the latter benefitted from the school's classical education and most would have left early. This was scarcely surprising given that a student at Oxford was reckoned to need £200 a year to live on, when the maximum working wage listed for Manchester in 1771 by Arthur Young was just ten shillings a week.

The school gathered together an eclectic social mix, with the sons of gentlemen, attorneys, merchants and clergymen studying alongside the sons of weavers, hatters, dyers, coopers and labourers, and this tradition continued under Lawson, who was High Master from 1764 until 1806. It was a characteristic observed by Thomas De Quincey who from 1800 spent two unhappy years at the school. He epitomised the privileged position held by boarders, having his own study-bedroom in Lawson's house, with money from his mother to subscribe towards the town's new library and to pay for piano lessons on the instrument that came with him. When he took part in the classical recitations held at Christmas, Lady Carbery, from the estate where De Quincey had lived before joining the school, came with her entourage, applauding him wildly.

De Quincey noticed how the boarders and day boys, a broad spread of social classes, all mixed together. Under Lawson, total numbers at their peak reached more than 200, with a corresponding increase in boarders. For De Quincey, the boarders set the tone of the school, partly because they were living together around the clock, unlike the day boys: 'The elder section of the School – those on the brink of manhood, and by incalculable degrees the more scholar-like section, all who read, meditated, or began to kindle into the love of literature – were boarders in Mr Lawson's home. The students therefore of the house carried an overwhelming influence into the School. They were bound together by links of brotherhood; whereas the day scholars were disconnected.'[25] There also seems to have been a certain degree of intellectual arrogance among the boarders, reinforced by the more limited achievements of day boys in the lower school. For De Quincey, the small group of older boys in Lawson's boarding house represented the cream of the school: 'What with our confederation through house membership, what with our reciprocal sympathies in the problems suggested by books, we had become a club of boys (amongst whom might be four or five that were even young men, counting 18 or 19 years) altogether as thoughtful and as self-respecting as can often exist even among adults.'[26]

The boarders continued to take the majority of university places. A typical example might be John Morritt, son of a wealthy

Pupils during Charles Lawson's tenure included the writer Thomas De Quincey (1800–02) and Frodsham Hodson (1784–7), who went on to become president of Brasenose College, Oxford and vice-chancellor of the University.

Right: Richard Pepper Arden (1752–61) rose to hold the position of Lord Chief Justice.

Far right: Statue of Cyril Jackson (1755–60) at Christ Church, Oxford.

Yorkshire landowner, later the patron and friend of Walter Scott, who progressed to St John's, Cambridge, graduating in 1794 and then spending two years with his tutor touring Europe. Or there was Frodsham Hodson, son of a Liverpool clergyman, who joined MGS in 1784 and left it in 1787 for a place at Brasenose, where he later became a distinguished president of the college. University places were not confined to Brasenose and St John's. Richard Pepper Arden, for instance, later Lord Chief Justice, joined the school in the 1750s and went up to Trinity College, Cambridge, in 1761. John Williams, another judge, was admitted to MGS in 1787 and in 1794 also went up to Trinity.

It seems that the overall tone of the school, rather than just its links with Brasenose and St John's, persuaded some prosperous fathers to use Manchester as a boarding prep school for their sons before they were sent to more distant and illustrious schools. Cyril Jackson, for instance, the son of a Yorkshire physician who later became a notable dean of Christ Church, Oxford, and his younger brother Francis, later regius professor of Greek at Oxford, and then bishop of Oxford, were both prepared for Westminster at MGS.

Among the fewer day boys who made it to university was Thomas Bancroft, the son of a threadmaker, born in Deansgate, Manchester, who came to the school at the age of six in 1762; he went up to Brasenose and became a clergyman and distinguished headmaster. Joshua Brookes, born in 1754, the son of a Stockport shoemaker, also left MGS for Brasenose and became a clergyman, returning to teach at his old school where he was an eccentric and unpopular master but regarded as an excellent scholar.

It was a growing group of well-connected and affluent former pupils. A number of them met on 24 September 1781, when Sir

Thomas Egerton, later first earl of Wilton, proposed 'an annual meeting of such gentlemen as have been scholars of the Free School'.[27] The meeting took the form of a dinner, held every year at Michaelmas, and advertised in advance in the local papers covering Manchester, Liverpool and Chester. It continues to this day, still as a separate organisation from the official old boys' club formed much later, and must be one of the oldest associations of former pupils in the country.

Most boys, of course, remained outside this influential network, spending their working lives within the steadily growing industrial town. Many families simply could not afford to have a productive member of the household in education rather than earning a wage, which was why there were usually many more boys in the lower school and why few of them ever made it into the upper school. Samuel Bamford, a weaver's son, had his education at MGS cut short when his father removed him after a year because he refused to allow him to learn Latin. Bamford spent most of his working life as a weaver or warehouseman but became a notable radical in an age of radicalism.

His autobiography includes a description of the school buildings, which had been rebuilt under Lawson in 1776:

The School was a large room of an oblong form extending north and south, and well lighted by large windows. At the northern end of it was a fireplace with a red cheerful fire glowing in the grate. The master's custom was to sit in an arm-chair with his right hand towards the fire and his left arm resting on a square oaken table, on which lay a newspaper or two, a magazine or other publication, a couple of canes with the ends split, and a medley of boys' playthings, such as tops, whips, marbles, apple-scrapers, nutcrackers, dragon banding and such articles.[28]

Financed partly by accumulated school funds and partly by the sale of land held by the trustees, the two-storey building, with the lower school below and the upper school above, lasted until its demolition in 1879.

On his first day at the school in 1799 Bamford brought with him two pounds of the best gingerbread, with a piece given to each boy in the lower school: 'This was a very acceptable introduction to the boys; it was the invariable custom of the lower school, and was always productive of a friendly greeting towards the fresh comer; for my part, in five minutes I had a score or two of new acquaintance, asking questions, giving me information, and ready to lend me a helping hand in anything.' He was taught by the Reverend John Gaskell, a young curate, neatly turned out with powdered hair. The boys were divided into six classes – introduction to Latin,

higher Bible, middle Bible, lower Bible, testament and spelling – and the boys were placed in order of merit, with those in first and second positions exercising 'considerable authority over the others'. The day began with assembly, when flogging took place, the master cutting miscreants once or twice across the shoulders with his cane, except the more frequent offenders, who were 'hit more severely, being often sent to their class writhing, to the amusement of their colleagues'. Promotion came once a boy had been head of his class for some time, when the head boy of the next class would lead him by the hand and ask the master if he might move up. Play times were on Thursday and Saturday afternoons and holidays were given at Easter, Whitsun and Christmas. Bamford counted among his friends John Pilkington, the son of the clerk at the old church, Jim Torkington, whose parents had a hat shop in Church Street, Dick France, whose father kept the Sir John Falstaff in the Market Place, and Henry Woodhouse, whose father was publican of the Bull's Head.[29]

Bamford knew nothing of the upper school, later described by Whatton as being

ninety-six feet in length, and thirty feet in breadth. This room contains four fire-places – is extremely well lighted with twenty-six large windows – and is furnished with desks and seats, which bear evident marks of long service, by the numberless initials of names which succeeding boys have carved upon them. The ceiling of the room is very lofty – a circumstance greatly favourable to the health of the master and the scholars. The Upper School Room is appropriated solely to instruction in the higher Classics.

Second Grammar School building in Long Millgate, constructed in 1776.

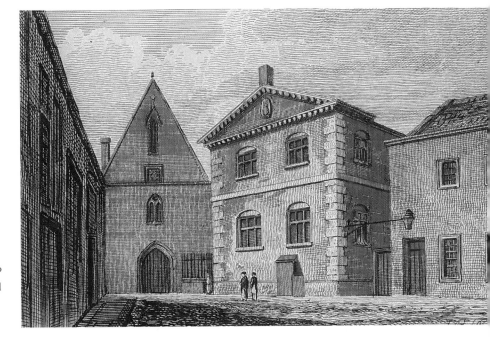

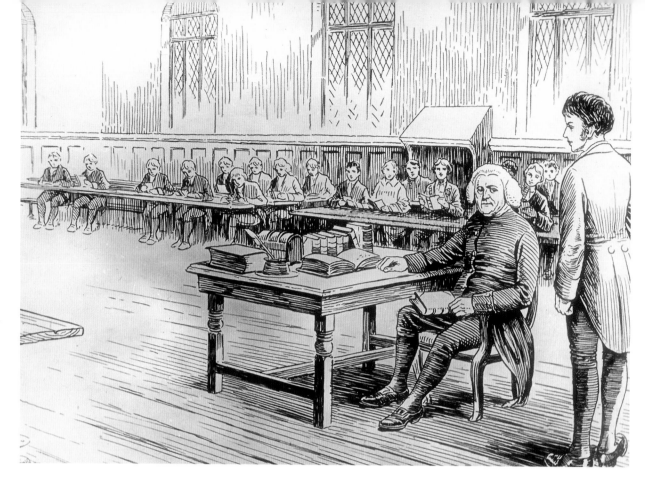

Right: Sketch of High Master Lawson teaching seniors in the upper school room.

Below: Oldham's owl, originally on the gable end of the second school building, now stands guard in the refectory at Rusholme.

He also noted on the front of the building the large stone medallion of the owl.[30]

De Quincey recorded the pattern of life in the upper school under Lawson. School began at seven for lower and upper school boys, with breakfast taken at nine. Lessons then ran through from nine-thirty to lunch at noon, with a three-hour break for lunch, recommencing at three and finishing at five. Lawson replaced Purnell's annual play with a speech day, held every October, when boys delivered speeches in Latin on classical themes, and former pupils at university were encouraged to submit verses for reading in public. There was an annual school feast, celebrated on Shrove Tuesday, with the boys taking part in archery before apparently adjourning to the adjacent Bull's Head in the Market Place.

Those boys who could afford it were able to enjoy a wider curriculum than permitted by the school's statutes. The trustees got around the ban on paying masters to teach anything other than the original classical curriculum by allowing the High Master and usher to employ resident boarding masters, whose costs were covered by boarding

fees. Since at least the 1750s writing, arithmetic or book-keeping, maths and French had been taught during the school's weekly 'holidays', on Thursday and Saturday afternoons. The fathers of those few day boys in the upper school wanting the same privilege were either charged an illegal fee or had to engage their own private tutors.

By the early 1800s MGS was typical of many other grammar schools both in being led by a master who was overdue for retirement (Lawson was aged 72 in 1800), and being constrained by its statutes from changing its curriculum to meet growing local demands for a more commercially oriented education. Only in its wide array of leaving exhibitions and closed college exhibitions and scholarships was MGS much different from other schools. But there were fewer boarders, partly because teaching standards were falling, resulting in fewer boys achieving university places, partly because of a revival in the fortunes of the long-established boarding schools where the sons of the wealthy had traditionally been sent and the foundation of others unhindered by ancient statutes.[31]

Mumford notes Lawson's growing conservatism in the school library, which, save for Bentham and several Scottish philosophers, was devoid of the writings of more recent authors. His willingness to wield a cane caused him to be known as Millgate's Flogging Turk. Yet Lawson earned the respect of several previous generations of pupils, who in 1797 presented him with his portrait, which still hangs in the school, and on his death in 1807 paid for a marble monument in his memory in the cathedral, with the surplus from the subscription applied to a gold prize medal.

Mumford also pointed out how the trustees had become a self-perpetuating oligarchy, their members drawn from successive generations of the same families, which he suggests made them out of touch with the changing life of the town. This was unfair. Their management of the school's endowments since the 1750s had been a success, financing the rebuilding of the school, higher salaries for the High Master and usher, the appointment of two more masters and an increase in the value of the school's leaving exhibitions. This position compared favourably with many other similar schools. And they had been ingenious in circumventing the constraints of the original statutes to meet an increasing demand for an extended curriculum, even if this satisfied only those who could pay for it.

Another reason why the school was less attractive to the sons of the wealthy was the steady deterioration in its surroundings as Manchester and its economy expanded. Between the 1760s and 1801 Manchester's population grew from some 20,000 inhabitants to more than 70,000. Even in 1772, when the town's first business directory listed 1,150 businesses, parts of the town were already in decline, with the river Irwell backed by squalid cottages and wasteland covered in waste or human bones from the overflowing nearby churchyard. Successive Acts of Parliament increased Manchester's powers to undertake improvements but the town's commissioners proved largely inept and growing hardship precipitated frequent rioting. The coming of the canals gave a further impetus to development, with warehouses springing up alongside the canal all the way into Deansgate, and by 1800 there were also 32 steam-powered mills in operation. The snobbish De Quincey was appalled by this industrialisation: 'I cannot stir out of doors but I am nosed by a factory, a cotton-bag, a cotton-dealer, or something else allied to that most detestable commerce.'[32]

The impact of this on the school was evident to the trustees, who noted in 1808 how the school was

closely surrounded by Old Buildings chiefly occupied by poor
people, in situations neither healthy nor comfortable. The street is
narrow and also serves as the Apple Market so that on two or three
days a week it is crowded with horses and carts, making it difficult
and dangerous to pass from the masters' houses to the school.
There is no playground so the boys have no other outlet but the

streets where they are prematurely exposed to temptations to the
great danger of health and morals. The resorting to taverns and
intercourse with women of the town becomes a fashion amongst
the boys in the higher classes of the school, which no vigilance of
the masters can suppress.[33]

Retaining boys in the upper school was a challenge for the trustees as the number of boarders declined. Poorer parents continued to send their sons to the lower school for a year or two to give them a basic education. MGS had little local competition. The Sunday school movement started in Manchester in 1784 and was educating 23,000 children by the early 1800s. In 1809 the British and Foreign Bible Society opened a school in Lever Street, where two masters and one mistress taught 1,000 children in one huge schoolroom. Some children had the misfortune to attend

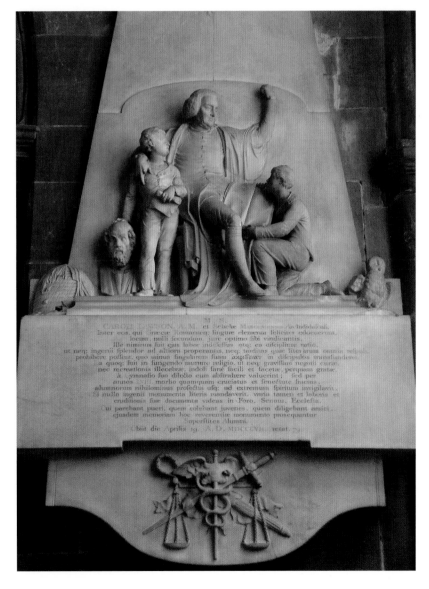

The splendid marble memorial to Charles Lawson in Manchester Cathedral, erected in 1810. Part of the Latin inscription, composed by old boy Dr Frodsham Hodson reads: 'So scrupulous also was he in the discharge of his duty that neither the weighty cares of business nor the seductions of social recreation – so alluring to an ageeable and witty disposition – could draw him away from his beloved school.'

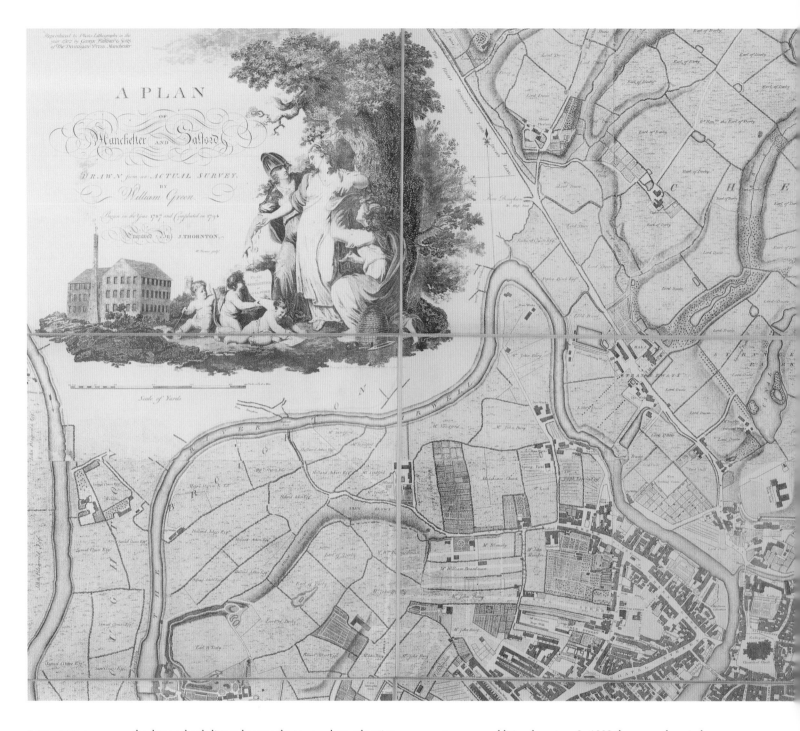

Extract from a map showing the location of the school (outlined in red) and the rapid development of the city in 1794.

the dame schools littered across the town, where education was almost entirely incidental. Most children, of course, had no education at all.

To improve numbers in the upper school, and attract more able boys, the trustees had two solutions. First, they wanted to move the school out of Long Millgate to a new site in the countryside; second, they wanted to make the extended curriculum previously enjoyed only by boarders available to day boys by eliminating fees and using the school's endowments to engage additional masters. In 1808 they were thwarted on both counts by the original statutes, the legitimacy of which had been restated by Lord Eldon, the conservative lord chancellor, in the Leeds Grammar School case of 1805, which limited the application of endowments to the purposes of the founding statutes. The trustees themselves also had misgivings about relocating the school since they believed a more distant location from the heart of Manchester would disadvantage boys from poorer homes.

The statutes also prevented the trustees from removing an unwanted High Master. Lawson remained in post until his death, at the age of 79, in 1807. Evidence of the pall of educational neglect hanging over the school came from Frederick Calvert, son of the duke of Norfolk's steward, who joined in 1803. Calvert and his brother arrived dressed in outfits converted from the scarlets, pinks and blues of his father's wardrobe, causing uproar among the boys, who were dressed in the severely cut uniform of tight-fitting jackets and short trousers of plain cloth. He wrote of the curriculum that

education at School was on a scale of the noblest simplicity. Nothing of vulgar mercantile element found entrance there. No writing, no arithmetic, no history or geography. We were not allowed to waste our time on such trifles as these. It was wholly and exclusively concentrated on two subjects, Latin and the Bible. Nothing was explained to us. We were given a grammar book, but even such words as nominative, genitive, dative, indicative, were left to our ingenuity to discover, stimulated by the powerful inculcation of the cane, for everything was thrashed into us.[34]

3 STRUGGLE FOR REFORM 1808–67

'One Connected Whole'

It would take MGS more than half a century to adapt to the changing times of the revolutionary 19th century. At first it seemed as if the school could simply carry on where Lawson had left off, and under an energetic High Master, supported by a buoyant income stream from the school's endowments, Manchester Grammar School enjoyed a revival that lasted nearly 30 years. But this only masked the fact that the school needed to find a new role in a town whose remarkable growth had seemed to diminish its status. This highlighted once again how the school seemed to be part of, yet apart from, the town, as they found themselves at loggerheads. Salvation came only when the school found a High Master with the forceful character and inner strength to take on, overcome and embrace local opinion, and in the process transform the school.

Jeremiah Smith, Lawson's successor, had been an exhibitioner at Corpus Christi College, which stood him in good stead when the post of High Master fell vacant. In recommending him, the college president would also have been impressed with his teaching experience gained from 14 years as second master at King Edward's School in Birmingham. One of his pupils, the novelist William Harrison Ainsworth, later wrote of Smith that he was

Right: Jeremiah Smith, High Master (1807–37).

Opposite: Extract from the 1862–79 admissions register showing the occupations of parents.

a spare man with large thoughtful features and a fine expansive forehead powdered at the top. He looked like a bishop and ought to have been one. His voice was particularly solemn and it was quite a treat to hear him read prayers. Under him, the boys began to give themselves the air of young men, wore well cut coats and well fitting boots, were very particular about the fashion of their hair and, above all, wore gloves. He was very quiet and controlled in manner, but very firm. He is only known to have used the cane once, and then it was very evident that it was more painful to himself than to the culprit. He had the faculty of at once inspiring respect and retaining it.[35]

William	Deceased	
Edward	Cott or Spin.	
William	Salesman	
Alfred	Cashier	
Robert W.	Foreman. Engraver	30 Clarence
Thomas as Rothwell	Cashier	12
Thomas as Rothwell	Clergyman	
John	Corn & Flour Dealer	
James	Tin plate Workers	
Patrick	Oil Merchant	
Benjamin	Bookseller	
Thomas	Law clerk	
Robert	Surgeon	
John	Solicitor	
Alfred	Market Colle	
Edmund	Cashier	
William	Groc	
John		
Valentine		

12
10
8
12
13
10
11
10
12
13
10
12
12

MANCHESTER HEROES

George Cruikshank's depiction of the Peterloo massacre 'showing the charge of the Manchester Yeomanry on the unarmed populace in St Peter's Field' on 16 August 1819. (The massacre was called Peterloo in an ironic comparison with the Battle of Waterloo, which had taken place four years earlier.)

True to the tradition of most of the ministers attached to the collegiate church, Smith was a conservative in religion, education and politics. Remaining in post for 30 years, he joined the school during a period of reaction in English politics and left it in the wake of significant political and religious reforms. He was High Master at a time when Manchester was undergoing a huge transformation socially and politically. The rapid industrialisation of the town, combined with a rising population,[36] not only turned Manchester into the king of all cotton towns, it created a social gulf between the richest and the poorest that led to growing political discontent. MGS would not be immune from the consequences of such dramatic change.

The Peterloo massacre of 1819 was one of the defining events in Manchester's history. The suppression of a peaceful mass demonstration in support of political change led to 11 deaths and injuries to more than 400 people. A former grammar-school boy, Samuel Bamford, was among the crowd, and later recorded the scene:

> *The Yeomanry had dismounted – some were easing their horses' girths, others adjusting their accoutrements, and some were wiping their sabres. Several mounds of human beings still remained where they had fallen, crushed down and smothered. Some were still groaning, others with staring eyes were gasping for breath, and others would never breathe more.*[37]

The High Master was directly involved, giving evidence against the radical leader of the protest, Henry Hunt, at the subsequent trial. The author of a short centenary history of the event described Smith's apprehension on the day itself:

> *The long-expected day came at last. The morning was fine, and later on the heat was considerable. In Manchester the magistrates saw fit to publish a notice recommending the peaceable and well-disposed inhabitants to remain in their own houses during the whole day, and to keep their children and servants within doors. The Rev. Jeremiah Smith, then the High Master of the Free Grammar School, afterwards stated at the Trial that most of the shop windows were closed, and that as there was a general feeling of apprehension, he dismissed his day boys after breakfast, and eventually went home and locked himself and his boarders into his house in Long Millgate.*[38]

The post-Waterloo depression lifted in the 1820s but the boom was short-lived, causing further discontent that had no democratic outlet as the town had no parliamentary representation. Manchester was a deeply divided place, a place of extremes, in wealth, class, environment and politics, where industrialisation had diluted traditional social relationships. The democratic deficit was remedied under the Great Reform Act of 1832, which gave Manchester two MPs.

But Jeremiah Smith was an enemy of reform, an opponent of both the Great Reform Act and Catholic emancipation that had preceded it. And his conservatism was evident in his leadership of MGS, for he based its revival on the template developed by Purnell and Lawson. The number of boarders began to rise again, forming more than 27 per cent of all admissions between 1806 and 1835, although they never reached as high a proportion as they had in the 1770s and 1780s. Boarding fees ranged from 40 to 120 guineas a year, the latter paid by so-called parlour-boarders, who had the privilege of their own rooms. John Slater of Cheadle entered the school in 1812.

> *Boarders came from various parts of England in order to obtain one of the school exhibitions. At that period there was no competitive examination. Those who occupied the first places in the highest forms were, as a matter of right, sent to the University with an exhibition, and nearly all were gentlemen's sons whose fathers were capable of supporting them at college. When I was a scholar, I do not remember more than one native who obtained an exhibition, and he was one whose abilities could not be hid. The boarders probably amounted to one-fourth of the scholars in the middle and higher schools; the lower school had not one.*[39]

As Slater implied, there was an overall shift in the social status of the boys. Mumford's analysis shows that of all the admissions between 1805 and 1835 the sons of the gentry, clergy, professional classes, merchants and manufacturers accounted for two-thirds, while boys from lower-middle-class backgrounds accounted for a quarter, with only just over three per cent drawn from artisan families. This reflected social change in Manchester, with the rise of wealthy manufacturers and merchants, whose sons now formed almost a third of all admissions.[40] The size of the lower school more than halved, suffering in part from the competition of the new elementary schools in Manchester, which drew boys from lower-middle-class and artisan families. It was still possible to find boys from lowly backgrounds in the 1830s, such as James Chapels, a joiner's son, admitted in 1834, Francis Ridall, a waiter's son, admitted in 1836, and John Sumner, the son of a post office clerk, admitted in 1837, but they were increasingly scarce. The school also began admitting boys from Manchester's growing Jewish community. One of the first was E. A. Franklin, who joined in 1837 and recalled that 'although always kindly treated by the masters, he had to overcome considerable prejudice among his school-fellows'.[41]

In 1818 the school had 140 boys in the upper school and about 40 in the lower school. The High Master was paid £420 a year plus a house, and was entitled to admit a limited number of boarders. The usher was now called the second master, earning £220 a year plus a house, and also entitled to admit boarders. There were three assistant masters, paid between £110 and £130 a year.[42] Smith took advantage of the reformed admissions system to Oxford, and one in five of his pupils entered careers either as clergymen, lawyers or doctors.

The development of the school under Smith led to growing local discontent, not among the poorest families, but among the prosperous mercantile families, who were also pressing for a curriculum better suited to the times, one that they were still denied in law. Further pressure for change came from the Charity Commission, which had made the first external inspection of the school in 1826. The only criticism of the commissioners was the indecision of the trustees in deciding how to apply their accumulated surpluses. The trustees had completed the rebuilding of the corn mills in 1821 and overhauled the operation of the malt mill, which, combined with the post-war boom, had seen substantial increases in revenue.

All this led the trustees to petition the Court of Chancery in 1827 to introduce a wider curriculum throughout the school and to build additional accommodation to house what would be called the English or Commercial School as an alternative to the classical

Boarder's invoice, 1826.

A grand event held to celebrate the election of the first two MPs for Manchester, Mark Philips and Charles Poulett Thomson, following the Great Reform Act of 1832. (The town of Manchester was deprived of its parliamentary representation in 1660 in reprisal for its support of the Parliamentarian faction during the English Civil War.)

or upper school for boys moving up from the lower school. One of the trustees behind the scheme was William Egerton, fifth earl of Stamford and a descendant of Lord Delamere, continuing an intermittent connection between the family and MGS that would span five centuries.

As the scheme went through Chancery, criticism of the school from another section of Manchester opinion was mounting. The Charity Commission had published for the first time not only the original statutes of 1515 but also details of the trustees' revenue, giving ammunition to radical leaders arguing that the school should do more to raise the level of education for boys from the poorest families in the town. Their argument was underpinned by hostility to the High Tory opinions of Jeremiah Smith. It was also entwined with opposition to the trustees' continuing malt monopoly. As one of the many pamphlets issued in this war of words summed it up, 'the working classes of Manchester are taxed, with every glass of ale they take'.[43] One of the leading critics was Mark Philips, one of the first two MPs elected for the town under the Reform Act. A successful merchant with radical leanings, he was particularly interested in educational reform. In 1833 the matter was raised in the House of Commons, when MGS was given as an example of a school so mismanaged that

its considerable income was spent on educating just 150 boys, many of whom came from outside Manchester and were strictly ineligible. The accusation of mismanagement was rather unfair, and the trustees rebutted the argument while inviting suggestions for the scheme. But an invitation to meet Philips and a local deputation came only after the scheme had been approved and was rejected by the trustees. Philips and his supporters appealed to the court to reconsider the scheme, dragging things out until 1849, and costing the school nearly £6,000 in legal fees.

What was the school like during the 1820s and 1830s while this dispute was taking place? One boy who joined in 1829 recalled making his way to school in the winter darkness of the early morning, illuminating his books in the gloom of the schoolroom with 'little wax taper cans'. When the class broke up for breakfast, the boys made for the back room of a milk shop towards Millbrow, kept by the widow of a soldier who had served at Waterloo. While she ladled out milk, her daughter served up hot rolls, spread on a table in front of a welcoming fire. The boys observed at first hand the great changes taking place in the country. The same boy remembered how, soon after the opening of the Liverpool and Manchester railway in September 1830, he and a few others extended their break one day to hang over a bridge from which 'they could see the train without horses puffing along the line at the terrific pace of 20 miles an hour!'[44] The school's surroundings were continuing to deteriorate. In 1824 one master complained that the warehouse next to his house had been converted into a power-loom factory, 'the noise of which is unbearable'.[45]

All the boys, whether in the dark and dismal lower school or the lighter, more airy upper school, were taught in separate classes within one space. The hubbub could become intolerable, and control was often exercised through the cane, as was so often the case in boys' schools. One master, Robinson Elsdale, who later became High Master, was described by Harrison Ainsworth as someone who believed that 'a knowledge of Latin and Greek can be driven into a boy, and that his capacity may be sharpened by frequent punishment'. Elsdale had a drawer full of canes of varying lengths and thicknesses, bound up to prevent them splitting, which he applied with vigour. 'Some boys were so frightened that they couldn't learn their tasks at all, and others so reckless of the punishment which they knew must ensue, whether or not, that they intentionally neglected them. I have seen boys with "blood blisters", as they called them, on their hands, and others with weals on their backs, but I do not recollect that the castigation did them any good, but the very reverse.'[46]

Some boys felt frustrated by the narrow curriculum. One, W. H. Herford, left the school after two years in 1835 to join a

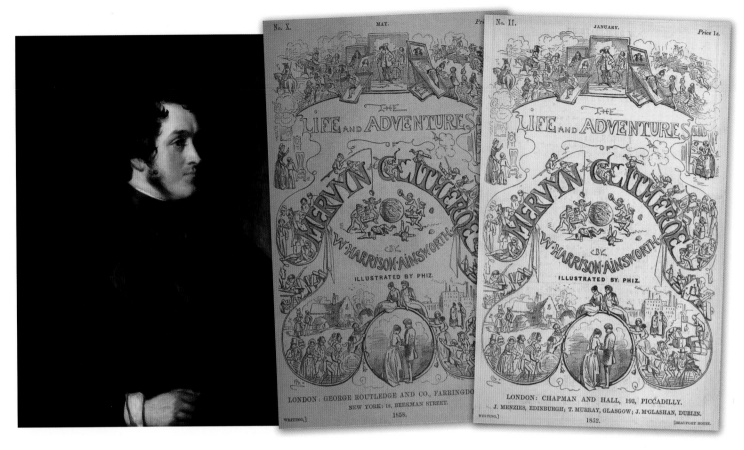

private school, later writing to the master of the latter how 'the introduction to literature, the rational geometry, and the natural sciences, which you provided for us, were all rich, rich feasts after starvation'.[47]

The Chancery-approved scheme formalised the teaching of English, French, arithmetic and mathematics, and also introduced German and natural philosophy, or science, a subject largely ignored in most schools. It specified an external examination every year by examiners from either Oxford or Cambridge. Most controversially, it proposed the addition of a new boarding house. Even as the legal wrangle over the scheme was still moving slowly through the courts, the English School was opened in January 1837, the year in which Jeremiah Smith was succeeded by Elsdale. Although it was quickly over-subscribed, it never met expectations. It was seen by many parents as little better than the lower school, a training ground for boys to acquire over no more than a year or two the elementary skills needed to fill a clerk's job. Teaching was reduced to the basics in most subjects, while few boys opted for maths or French. As a result, the experiment was criticised for delivering an education that was either too simple or too advanced.

The court case was decided by degrees. Over the course of ten years the court torpedoed the strategy pursued by successive High Masters and supported by the trustees since the 1760s. First,

it effectively ended the boarding side of the school. Boarders were declared ineligible for leaving exhibitions in 1839, and in 1849 a further ruling banned masters from taking boarders. Second, the English or Commercial School was given equal status alongside the classical school. While the court reaffirmed the central importance of the classical school, rejecting its replacement with a commercial school, it also decided that any surplus funds after paying the salaries of the classical masters should be applied to extending the English School. Since the demands of the latter seemed infinite, this also put an end to leaving exhibitions.

By 1849 the Reverend Nicholas Germon had been High Master for seven years. An assistant master at the school since the 1820s, he found himself out of tune with the new arrangements. He lost his boarding house, and therefore a large part of his income, and was expected to assume responsibility for the entire school, now formally known as the Manchester Free Grammar School, rather than concentrating on the preparation of the most able boys for university. He resisted a more liberal curriculum, believing that additional subjects distracted boys from concentrating on the high standards in classics they required for university entrance. His antipathy towards change was supported by other masters, by the dean, who was the school's visitor, and many old boys. But Germon could not afford to resign and the trustees were unable to remove him.

William Harrison Ainsworth (c.1816–21) began writing melodramatic gothic plays when he was at school. During his prolific career he was known for turning out historical romances. A contemporary *Punch* cartoon of him is dedicated 'To the greatest axe-and-neck-romancer of our time'. Today, Ainsworth is remembered chiefly for popularising the story of the highwayman Dick Turpin in *Rookwood* (1834).

Above: 'Manchester from Kersal Moor' by William Wyld was commissioned by Queen Victoria after she visited the city in 1851. The Queen noted in her Journal: 'The mechanics and work-people, dressed in their best, were ranged along the streets in their button-holes ... a very intelligent, but painfully unhealthy-looking population they all were, men as well as women.'

Right: Early photograph of Long Millgate.

Germon had become accustomed to maintaining order through violence, and for many boys this was the sharpest recollection of their days at the school. As one old boy later put it, 'we were still in the age of the stick. The very generally received practice was to bring up children by cane', yet even in such an era he could write that 'I often wonder that so many of that generation turned out so well, when I reflect how positively brutal was often the system of their bringing up'. Two of his contemporaries, J. S. H. Atkinson and J. C. G. Parsons, both recalled the free use of the cane by masters. Often it bred only stubborn resistance, epitomised by the case of one boy, thrashed and then expelled by Germon for carving his name on a desk, who simply refused to leave the school until he walked out at the end of the day, saying that one more stroke of the cane, and he would have assaulted the High Master. In spite of all this, discipline was often lax. One

master was so short-sighted that cribs were used openly in class, and he would fail to notice that half the boys would often slip away to the playground to prepare for their next lesson. Annual prize-giving in the schoolroom was an opportunity for boys to use pea-shooters prior to the arrival of guests.[48]

The school buildings were 'often miserably cold. There was no gas in the building and sometimes on a foggy day the room became so dark that the pursuit of knowledge by means of books was impossible … If fog prevailed in the afternoon, an early dismissal was the result'. Outside in the playground the boys played games including 'relievo' and 'staggett', whose rules have long since been lost, as well as whip and spinning tops, darts and marbles. Here too was found the school's inadequate and insanitary toilet block, with no provision for the boys to wash their hands, nor even a tap for a drink of water. All the boys wore square caps, which were generally hated, and to avoid wearing them on the way to and from school they each paid a penny every week to the school porter to keep them in his small shop.[49]

Nevertheless, external examiners concluded in 1859 that the overall standard of education was 'very favourable', although there were variations from subject to subject. The teaching of classics, English and French was largely satisfactory, if under-staffed, but the teaching of maths was criticised for giving simultaneous lectures to boys of varying abilities in classes that were much too large in too little time.[50]

The resistance of the High Master and assistant masters towards change must have been frustrating for the trustees. They were all newcomers, as their predecessors had decided that since the Chancery judgement had changed the school so fundamentally, their resignation would be an opportunity for others to make a fresh start. The new trustees were drawn from leading merchants in Manchester and Salford, half of them nonconformists, half of them churchmen, united in their belief that a purely classical education was no longer sufficient for the sons of the rising middle classes.

The chairman, Sir Elkanah Armitage, was a man of his times. The son of a weaver, he was a self-made man, a successful industrialist and an influential local politician of liberal instincts, who had been mayor of the now incorporated town of Manchester in 1846. Armitage was fully behind the changes made by the Court of Chancery. He believed that the equal status of the English School demanded that the subjects it covered (English literature, French, German, mathematics and the 'Modern Arts and Sciences') should be taught to the same standard as Latin and Greek. This was easier said than done. By the mid-1850s, as the trustees completed their third thorough review of the school's organisation and finances since 1849, it was clear that

Sir Elkanah Armitage, industrialist and politician, served for many years as chair of governors.

the way in which the English School was run had changed little since it had opened, even though it now catered for 150 boys. In particular there was too much learning by rote, which the trustees considered was ineffective 'in giving interest, rousing the intellect or in cultivating taste. The boys are ready in answering questions of fact, but have little or no comprehension of any question involving thought and not directly based on their books'.[51] There was, however, recognition that such methods were one of the few options for a master faced with teaching history, geography, grammar and other subjects to 150 boys aged between eight and twelve. As for the 100 boys in the classical school, few took the opportunity to study French or maths as well as Latin and Greek. The loss of boarders had reduced standards in the upper forms, and things were not helped by the practice of filling the gaps with younger boys promoted too early from lower forms.

The school's finances were in a much worse situation than they had been prior to the 1833 petition. As well as legal costs, and the cost of building the English School and the new boarding house, there was a steady and irreversible decline in revenue from the trustees' monopoly on grinding malt, partly through the rise of the breweries, which could avoid the monopoly by locating outside the town boundaries, and partly through a decline in the number of publicans brewing their own beer. From £3,500 in 1839, revenues had fallen to less than £1,000 in 1849, forcing cuts in salaries,

already reduced because of the decline in boarding. Attempts to improve the management of the mill failed to increase profits and by the mid-1850s the malt mills were losing money. Both mills were let in 1857, one as a warehouse for cotton waste. Later the railway companies would pay the trustees rent for running their lines across the properties once occupied by the mills, but by the end of the century this income, the sole source of revenue for the school, was no more than had been available to the trustees for spending on the school in 1849. In other words, the trustees, in attempting to make improvements, were strapped for cash.

Germon was finally persuaded to resign in the spring of 1859, after the trustees agreed to grant him an annual pension of £200. In his place the trustees chose wisely. They appointed a young man, aged just 27, a fellow and tutor of Corpus Christi College, Oxford, called Frederick Walker. Born in London, and educated at grammar school in Southwark, followed by Rugby, he shone at Oxford, gaining a first in Greats and a second in mathematics, as

well as scholarships in law and Sanskrit, before studying philology in Dresden. He also became a lifelong friend of Benjamin Jowett. Called to the bar in 1858, he had intended to make the law his career but was persuaded against his better judgement by the president of Corpus Christi to take up the High Mastership. In terms of scholarship, intelligence, forthright character and youth, the trustees brought to Manchester the ideal man for creating a new school that would both meet the demands of the town and establish an outstanding national reputation.

Walker lost no time in implementing the recommendations of the report made by the trustees in 1856, and welding together the two parts of the school to create the organisation implied by the settlement of 1849. He weeded out weaker staff and raised the standards of the top form simply by moving the boys out of the schoolroom and into a separate classroom. On the resignation of the lower-school master, he appointed new staff and overhauled the teaching, commenting to the trustees in March 1860 that

'Under this arrangement, the children, I hope, learn writing, Arithmetic, Grammar, history, geography, etc., as much as ever they did, while in addition they receive a tincture of Latin. Thus too the so called English School becomes the principal feeder of the Upper School'.[52] He stressed that he was working 'towards the amalgamation of the separated parts of our foundation into one connected whole'. He drew up a modern timetable for both schools, creating a 30-hour week divided between Latin, Greek, English, French and maths, which were all now taught throughout the school. He created maths sets based on ability, indicative of his belief in high academic standards, which he further emphasised through the introduction of class lists and university honours boards. He adopted the newly introduced Oxford Local Examination, of which Manchester became an examining centre in 1860, to set a benchmark. (The school moved to the Oxford and Cambridge Joint Locals in 1874.) Unlike some schools, Walker entered every eligible pupil, numbering 40 each year. In 1860, drawing was added to the curriculum, and the school quickly developed a leading reputation in the subject under the drawing master, Mr Evans, which led to a visit by John Ruskin to address the boys in 1865. (One boy later recorded of Ruskin's lecture, 'I don't think I understood and enjoyed what Mr Ruskin said as I ought – for one thing his speech was far too rapid.')[53]

All these changes placed Walker at the heart of those already implementing educational changes in a select few grammar schools and public schools, but it must also be remembered that he was introducing these innovations before the great reforming inquiries of the 1860s.

His changes brought speedy results. In October 1861 the reports of the external examiners were wholly complimentary on every department as standards began to rise. By Easter 1862 the English School had effectively been merged with the classical school, with boys entering Lower I and working their way through to Form VI. In October 1862 the examiners concluded, 'The general management and arrangement of the School appears to be very good, and its discipline perfectly satisfactory. In this respect its present condition, as compared with former years, shews a distinct improvement.'[54] Although numbers dropped briefly when Latin became compulsory throughout the school, they soon revived, and by 1862 there were more applicants than places. This allowed Walker to introduce the first entrance examination,

overcoming previous criticism from the examiners about the deficient educational standard of new boys, but generating further controversy in the correspondence columns of the local newspapers. Walker himself was always on the lookout for able boys whose parents could be persuaded to send them to MGS. Often he plucked them out of the evening classes he held at Owens College, the precursor of the Victoria University of Manchester, giving them private tuition for a term before placing them in the sixth form. In 1863 all 12 boys in Walker's classical sixth were elected to open scholarships or exhibitions in classics at Oxford and Cambridge. The Taunton Commission, which investigated English secondary schools in the 1860s, recorded in 1866 that the school had 39 boys up at either Oxford or Cambridge, of whom 20 were open scholars or exhibitioners. 'As much as this cannot be said of any other school in England, and it is all the more remarkable because this School is purely a Day School.'[55]

Parents were now clamouring to send their sons to the school. Walker's rapid success posed a problem for the trustees, whose resources were simply insufficient to fund any expansion to cope with the demand for more places. The school was overcrowded and understaffed, with classes numbering 40 or 50 boys, a situation made worse because the trustees could not afford to pay realistic salaries. This made it difficult to recruit talented new staff while existing staff, the trustees noted, 'by way of increasing their income devote so much of their spare time to

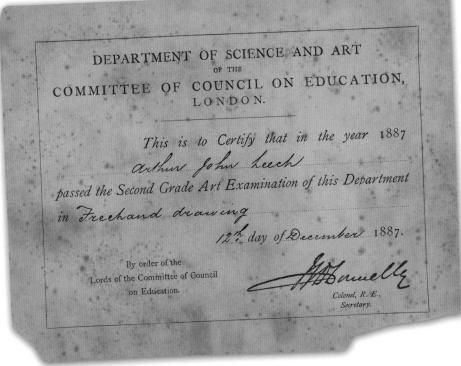

Clerical work and private teaching as to come to their School duties with impaired energies'. Lack of funds also made it impossible to begin the teaching of either modern languages or science, both of which Walker was eager to introduce. The solution, the trustees agreed, was for every boy to be charged moderate fees (four guineas was suggested), excepting some 'whom the Trustees may deem it necessary on account of their poverty to admit gratuitously', and consent would be sought from the Charity Commission.[56]

This decision opened up a fissure between school and town even deeper than the one that had appeared in the 1830s. The old boys were outraged, organising a petition that was also signed by several masters who disliked the changes Walker was making. Rather vindictively, the old boys refused to hold another annual dinner until Walker left the school. The town council also opposed the idea of charging fees, as did a public meeting held in October 1863. The trustees refuted the accusation that poor boys were being deprived of a free education, pointing out that most boys had come from the ranks of those who would not be deterred by paying fees. Many grammar schools were in any case already charging fees. When James Bryce, assistant commissioner of the Taunton Commission, visited MGS in 1866, he confirmed the trustees' views on the social composition of the boys.

> Manchester Grammar School is used by all classes, but the really poor are scantily represented. A third of the boys are the sons of shopkeepers, clerks and warehousemen. Another third are the sons of the better shopkeepers, and merchants of moderate fortune. The rest are the sons of professional men, for owing to its classical character the Manchester school is par excellence for clergy, doctors and lawyers.[57]

Walker was the subject of personal attacks, and the trustees were relieved to hear that he had failed in his application for the headship of Charterhouse. This personal animosity delayed serious consideration by the trustees of a compromise suggested by a committee of the town council, that school funds should support 250 free places, compensated by charging pupils over this number higher fees of 12 guineas. The trustees eventually backed this idea, which gained the support of another public meeting in early 1865, although controversy still raged in the newspapers, and new proposals were submitted to the Charity Commission at the end of 1865. The Commission approved the new scheme but its remaining opponents were sufficiently encouraged by a change in government in 1866 to appeal to the House of Lords, which finally decided in favour of the scheme in April 1867. The foundations for the modern school had at last been laid.

Photograph of Long Millgate, 1900. The two older boys may have been pupils.

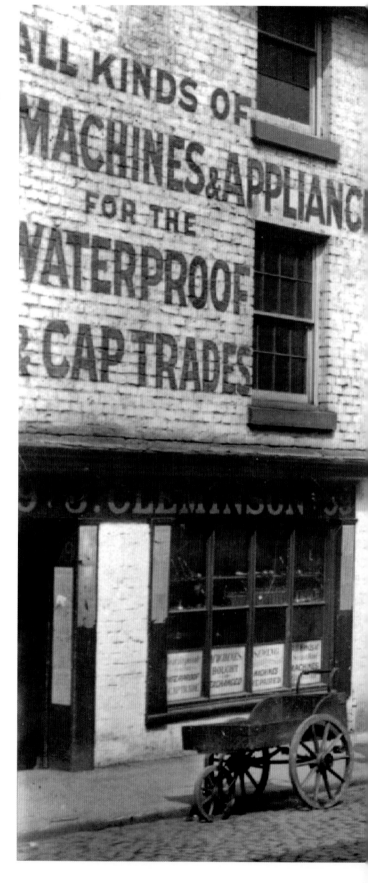

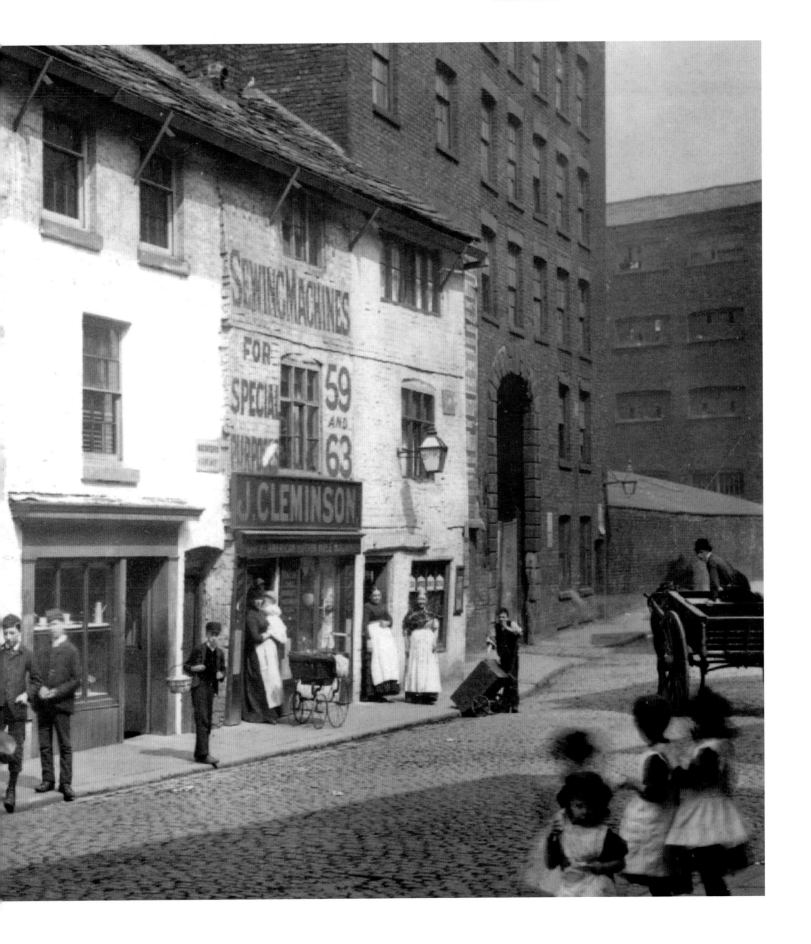

THE MODERN FOUNDATION 1867–1903

'Boys of All Classes and Creeds'

The 1867 scheme had three main consequences, and all three became defining characteristics of the school. First, the school was organised into classical and modern sides (later followed by a science side), a structure that would remain in place for nearly a century. Second, it created 250 foundation scholars, supported by the school's endowments, demonstrating the school's commitment to providing a free education to the most able boys, regardless of income. Third, it left the school's finances in a parlous condition: with the foundation scholars absorbing all the endowment income, income from fee-payers was scarcely sufficient to run the school on a daily basis, let alone invest in capital developments. Yet if additional subjects were to be taught to the same high standards as classics to more boys, it was reckoned that only a school of 1,000 boys would be viable. The conundrum was that the school required the facilities to cater for so many more boys in advance of their arrival. It was a task that would tax the trustees, the High Master and the receiver (as the bursar was known) for decades to come.

Right: A view of the river Irwell in the 1850s at Albert Bridge. The image shows the changing use of the river within a matter of years as the Industrial Revolution accelerated.

Opposite: The main entrance of the Long Millgate site.

The school was fortunate to be able to call on the aid of Edward Langworthy, the vice-chairman of the trustees, and one of the authors of the 1856 report on the future of the school. Extraordinary wealth had been created in and around Manchester and Edward Langworthy was an extraordinarily wealthy businessman. His money came from the profits of the cotton business he had set up with his brothers in Salford in 1840. For Langworthy, wealth brought responsibility, and he was active in local politics and a considerable philanthropist. On his death in 1874, his generosity to the school earned him the title of 'our second founder'. To fund new school buildings a public appeal had been proposed but this had to be postponed because of a recession in trade. Instead, Langworthy provided the site adjacent to the existing school buildings in Long Millgate and subscribed funds along with his fellow trustees. The new buildings would accommodate 500 boys, double the existing number,

Entrance
Manchester
Grammar School.

Harry A Morist

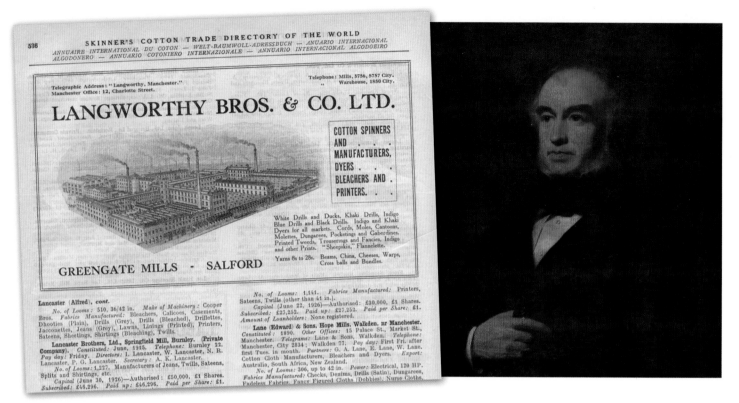

536

Telephone: Mills, 5756, 5757 City.
Warehouse, 1850 City.

Telegraphic Address: "Langworthy, Manchester."
Manchester Office: 12, Charlotte Street.

LANGWORTHY BROS. & CO. LTD.

COTTON SPINNERS
AND . . .
MANUFACTURERS,
DYERS . . .
BLEACHERS AND .
PRINTERS. . .

White Drills and Ducks, Khaki Drills, Indigo
Blue Drills and Black Drills. Indigo and Khaki
Dyers for all markets. Cords, Moles, Cantoons,
Molettes, Dungarees, Pocketings and Gaberdines.
Printed Tweeds, Trouserings and Fancies, Indigo
and other Prints. "Sheepskin," Flannelette.
Yarns 8s to 28s. Beams, China, Cheeses, Warps,
Cross balls and Bundles.

GREENGATE MILLS - SALFORD

Caption for portrait photograph:

Edward Langworthy's benevolence led to him being regarded as the school's 'second founder'. His wealth came from the cotton mills that he set up with his brothers.

and provide dedicated teaching facilities for art, maths and the classics, allowing the old building to be converted for teaching science. By the time the public appeal was launched by the bishop of Manchester in May 1870, Langworthy's total contribution, including the value of land, had risen to the massive sum of £10,000. On his death he left a further £10,000, alongside similar donations to other local causes, to create scholarships for boys who otherwise would have left school at 14.

Once again the idea of relocating the school was considered, and a site was identified in leafy Ladybarn, four miles away in Rusholme. But the trustees were conscious of their reliance upon the railways in their objective of building up a thousand-strong school full of able boys, who the railways could deliver into the heart of Manchester from a 30-mile radius. It was considered impractical to ferry the boys out to Rusholme, and the trustees of Manchester Grammar School were nothing if not practical: the go-ahead was given for new buildings in Long Millgate. The importance of the railways more than outweighed the continuing decline of the school's immediate vicinity, next door to pubs throwing out drunks who stumbled past the school door, backed by a river so dank that the stench sometimes compelled the evacuation of the overlooking classrooms.

Attempts to calculate the rate at which the school would fill up proved hopeless. The resurgent popularity of the school meant that the buildings were already too small by the time they were opened in October 1871, making it necessary to hire every other

available room in the street as temporary classrooms. But the imposing new buildings, dominating Long Millgate, expressed the school's confidence in its future, and reasserted its presence in the heart of a great city. The city happily embraced the school, with the banquet celebrating the opening hosted by the corporation in the town hall, presided over by the earl of Derby, the latest representative of the Stanley family and then prime minister, with Dr Benjamin Jowett, a friend of the High Master, as guest speaker.

This outward confidence was supported by the school's academic results. One of the most striking developments was the school's rapid rise to prominence in science, a subject still largely ignored in many schools. Walker, a man steeped in the classics, had told the Taunton Commission that, 'If an orderly and comprehensive system of scientific education could be constructed, it should hold the first place in a boy's education, literary training the second',[58] and he set about doing exactly that. He recognised that able boys without a taste for the classics might well have an aptitude for science. The first chemistry teacher, Dr Marshall Watts, appointed in 1867, was succeeded by Francis Jones in 1872, while the first physics teacher, Mr Angell, arrived in 1869. In 1873, after the conversion of the old school into a laboratory, middle-school boys were being taught nine and a half hours of science every week, and sixth-form scientists 17 hours. Only Clifton College and Cheltenham College came close, with Clifton and Manchester almost monopolising science scholarships at Oxford and Cambridge. It was a record the school would sustain throughout the rest of the century, producing many fine scientists.

Among them was Lazarus Fletcher, later Sir Lazarus, fellow of the Royal Society, distinguished mineralogist and director of the British Museum. He was the first boy from the school to win an open science scholarship (the Brackenbury) to Balliol, and in later life recounted the very personal interest that Walker had taken in him. Fletcher, having joined the school in 1865, had reached the classical sixth and was uncertain of his future. Walker encouraged him to stay on but recommended that he should transfer to science, a subject he had never been taught. Moving down to the science fifth, Fletcher had to give up the tassel on his square cap that denoted sixth-form status, giving rise to rumours that he had been demoted. Walker helped Fletcher through his extended studies by paying him to correct exercise books from the lower forms and assist in the chemistry lab, which also gave him great practical experience.

Recognising the need to support many able boys during their school studies, Walker did not hesitate to engage in what today would be called networking, introducing himself to wealthy Manchester merchants and persuading them to endow scholarships or exhibitions for the school. One merchant, C. F. Beyer, was so struck by Walker's forceful and direct approach that

he left the school £10,000. Walker was also successful in finding benefactors to endow new leaving exhibitions, which the school could no longer afford to fund. Mumford in his history records the foundation of 27 scholarships at the school between 1874 and 1878. For many years this number by far outstripped the provision made by the local authorities.

Walker believed that the full potential of a boy's natural ability could be properly developed only in alliance with hard work and self-motivation. At speech day in 1873 he told the boys, 'The chief requisite for success is a determined will, without which genius itself is powerless, but, armed with which, the dullest boy may achieve success.'[59] As a former pupil later recalled, 'A boy was made to act for himself, think for himself, and read for himself.'[60] For Walker, hard work, self-motivation and ability produced the outstanding results, principally measured by Oxbridge awards, that he believed to be the only worthwhile riposte to the school's critics. He was a hard taskmaster. John Hamilton, later the first Viscount Sumner and a distinguished law lord, entered the school in 1870, and characterised Walker as 'a tyrant', 'brought there to have his own way', who impressed on boys 'the importance of getting on'. He remembered how Walker confronted one boy who had suddenly changed his mind about Oxford half-way through his entrance exam. 'Mr Walker looked at him and said: "Go home to

The school built in 1871 was financed largely by Edward Langworthy.

Manchester Grammar School.—Time Table.

Science fifth, 1898, and a timetable from 1870.

price to pay for this, with one later saying that 'it must be admitted that the School was to a great extent a mere forcing-house for exceptional brains'.[61] The temptation was to move able boys too quickly through the school, since there was always room at the top. One boy found himself moved up seven forms in his first year and three in his second. Another observer noted that 'the physical cost at which the successes of MGS boys had been attained was hardly yet realised. Walker had stoutly refused to believe in the possibility of overwork … but experience has tended to show that over-pressure in boyhood may have disastrous consequences in later years'.[62] This would give rise to the myth that MGS boys never reached their potential at university, one that the school was still battling to overcome in the 1950s.

Charles Hughes' sister recognised that Walker's sixth form produced 'some remarkably fine-minded scholars'.[63] John Hamilton was one of those scholars, finding the High Master 'a wise and resolute autocrat', and sailing through Walker's classical sixth, which inculcated in Hamilton a love for the beauty of speech and exactness of thought and led him to win a classical scholarship to Balliol.[64] Walker's friend Jowett, master of Balliol, greatly valued the calibre of the boys from Manchester who won places at the college, regarding them as 'among the best of our Oxford students'. He would describe the school as one 'which by merit has won its way to a place among the great public schools of England', and marvelled at the affection so many boys had for Walker, causing him to ask the High Master why it was that his boys worshipped him as no other head of an English school was worshipped.[65]

Another former pupil, quoted in Walker's 1910 obituary in the *Manchester Guardian*, agreed Walker could be fierce but noted how this masked a more compassionate side. He was, he wrote, 'a man of the most severely sarcastic, almost brutal exterior, but his bark was worse than his bite, and he had the gentlest heart under his rugged hide. If his rebuke was irony in more senses than one, his praises were golden, and not stinted when deserved.'[66] Testament to this compassionate side of the man comes from a note preserved in the school archive, written by Walker in response to kind words from a father grieving the loss of his 17-year-old son, William Kelly, a pupil at the school. 'I am deeply touched. This is the first death I know of a pupil under my immediate care. A year ago he was a playful light-hearted boy. I have watched with interest and pleasure his gradual passage into the thoughtfulness

your father, boy, and tell him I never wish to see your face again." The boy went and but for the fact that he was a person of some strength of mind, I think he would have gone away and hanged himself.' The sister of Charles Hughes, who joined the school in the early 1860s, writing after his death in 1917, pointed out the pressure placed on sixth formers, describing her brother's 'incredible' reading list, and reporting how 'he used to say that three months of it would have killed him'.

Undoubtedly boys were under pressure, and those under most pressure were the most able, those who would make a mark for the school, whose achievements would fly the flag for the school not just in Manchester, not just in neighbouring boroughs, where there was growing parental clamour for places, but also in the nation as a whole. Some of Walker's pupils believed there was a

By 1872 the school had grown so large that Speech Day was moved to the Free Trade Hall.

and conscientiousness of manhood … you had a son of whom with reason you might be proud.'[67]

While no doubt a few less than adequate masters felt the lash of Walker's tongue, by and large he was regarded by staff as encouraging, patient and supportive. One colleague recollected Walker's innate understanding that the revival of the school depended upon both winning the support of staff and making them realise that they shared that responsibility. Walker publicly praised the commitment of his staff, lamenting that their salaries were limited by the difficult state of the school's finances, and expressing the hope that one day the post of assistant master at MGS 'would not be one of barren honour but of adequate emolument'.[68] The lessons many staff learned from Walker helped them to move on to higher positions elsewhere. He also revitalised the careers of existing staff, including the Reverend George Perkins, a former pupil, who had been on the staff since 1848 and became Walker's second master.

As a further part of his strategy for enhancing the school's status, Walker set about giving the school new or revived traditions. In 1860, after an absence of 22 years, speech day was reintroduced, and in 1872, as the school grew larger, it was held for the first time in Manchester's imposing Free Trade Hall, another sign of the school's determination to become an integral

part of the city's fabric once more, but also a platform for the High Master's views. In the same year he also raised the status of Founders' Day, regularly held each year on 1 May in the cathedral, by inviting a guest preacher for the first time.

But what of the vast majority of boys who never reached university, those who left early for careers in trade and commerce, who populated the lawyers' offices and the trading exchanges and the factories, whose efforts kept their great city's economy purring away? Walker, like so many heads of similar schools, had to contend with the early departure of many boys, a fact noted by the examiners in 1868, when they reported that, 'There is unusually good material in the boys and we think that under the management of the present head Master all that is wanted to secure great results is that the boys should remain longer so as to obtain the full benefit of the instruction.'[69] And while the annual examination reports recorded consistently favourable opinions in almost every subject on the quality of the teaching and the

Right: Staff and boys, *c.*1900.

Below: Today's visitors are welcomed by the bust of Frederick Walker, located in the reception area of the school.

ability and industry of the boys, there was evidence that the level of attainment outside the highest forms was less consistent. One examiner covering the classics pointed to the lower classical form, Transitus, where 'in the lower part of the Form, there was still in most cases evidence of work, [but] the proficiency actually attained was small'. As for those candidates entered for classics in the local board examinations who were not members of classical forms but mainly studying maths and science, 'I cannot give a favourable report. The greater number of them failed entirely in their classical work.' This was echoed in the report covering maths, where the highest forms were outstanding, and the general standard was much above the average, but those boys 'merely candidates for Certificates seemed very unequal in merit; while some few did well, others knew but little and that little very imperfectly'.[70] One boy later observed that in his time 'those of more slowly maturing abilities were disheartened by finding themselves left behind and were apt to be neglected.'[71]

Nevertheless, Walker's policy of entering every eligible boy for the board examinations (which he also used as a de facto entrance exam for the sixth form) at the very least

provided those who were successful with a valuable qualification that opened the door to various professions, while the fact that they had entered by entrance exam the increasingly intellectual portals of a school whose reputation was rising also counted in their favour with employers. Walker welcomed able boys from all backgrounds into the school, and was blind to social status, telling one more affluent mother in his usual blunt manner, 'Madam, so long as your son behaves properly and the fees are paid, we shall ask no embarrassing questions about your social status.'[72] (Conversely, the growing stature of the school was encouraging some boys to see themselves in a more superior light, with one anonymous contributor to the school magazine in 1873, lamenting the lack of a school cap, observing that 'the greater number of us might be taken for National School Boys'.[73])

Walker's concentration on academic success led to criticism that the education he offered the most able boys was too narrow. Charles Hughes' sister wrote that 'there were no songs, no games, no playing fields, no physical exercises of any description, and I do not think that any of the masters took the least notice of the boys outside of school hours'. But Walker's challenge was immense, he was starting with very little, and for him the most immediate way to revive the school was to raise its academic stature. And the school was constantly striving to keep pace with the growing number of boys; the new buildings, built for 500, were filled with 750 boys by the end of Walker's time.

Nevertheless, efforts were made to build up activities outside the classroom. In June 1873 the first athletics sports took place on a ground at Heaton Park, four miles north of the school. The lack of playing fields hindered sporting development but rugby matches were arranged, with two sides playing against opponents such as Huddersfield College, Wellington College and Broughton Wasps, initially using a ground at Kersal, a similar distance from the school, and efforts were made to keep school cricket alive. Several boat races were held between teams of boys and masters on the insalubrious waters of the Irwell, a boxing club was formed and the first gym master was appointed in 1869. The first overseas school trip was organised during the summer of 1873, when a dozen boys spent a fortnight in France, and a party of senior boys under the science master, Francis Jones, were taken on an excursion into the Derbyshire Dales in the summer of 1875. A debating society, that stalwart part of so many schools, was initiated, whose early debates hinted at a conservative cast of mind among the participants, as they voted against independence for the colonies, were in favour of Napoleon III, and agreed that 'the average culture of the working classes does not qualify them to take a direct part in the task of legislation'.[74] There was a philosophical (or science) society and in the spring of 1874 a chess

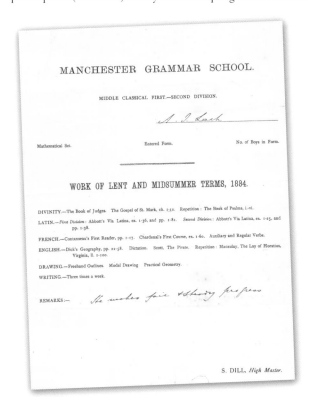

club was formed. Under an energetic and talented art master, Zachariah Pritchard, appointed in 1869, drawing was taught to all but the most senior boys, annual exhibitions were begun and many pupils won prize medals. Pritchard extended art into the wider community, beginning very successful day and evening classes, which won for the school recognition as a school of art by the national examining authority based in South Kensington.

Walker was an ambitious man, and had applied for headships at other schools. He was appointed High Master of St Paul's School, London, another leading day school, in 1876.[75] The trustees parted with him only reluctantly but he went with their best wishes. He would spend the rest of his life at St Paul's, remaining as High Master until 1910, and making as much of an impression on that school as he had at Manchester.

He left Manchester as the trustees were preparing to adopt a revised scheme of governance. This stemmed from the precarious state of the school's finances. The school was regularly running at a loss, and its limited endowments were no longer sufficient to support the large number of free places. The scheme proposed by the trustees in 1874 and approved by the Charity Commission in 1877 reduced the number of free scholars to 150 to match the resources available, while reserving half the places for pupils from

Above: A junior class, *c.*1910. In 1919, the Bulkeley-Allen Collection, comprising over 95 cases of birds, was loaned to the school and eventually gifted in 1959.

Left: Letter home outlining the study schedule for the Lent and Midsummer terms, 1884.

Right: Statue of Oliver Heywood in Albert Square, unveiled in 1894. The inscription on the pedestal states that Heywood's life had been one 'devoted to the public good'.

Below right: Sir Samuel Dill, High Master (1872–88).

Christi. He would later achieve a leading reputation as a classical scholar, and would be knighted for his work in transforming Queen's College, Belfast, into a university.

Dill was a shy and sensitive man who found the frequent comparisons made with Walker difficult. He himself confessed that Walker's stature made him feel that in taking over as High Master he was 'doing a daring thing. I confess that at times the magnitude of the task of maintaining the efficiency and distinction of this School almost overwhelmed me.'[77] The burden of his post would bring about a breakdown in his health that would cause him to be absent from school for several months during the second half of 1882.

Dill was taking over MGS as it was facing external challenges. There was competition from the new higher grade schools run by the local school boards, which were taking more of the able elementary pupils once destined for MGS, offering what many parents considered an education more appropriate for sons whose futures lay in local trade and commerce. Walker had left behind a school that had concentrated on the classical and science sides. This had the no doubt unintentional effect of making the modern side feel less of a priority, for which one reason may well have been that neither Oxford nor Cambridge at that time awarded scholarships in modern languages. But entry into one or other of the sides also determined how much or how little of any particular subject a boy studied, which, for instance, meant that boys on the classical side learned little science, with obvious adverse effects on their overall education.

local elementary schools, and raised fees to 20 guineas a year. The opportunity was also taken to transform the trustees into an enlarged body of governors, while the president of Corpus Christi lost his right to appoint the High Master, and later his right to lifetime tenure. The new board of governors included several representative appointments, strengthening links with the universities of Oxford and Cambridge but also with the local community, with places for the nominees of local councils and the school boards of Manchester and Salford. The first chairman was Oliver Heywood, a wealthy and prominent local banker, a man of liberal sympathies, and a generous supporter of local charities and other causes. As the school said farewell to Walker, Heywood announced the governors' ambitious building plans, aiming to create over the next few years 'a great and good central School for 1,000 boys'.[76]

Walker's successor was appointed prior to the implementation of the new scheme and, as such, was the last High Master chosen by the president of Corpus Christi. Samuel Dill, aged 43, was a classical scholar like his predecessor and had been dean of Corpus

Dill recognised the achievements of his predecessor, and wanted to build on them, but he also wanted to broaden the scope of the education offered by MGS inside and outside the classroom, partly to win back some of the boys being lost to the higher grade schools, but also because he was convinced that a more all-round education would better equip boys for their future lives. At his second speech day in 1878, while he praised the continuing achievements of boys in passing exams and winning awards, he also indicated that he was aware of the dangers of overwork and of 'treating knowledge as material merely for immediate use'.[78]

He saw how much MGS brought to the life and work of Manchester, and worked hard to make the school a more integral part of the city. The fund-raising appeal for the new buildings, which once again elicited several substantial donations from generous local benefactors, sought to strengthen these ties. As the school magazine noted, 'A School of 850 or more boys, drawn from all classes alike, must be doing no small work and taking no small part in equipping the minds and moulding the characters of the Manchester men, or rather the Lancashire men of the future. To many our School furnishes the only, to many more the best attainable means of obtaining a liberal education. Recent changes have broadened its already broad basis, whilst at the same time they have rendered it more definitely a civic institution.' Dill stressed the importance of the school's free places and the more than 50 scholarships available to support boys both while they were at school and while they were at university, which meant, he told parents, that 'their School was now open to boys of all classes and creeds in the kingdom, and by means of these scholarships any boy of industry, ability and good conduct might make his way from the humblest elementary schools to the older universities'. The prime importance of the school, he insisted, was 'preparing these boys to take their places as useful citizens of this great community'.[79]

But the importance Dill placed on education for the sons of Manchester was not entirely shared by those in charge of organising education across the city. Throughout this period there was a constant shortage of school places within the city, as the efforts of the local school board to set up more schools met with opposition. First the opposition came from churchmen appointed to the board who were more focused on protecting the interests of denominational schools; and second from a body claiming to represent the interests of poor parents deprived of the earning capacity of their sons and daughters, but actually a vehicle for ratepayers seeking cuts in the education budget. MGS suffered from the weaknesses of the city's education system. Despite what he had to say about overwork, Dill emphasised the extraordinary effort made by the typical MGS boy, noting that whereas a boy

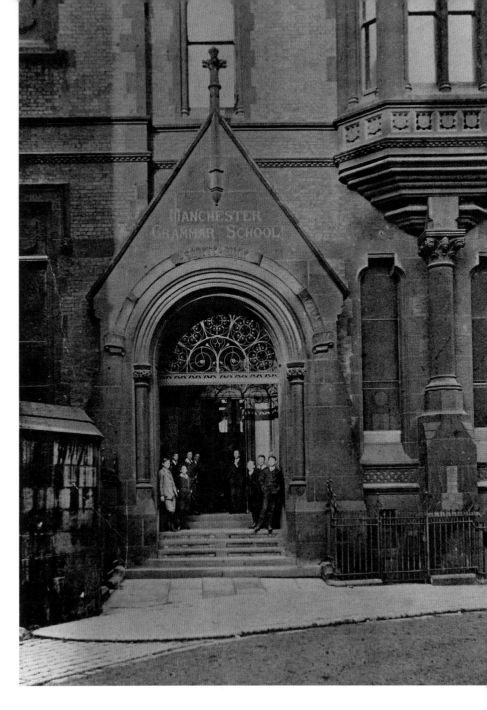

prepared for Harrow or Marlborough was in educational terms years ahead on entry, Lancashire boys joining MGS at 12 to 14 had to achieve in three or four years the work of six. He warned that 'if the Manchester boys are to compete with the boys from the Public Schools without injury to health, they must start early in the race, and our Secondary Education must be organised'.[80] MGS seemed to be an isolated island within the city and, despite the school's best efforts, often ignored, leading Dill to criticise the lack of support from the general public and the city's leaders, and lamenting that the school's 'capacities of service to the community were quietly ignored'.[81] This had some effect, resulting in a short-lived arrangement between the school board and the school for joint scholarship examinations initiated in 1887.

Boys on the front steps of Long Millgate, c.1900.

A gym team and boys in the new gymnasium
which was situated in the extended school
building of 1880. The master is John MacAuley,
who drilled boys from 1898 to 1945.

The extended school buildings were completed in 1880.
Providing additional classrooms, a gymnasium, a modern chemistry
laboratory and a lecture theatre, they enabled the school to welcome
more boys. Under Dill, numbers peaked at 953 in 1883, although
the effects of competition with other schools saw a fall to 831 by
the time he left five years later. Twelve hundred guests attended the
reception for the opening of the new buildings in December 1880.
The venerable old owl almost became a casualty of modernisation,
following the demolition of the old school building, but it was
rescued from a heap of debris by Francis Jones, the science master.
Despite rivalry from the city's higher grade schools, demand
for places remained high, and foundation scholarships were
oversubscribed (in 1880, 346 boys applied for 70 places).

Nevertheless, for some families the financial implications of
sending a boy to MGS made it an almost impossible aspiration.
Ernest Barker, a labourer's son, later a distinguished political
theorist, was able to take up his scholarship in 1886 only because
his grandfather paid for his railway season ticket into Manchester.
Clothes were also a costly problem for a boy unused to wearing
collars and who had only ever worn clogs. He could never afford
lunch, sometimes taking his own, sometimes going to a little
basement eating-house among the nearby warehouses, where

there was meat and potatoes for fourpence. A limited number of
maintenance allowances, worth up to 20 shillings to cover incidental
costs, were introduced in the following year by the governors, but
only in response to the school boards, whose own scholarships
included such a sum. Even then, some families still struggled.

Within the expanded buildings and improved facilities,
Dill sought to achieve a more balanced curriculum, one that
not only provided for those seeking places at university, but also
gave an education to equip the many boys leaving the school for
work. So, for instance, boys on the classical side were taught
more science, a course in practical physics was initiated, and a
practical commercial course was introduced, although the latter
had as little success at MGS as at the other secondary schools
where such courses appeared. Most importantly, perhaps, was
Dill's reorganisation of the modern side, and the creation of the
modern sixth form out of a form for boys applying for the civil
service. Between 1879 and 1888 the modern side grew from just
over one-third of all boys to almost half. It was a popular move,
and without it the school's numbers would probably
have dropped further. Dill was visionary in insisting that most
of the staff teaching modern subjects should be specialists rather
than generalists as was common at the time. All this led one

Tug of War junior cup, first awarded in 1890.

examiner to remark in 1883 that the school 'bids fair to have the most complete and best organised modern side of any school in England'.[82]

None of this was achieved at the expense of the school's academic reputation; in fact, in 1886, MGS boys achieved a record 18 open scholarships and exhibitions. The bishop of Manchester in his address at speech day in 1881 had already compared MGS favourably with Eton, adding to applause in the Free Trade Hall that 'Manchester boys were not afraid to meet Eton boys in fair competition and upon even terms'.[83] One of Dill's great successors, Paton, would later defend Dill against his detractors by citing as his greatest achievement the reform of the modern side, which he believed was the first in the country to gain recognition from the universities. Dill believed just as much as his predecessor in pushing the most able boys, which led to similar complaints of over-working and hot-housing. The brightest boys were still moved through the school at a rapid rate. Ernest Barker, for instance, found himself moved from upper classical first to upper classical remove within five terms.

But Dill also wanted to bring boys together outside the classroom and broaden their interests. One of his aims was to break down the boundaries, social as well as academic, between the classical and modern sides. He began a termly series of lectures and encouraged a number of new clubs and societies, including the literary society, the natural history society, the photographic society, the modern languages society, the dramatic society, the glee club and the rifle corps. The debating society began a tradition of annual summer picnics in the Derbyshire countryside, and the natural history society made regular excursions to destinations like Ashley and Delamere. The boxing competition was held every year, the new gymnasium proved a great motivator for the boys, and school hours were changed to permit afternoon games. In 1881, a seven-year lease was taken on a cricket field, at last

Below: The library that was home to the classical sixth in the building of 1880.

Michael George
Glazebrook, High
Master (1888–90),
with masters.

allowing a cricket club to be formed on a permanent basis, and the first swimming competition was held at Blackfriars Street baths in Salford. In February that year the school gained its first rugby international, when W. R. Richardson, who was still at school, appeared for England against Ireland. By 1887 more than half the school had joined the athletic club and football was proving popular, with the first school matches taking place. A lacrosse club was formed, with matches taking place on the South Manchester ground, the first against Cheadle Hulme being tied 4–4. In the same year the rugby teams were supplied for the first time with jerseys in the school colours, the first team jersey distinguished by the school arms on the left breast. By 1888 Dill felt able to say that the school's 'great weakness – the absence of a common life outside the classroom – is in the process of being cured'.[84]

Dill opened up the school to the outside world in two distinct ways. The first was another attempt to bridge the gap between school and city. The Hugh Oldham Lads' Club was formed to give recreational and educational opportunities to boys from poorer homes around Rochdale Road and Oldham Road, not far from the school. Such clubs were supported by boys' schools across the country, and the initiative was suggested by a former pupil who had been involved with a similar venture organised by Westminster School. It received Dill's whole-hearted support, and was up and running by the summer of 1888, based in a vacant police station in Livesey Street, just off Oldham Road. MGS boys raised more

than half the funds and sixth formers played an important role in running the club. It was formally opened by Prince Albert Victor, the duke of Clarence, on 20 October, shortly after Dill had left the school, by which time there were more than 1,200 members.

Dill's second initiative was the introduction of open days, although the term did not yet exist, and they were described as 'conversaziones'. The first, held in December 1885, was attended by 800 guests, and featured a musical entertainment, a gym display and several exhibitions. It was a great success and became an annual event.

Even under the fearsome Walker, discipline had left something to be desired. By comparison with his predecessor, Dill was a much gentler character; it was said that boys sent up to the High Master for corporal punishment were caned by the janitor since Dill could not bear to carry out the punishment himself. One boy recalled that he and his peers behaved like 'young hooligans' and masters used the cane freely to rein them in. MGS was undoubtedly a rowdy school. Generally good discipline in the classroom contrasted with near anarchy outside. The din from the boys forced masters to shout to make themselves heard, and no doubt this was not helped by the school's physical situation, with the constant hubbub from Long Millgate, a combination of rumbling horse-drawn traffic, brass bands, organ grinders and concertina players, that in summer made it almost impossible to conduct lessons with the windows open.

Into this riotous atmosphere arrived Dill's successor. A Balliol graduate and a distinguished scholar, Michael Glazebrook was 35 years old when he became High Master. He took immediate action over discipline, removing in his first year 40 'undesirable members of the School' following 'frank reports' sent to their parents. This had an instant effect and allowed Glazebrook to reduce the number of punishments of all kinds while raising standards of behaviour. He also produced the first version of a handbook, *Customs and Curricula*, that would go through many revisions under his successors. Good discipline raised the tone of the school, he believed, and engendered courtesy, public spirit and self-control.

Influenced by his education at Dulwich College and ten years spent teaching at Harrow, he aimed to bring the traditions of the public schools to a city grammar school and strengthen the school's identity as a corporate body. To assist him, he appointed a man who had been on the short-list for the High Mastership; A. T. Pollard, a former headmaster of Oxford High School, became the school's first vice-master. Glazebrook fostered the idea of pastoral care, encouraging form masters to take responsibility for their boys and to interview parents. They also became responsible for the general supervision of a boy's homework, bringing coordination to an area where hardly any had previously existed. Fortnightly form lists sent home to parents encouraged boys to pay greater attention in class. This was part of Glazebrook's belief that school and home must work in partnership; he had stressed from the outset that a boy's education in school was incomplete without supportive parents at home.

Glazebrook took a more collegiate view of school management and established regular staff meetings. He believed that the schoolmaster 'is not merely a teacher of boys; he is a maker of men, and it is not the few, but the many, that he desires to influence' and, like many High Masters, influenced a number of junior staff to aim for greater things, such as Alfred Hughes, later professor of education at Birmingham.[85] He valued teaching as a profession and was an active member of the Manchester branch of the Teachers' Guild, becoming president in 1890, when he gave an address on specialisation at universities.

Glazebrook considered that the sixth form had gained a reputation for Olympian aloofness that was unhealthy for the unity of the school. He tackled this partly by giving selected sixth formers responsibility as prefects. Some, like Ernest Barker, believed in retrospect that this was the High Master bringing to MGS his 'public school ways', which also included new school caps and hats, with boys below the sixth form given caps striped in dark and light blue with a little silver owl, while sixth formers wore a hard black straw hat with a riband of similar colours, and prefects donned mortar boards. Barker was not unhappy. 'The little uniform gave me a new sense of dignity, and a new consciousness of membership of the school: indeed its coming coincided for me with the beginning of a corporate sense, or a feeling of esprit de corps.'[86] But the straw hats were never popular, largely because of the ridicule they provoked outside the school, with arguments for and against their retention regularly recurring in the pages of the school magazine.

The High Master told parents at his first speech day that 'a few successes of clever boys cannot redeem a school from the charge of failure, if it does not do well for the rank and file'.[87] He wanted to broaden the intake in terms of aptitude, and amended the foundation scholarship examination so that a boy was judged on his general merits rather than on his standard in classics alone. This led to greater prominence in the curriculum for modern languages, maths and English literature. The modern side continued to outstrip the classical side in numbers, yet still the universities refused to offer scholarships in most modern subjects. But Glazebrook also recognised the value of the modern side in preparing those boys leaving for commerce and industry, and he made available to the city's employers a registry of boys seeking various types of employment.

The school song, 'Hugh of the Owl', was first sung in 1889.

John Edward King, High Master (1890–1903), and a book given as a prize signed by King.

club, and oversaw the formation of a harriers' club and hockey club. He lamented the lack of a permanent playing field, and wondered if the reason more of Manchester's wealth did not come in the school's direction – 'while it rains gifts and legacies all over the city, there is always a dry spot in Long Millgate' – was because of the misconception that it was a wealthy institution.[88]

Spinning through the school like a whirling top, Glazebrook was gone in three years, leaving to become headmaster of Clifton College in 1891. Coincidentally, his successor, John King, had been educated at Clifton before taking up classics at Lincoln College, Oxford, but the thing that probably counted most in his favour with the governors was that he had spent part of his career teaching at St Paul's under Frederick Walker, who gave him a glowing reference.

Like his immediate predecessors, King believed strongly that the school should provide 'a ladder' upwards for the brightest and poorest boys. This was epitomised in his first year by the fact that the first three names in the list of university honours were those of foundation scholars from elementary schools.[89] His views were shared by the chairman of governors, H. J. Roby, who later became King's father-in-law. Roby had a reputation as an educational reformer, having been secretary of both the Taunton Commission and the Endowed Schools Commission. But he expressed his views, when giving evidence to the Royal Commission on Secondary Education in 1894, in more trenchant class-based terms, saying that he believed that education was a luxury that the poorer classes might do without, although it was only right if a boy of exceptional ability appeared, that he should lifted out of his class. 'I should be most sorry that any boy who really had the capacity and industry should not obtain a very high education but I do not think such boys are very common.' He considered that for poor boys in general 'the study of the humanities was more likely to unfit them for their future sphere than to help them rise out of their present sphere'.[90] These views did nothing to deter the commission from concluding that MGS was foremost among the great English day schools.

With the opportunity for boys to win scholarships not only to the established universities but also to newer, more local institutions, such as Owens College and Victoria University, King believed MGS was a principal pathway to these institutions for local boys. They provided scholarships in a broader range of subjects, but the older universities, too, were extending

2nd Prize

MANCHESTER GRAMMAR SCHOOL.

Prize awarded to

A. D. Markland

Subject Modern Languages

Form Modern Upper Second

Midsummer 1891

J. E. King

High Master.

Glazebrook brought a colleague, John Farmer, to the school, initially to encourage singing, but later as the first director of music in 1890. It was Farmer who wrote the music for the school song, 'Hugh of the Owl', sung for the first time at speech day in 1889. Glazebrook, a fine college athlete, encouraged the athletics scholarships to subjects such as natural science and modern languages. There was still a feeling that the school was more valued in districts such as Salford than it was within Manchester itself, but King also emphasised MGS's wider role, that 'they were not a school for Manchester alone. They were not even a school for Lancashire alone. Many of their boys came from Yorkshire, Cheshire and Derbyshire.'[91] By 1900 62 per cent of boys came from outside the boundaries of Manchester and Salford.[92]

As ever, the main obstacle preventing such boys from ascending the ladder of opportunity was the tendency for parents to send them late and take them away early. The local board examinations may have helped boys to enter the professions but employers were never really satisfied with these qualifications, leading the High Master to complain in 1898 that 'in this country there was no generally accepted test of a modern side education either for parents or employers. The consequence was that few boys remained at school long enough to reach any high degree of proficiency.'[93] Even so the school, King had stated in 1894, strove at all times to offer 'a training which was in the best sense liberal and humanising'.[94]

King's major battle was to sustain numbers. He took over the school when it had 860 boys; by the time he left numbers had fallen to 737. One reason was boys spending too short a time at the school. Another was continuing competition. Partly this came from the extension of science teaching in other schools, supported by legislation and local authority grants. MGS itself benefited from such support, largely from the city council's technical instruction committee, which helped to modernise the school's own facilities, strapped for cash as it was. In 1901 the school also satisfied the conditions for the continuation of science grants from the Board of Education that would also bring the school under the Board for inspection. In the following year Francis Jones, a master at the school, was rightly recognised for his services to the teaching of science when he was awarded an honorary degree from the Victoria University. But the school's pre-eminence in this field was now being challenged.

The impact of competition showed in the composition of the boys admitted to the school between 1888 and 1894, when elementary schools supplied only slightly more than 40 per cent of entrants. By 1895 the High Master was already asking the governors for consent to set up a prep school to feed boys into MGS, and a property was identified in Dover Street. Although this plan petered out, numbers continued to fall, with a noticeable decline in boys applying from Oldham and district, as a result of the foundation of Hulme Grammar School in that year. The proposal for a prep school was revived, with two aims in mind: to halt the decline in numbers and to better prepare boys from local

MGS opened a prep department, South Manchester School, in 1897.

elementary schools prior to their admission to MGS. In January 1897 MGS re-opened the former Chorlton High School as South Manchester School. In the following year, as the school refused to fill all its foundation scholarships because of a decline in the calibre of applicants, a prep form was also started within MGS for boys who were still arriving under-prepared for work in either the classical or modern sides. King was eager to see MGS open prep schools on all sides of the city. He also persuaded the governors to increase the fees for boys entering after the age of 14 to encourage parents to send them earlier. Without this combination of measures numbers might have fallen even further.

Falling numbers, and the tendency for many parents to send their sons to the school for just a couple of years, played havoc with the modern side of the school. The curriculum included French and German (instead of Greek and Latin), English, maths, science, history, geography, divinity and drawing. But the modern side troubled H. W. Eve, the distinguished former head of University College School, who inspected MGS on behalf of the examination board in 1899. He found that the average age of all except one form below the sixth form was just 15 because so many boys entered late, 'many of them to stay a short time only, to "finish" an education scarcely begun. Many of them, too, come from illiterate homes.'[95] Nevertheless he was impressed by the teaching, as indeed he was by the teaching in the much better-organised classical side. But he highlighted the quirks of the system, which meant that boys on the classical side were taught neither history nor geography beyond

From the top: A school visit to the park; passing the relay baton at Sports Day and the cup awarded in 1899 to the winner of the 220 yards race.

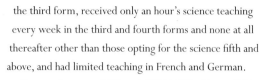

the third form, received only an hour's science teaching every week in the third and fourth forms and none at all thereafter other than those opting for the science fifth and above, and had limited teaching in French and German.

Even so, between 1891 and 1903 MGS still sent 178 boys to Oxford and Cambridge, while another 402 boys either matriculated for the University of London degree or took up places at Victoria University. If the sixth form averaged 62 boys, the number given in an inspection report in 1899, then this accounts for nearly three-quarters of all sixth formers. It was a remarkable performance.

Ernest Barker, who joined the classical sixth at the age of 15, painted a lively portrait of sixth-form life in his autobiography. He was one of a half a dozen young scholars in his form who would soon win Oxbridge scholarships: 'We came from all sorts of homes; several of us came, as I did, from an elementary school; but we all went forward together,

and each of us found a job and did something "to maintain the state of the world".' He wrote of the spirit of competition among boys with lively minds, a rivalry of mental achievement, as they developed style as well as accumulated knowledge. But, taught some German and little science or maths, his experience in the classical sixth corroborated Eve's impression: 'I was highly educated; and yet, perhaps, at best, I was only half-educated.'[96]

Outside the classroom the pattern of life remained much as it had under Dill and Glazebrook. Music and drama, not regarded very seriously in boys' schools for many years, progressed little more at MGS than anywhere else, although King persuaded the greatest actor of the day, Henry Irving, to give some coaching to the boys in 1891. On the sporting side, water polo was introduced, but the most important event was the acquisition of a five-acre field in Lower Broughton Road in 1897. With the craze for cycling, bicycle races were a popular part of sports days during the 1890s, alongside barrel races and sack races. In 1901 an old boy, working for the Edison Company, organised the filming of the event, which was shown to the boys, and for a short while to the

MODERN REMOVE REVIEW

FEB 18   1902

No.2   VOL1

TO BE PASSED ROUND THE FORM.

public in St James's Hall. The school was building up its reputation for outdoor activities. The natural history society continued to organise visits to the Derbyshire Dales, while in the summer of 1895 a group of boys spent the summer in the Lakes at the invitation of the headmaster of Hawkshead Grammar School. A handful of boys joined the Universities' Camps for Public Schools in 1898 and 1899, at a cost, however, of two guineas a head. In August 1902, 29 years after the last overseas excursion, S. E. Bally, the modern languages master, took a party of boys on a walking holiday of Switzerland, and followed it up with a further visit in 1903, both, it was said, at a very moderate cost. In the same year he also took a Whitsun cycling party on a journey of more than 500 miles, cycling from Withington via Birmingham and Stratford to Oxford, then towards Southampton (where unexpected storms prevented their embarkation for France), into the New Forest, along the coast to Sherborne, then on to Bath, taking the train to Chepstow before riding to Tintern and the Wye Valley, and on through Ross, Ludlow and Shrewsbury, returning via Alderley to Manchester. Bally would leave the school in 1904 to found his own school in Switzerland.

In 1899, shortly before the Boer War began, there was pressure from the boys to establish a cadet corps, but MGS had never had strong military links, and the appeal was quietly ignored. It was perhaps unsurprising that when the war did start, the school had little idea whether any of its former pupils were on active service. The boys shared in Manchester's celebration of the relief of Ladysmith in March 1900, although jubilation at the relief of Mafeking three months later was muted, largely because the news came through late on a Friday evening and was old hat by the Monday morning. The school magazine included reports from pupils serving in South Africa, including one from John Sheldon, based at a hospital in Pretoria, who recounted a poignant tale of admitting a young private suffering from enteric fever: 'You need no thermometer, no stethoscope, to diagnose his case. You see the hectic flushes on his sunken cheeks, his dry, parched lips; you feel his pulse irregular. He is at the end of his second week of enteric fever. You transfer him to hospital, knowing that in a few days he may be on the way to recovery, but will most probably be dead.'[97] One old boy, Lieutenant W. H. N. Nickerson, serving with the Royal Army Medical Corps, was awarded the Victoria Cross, gaining an extra day's holiday for the boys at half-term.

In 1903 John King was appointed headmaster of Bedford Grammar School, where he remained until 1910. He had served the school well during a challenging time. Sandwiched between two great headmasters, Frederick Walker and John Lewis Paton, Samuel Dill, Michael Glazebrook and John King tend to get overlooked, yet they each helped to secure the foundations built by Walker that Paton would take to new heights.

Above: Front cover of a handwritten magazine produced by the modern remove form containing creative writings, competitions and reviews.

Centre: Joint trip between MGS and South Manchester School to Kinder Downfall in the Peak District, *c.*1910.

5 WANDERBIRDS 1903–14

'The Chance of Becoming the Best'

John Lewis Paton was an extraordinary man who made an extraordinary impression on an already outstanding school. He had turned his back on a famous school in the south to come north, where he felt more at home and became revered by successive generations of boys. His charisma and ability transformed the school at a time when secondary education was itself being transformed nationally; he achieved this when the school was still seriously underfunded, and increasingly reliant on state aid.

The son of a famous father, the theologian and missionary John Brown Paton, John Lewis Paton inherited his father's strong Christian faith, which influenced his own philosophy of education. He had been schooled first for a year at a gymnasium (or grammar school) in Halle, which gave him a lifelong love of Germany, its land, people and culture. After three years at Nottingham High School, he went to Shrewsbury School, where he became head boy. Winning a scholarship to St John's, Cambridge, he achieved a first in classics with special distinction, and won the chancellor's medal. Elected a fellow in the year he graduated, he immediately took up teaching, joining the staff of the nearby Leys School. He spent ten years as sixth-form master at Rugby before he was appointed as headmaster of University College School (UCS), succeeding H. W. Eve, who would soon afterwards inspect MGS. UCS was, like MGS, a school with a distinctive and off-beat character, well matched to its unconventional and lively new head, who would cycle to school in a morning coat and plus-fours, his frock trousers wrapped up in a paper parcel. He had an extraordinary rapport with UCS boys. As his obituary recorded, he 'understood the boys' overflowing spirits, joining them in their open-air recreations, sympathising with their foibles, confessing his own youthful delinquencies, understanding their temptations,

tactfully guiding their spiritual troubles, and at the same time denouncing with fierce wrath anything that savoured in the least of meanness and, above all, of impurity'.[98] He won the affection of the boys and the respect of the staff, of whom he had high expectations, though he never asked them to do anything he would not do himself. He sought to broaden boys' interests inside and outside the classroom, encouraging a love of art, music and craft, running school camps, pioneering overseas visits, joining in the working parties of boys he organised to carry out work around the school so they should value manual labour. In many ways Paton's headship at UCS proved to be a trial run for MGS, where he would repeat many of these initiatives.

But Paton became frustrated both by the middle-class prejudice that arose from his efforts to open up the school to the sons of poorer parents, and, ironically, in view of his later experience at MGS, by the tardiness of the governors in moving the school out of its unsatisfactory surroundings in the grimy heart of the capital, and in 1903 he left.

Perhaps he felt that his non-conformist, unconventional approach would be more suited to and better appreciated by the more down-to-earth, direct northerners of MGS. When he was introduced by his predecessor to the boys in the drawing hall on

Bronze of John Lewis Paton, High Master (1903–24), now in the Paton Library.

J. L. Paton in his study.

Founders' Day 1903, he was received with loud and sustained cheers, which took him aback, but must have confirmed that he had made the right decision. He already knew Lancashire through his friendship with Arthur Leonard, who had been a congregational minister in Colne. Leonard was the influence behind Paton's introduction of camps and expeditions at UCS, which Paton would extend to MGS.

Paton would spend more than 20 years at MGS, leaving an indelible mark upon the school. He arrived, one writer later recorded, 'with his brisk, eager step, his firm mouth set in a half-smile, and the characteristic upward lift of his head', his voice clear and his speech 'crisp, succinct and decisive'. One pupil would describe him as 'this short, stocky figure, red-faced, mortar-boarded, stern of expression, until he lit up into a deep smile on speaking to an individual', with a platform presence that gave off 'a charge of electric energy'. Clean-cut, with a high forehead and penetrating blue eyes, he was indifferent to convention and although he could be quick-tempered he was innately fair.[99]

For many boys, his was the dominating influence of their adolescence. As one later recalled, 'the stamp of his glowing personality, put on us when our minds were plastic, determined the outlines of our social and intellectual pattern'.[100] George Clark, later Sir George Clark, the illustrious historian, provost of Oriel College, Oxford, and president of the British Association, would describe Paton as 'one of the most powerful personalities I have ever known'.[101] He had the ability to make every boy feel he was the most important in the school, and could recall their successes and failures, hopes and ambitions whenever he met them, either as school boys or in later life.

Often autocratic, Paton was never universally popular, yet for many boys, he was a hero. He was unafraid to motivate them by mixing with them, for instance, when he led parties of staff and boys in levelling the addition to the school playing field, or by inviting them on one of his regular morning runs. There were a few who refused to fall under his spell. Geoffrey Jefferson, for instance, later a distinguished neuroscientist, a shy and sensitive boy, small, weak and easily tired, detested Paton, never forgetting how the High Master had described Jefferson's matriculation form 'as the refuse dump of the school'. Paton had unfairly accused Raymond Streat of cheating, the boy's tears of frustration eventually convincing the High Master that his accusation had been misplaced. It was not his admission of error that Streat resented, but the form it took: 'He proceeded to abase himself on innumerable occasions by introducing me to visitors as a boy he had misjudged – a lesson to him to use his schoolmaster's power more carefully and all that sort of thing. This caused much teasing and misery for me and eventually prompted me to ask my father to let me leave school and start work as an office boy instead of going in for a scholarship.'[102]

Rather like the Three Musketeers, Paton believed that MGS should be about 'each and all'. The school should 'consider each and all alike, to get at each individual boy and capture his heart, so that though there were so many, none should feel lost in the crowd. At the same time they wanted each boy to regard himself as a member of the corporate whole, in which he had his part to play, for which he had his duty to fulfil. The life of each could only have its fulfilment in the life of all.' He had no time for schools where 'each was sacrificed to all', with 'seldom any living, human, personal interest taken in each boy', where 'boys were graded out with mechanical regularity, were taken at a regulation step through a regulation syllabus of instruction, none being allowed to go on ahead, however clever, none to lag behind: [where] all boys were treated as average, or rather sub-average, for a squad must move at the pace of the slowest'. But neither did he have time for schools where 'all are sacrificed to each', where 'they were always preparing for examinations, longing and struggling to swell records, and clever boys were fattened and primed for the scholarship market'.[103]

For Paton, education at MGS was all about building up a healthy and intellectually curious individual, developing his capacity of leadership in society, and making him more aware of the world at large, whether close at hand or through experience of foreign cultures. He wanted to find out where a boy's interests lay and make the most of his potential. 'We are', he said, 'responsible for making the best of them'.

with bad and excessively small print should be vigorously condemned.

9. Adolescence.—It may be well to mention here that a boy's brain often "stands still" for a time at the age of puberty, because of the demands made on his physical nature at this period. The result is that he makes no headway with his studies, and is apt to lose heart. The remedy is patience and encouragement, not punishment or reproof. The intellectual crop is often all the heavier after such a space of "lying fallow." Between 14 and 16 a boy's brain rather mounts by steps, with halts upon each step, than climbs, without stopping, a gradual slope.

As to instruction in private matters which a boy needs at this time of life, it is better he should be told it by his father, as part of God's great law of natural process, than be left to pick it up from some dirty-minded companion.

He had high expectations. 'We believe at the Grammar School that there is nothing so difficult, nothing so high, that Manchester boys cannot achieve it.' He particularly wanted MGS to give 'every boy, however poor, the chance of becoming the best and doing the best that he had it in him to become and to do'. He would seek out the brightest boys at the poorest schools and encourage them to apply for MGS. To encourage the poorest parents to keep their boys at school as long as possible, his ambition was always that their education should cost less the longer they were at school, and be free after the age of 16. He was always pressing for more funds for maintenance allowances and bursaries, and successfully persuaded the governors to remove the previous three-year limit on scholarships. He quietly helped poor boys, often failing to charge them for books or stationery or examination fees, and paying for them to join their peers on school outings. He continued the fight of his predecessors against the tendency for many boys to leave school too early, when for many of them he was convinced that 'the chance of a boy's lifetime was the chance of higher education'.[104]

There was a moral purpose in all this. In his first speech day address in 1903, he emphasised the importance of rectitude, personal honour and public spirit. Appealing directly to the boys from the platform of the Free Trade Hall, he continued: 'We cannot do without your help. With you there is nothing we cannot do. Uphold the good name of your school; keep the tone high; set your faces like flint against anything that is low or unworthy of your school; cut it down, sweep it away; overcome evil with good;

13

4. Fresh Air and "Fresh" Bodies.—In order to secure freshness at School, arrangements must be made for the boy to learn early in life and through home customs the value of fresh air and open windows, and to realise how much easier it is to work his brain or rest his body under such conditions. Not only should he sleep in a properly-ventilated bedroom, with the windows open, but the room in which he does his home-work should always be kept at the right temperature—between 55° and 65°, preferably about 60°. If he sleeps with his bedroom window open, his sleep will be much sounder and more refreshing, and it is obvious that work done in an over-heated room, with its atmosphere vitiated by the products of burning gas, will be of inferior quality. A boy's study should therefore be provided with a thermometer, for regular consultation. Moreover, if he is of normal vigour, he should accustom himself to a cold bath every morning throughout the year. Nothing is equally tonic and bracing for the day's activities, or a better safeguard against catching cold. If the boy's circulation is subnormal, he should sponge himself down with cold water instead. A hot bath should be taken at least once every week. Particular care should always be given to cleanliness of teeth, particularly in the form of mouth-washing on rising and retiring, and when possible, after meals.

5. Clothing.—The essential point about a boy's clothes is that they should be light and warm in the winter, light and cool in the summer, and always loose and airy enough to let

turn bad to good, and better good with best, so that we may be able to claim for our school in this great city what the prophet of old claimed for the ideal city of his vision – that she is an eternal excellency and a joy for many generations.'[105]

These were not just words. For example, Paton's drive to ensure boys cultivated a wide array of interests beyond the classroom would help, he said, 'to distract the boys' minds from more serious pursuits, and those distractions would perhaps save them from developing diseased livers, running away and making a mess of their lives'. Games were important because, he said, they offered 'a lot of training for character as well as muscle', developing courage, equanimity, selflessness and 'comradeship'. He wanted his boys to lead moral, ordered, almost puritanical lives, much in the way he lived his own (he always, for instance, took a cold bath before breakfast). In two small booklets he wrote, taking the form of letters to boys either at or leaving school, he exhorted them to abstain from alcohol, tobacco and gambling; cherish their homes; be courteous towards women; spend frugally and carefully; know their own minds; pray and read the Bible every day. They should take regular outdoor exercise: 'Remember, your body exists for the sake of your mind and soul; don't let the affairs of the body invade and engross the higher levels of your nature.' And they should choose friends carefully and avoid being led astray; he warned them to 'beware of any fellow who carries about shady pictures in his inside pockets'.[106]

He could be ruthless in stamping out anything that smacked of immorality. Often it involved pornography or sex. In two years, 1905 and 1906, four boys were removed for circulating 'an indecent photograph' within school, another four were expelled for indecent behaviour, and two more were thrown out for 'having indecent pictures and writing on their person'. He told the governors in 1907 that while he would never rule the school with fear, 'fear is needed to inhibit summarily certain low propensities which cannot be allowed to gain a footing. The things that injure a school come not from without, but from within.' He made his remark in response to complaints from parents about the beating (five strokes of the birch, which had been adopted by Paton in preference to the cane on the grounds the birch left no permanent marks) he had given their son for injuring another boy and subsequently lying. For a while it became a cause célèbre in Manchester, an issue raised in a meeting of the full council, a matter that the boys' parents threatened to take to court, prompting the governors and the staff to express their full confidence in the High Master, noting that the incidence of corporal punishment had been falling. Paton also despised idleness, which cost several boys their scholarships.[107]

The extensive *Parents' Handbook* (1921) gave strict advice on every imaginable aspect of a boy's upbringing.

Caricatures of masters drawn by W. D. Rownley (1911–15) during his time at MGS; Art class c.1910. Freddy Garnett, the art master, was assisted by two ladies, one of whom, 'Ma Whitworth', is seen here.

As for their place in the world once they had left the school, he wanted old boys to think for themselves, be their own person, resist uniformity. He wanted them to fight not only their own battles, but those of others as well. While he did not want them to be cocksure in the righteousness of their own opinions, contemptuous of those who held different views, neither did he want them to acquiesce for the sake of politeness and good manners. He preferred to translate the school motto not as 'Dare to be wise', but rather as 'Distinguish yourself through knowledge'. He wanted boys to challenge through their own knowledge what too many without knowledge accepted as fact. One example he took was the London clubman comfortable in his view that every trades union leader was no more than an agitator. 'What a crying need there is for a man who will call a spade a spade, and who will remind these people in their gilt-edged security that a man is not a lout because he lives perforce in a slum.' He insisted, 'It is only by discussion that we test out the validity of our own views and the invalidity of other people's, or vice-versa. It is only by discussion that we learn, because it is by discussion that our minds are deepened.' He felt that Hugh Oldham 'meant us not merely to be wise, but to be wise with a mind of our own and with a feeling of our own, thoughts and feelings that are real and not merely borrowed from other people however estimable, not camouflaged so as to pass muster in our social circle, but based upon our own inward choice, a choice made seriously, *sub specie*, a choice tested out and found true and trustworthy in an experience among our fellow men and the facts of life as we know them'.[108]

When Paton came to Manchester, in the words of one academic, 'the modern system of state secondary education in England was in its most crucial stage of development'.[109] The Bryce Report on secondary education recommended that order should be brought to the hitherto fragmented system of provision and administration. The result was the creation of a central authority, the Board of Education, in 1900, followed by local education authorities under the 1902 Education Act, which replaced the school boards. More importantly, the reforms defined a form of academic secondary education that still prevails

school and school of art, it received grants not only from the Board of Education, but since 1903 also from Manchester and Salford councils. In 1907 under the free places scheme (the school agreed to reserve not less than 15 per cent of its annual intake as free places for elementary school boys) MGS also began receiving additional grants from the Board, which by 1910 accounted for nearly three-quarters of all the grants paid to the school. By then, while capitation fees were regularly raised, and were actually the highest charged by a boys' school in the area, grants accounted for a third of the school's revenue. The Board's inspection report that year noted the low average spend per pupil, with the consequence that the school was overcrowded (951 boys) and understaffed (43 staff). Many classes were at the prescribed maximum of 30, something that altered little over the next half-century. Without endowments to fund running costs, the school depended on economies of scale to sustain standards, and any reduction in numbers could be accommodated only by increased fees or other income.[110] Once again the school felt a lack of support from its nearest local authority. While Manchester generously supported Hulme Grammar School, whose endowments accounted for nearly half its income by comparison with MGS's 12 per cent, it was positively mean in its treatment of MGS, an attitude that seemed incomprehensible to the Board, which described the corporation's approach as 'almost wholly destructive'.[111]

MGS boys taking a walk, pre-1914.

today, with the 1904 Regulations for Secondary Schools defining an academic curriculum intended to cover a child's education from 11 to 16. Secondary schools still charged fees but their income was supplemented by a system of grants. In 1907 a free place scheme, reserving up to a quarter of the annual intake for elementary school pupils, was introduced. By 1911 elementary school pupils would account for some 60 per cent of pupils in secondary schools, and about a third of them were receiving free education. But the divide that these reforms, bitterly fought over at the time, had intended to bridge, between elementary and secondary education, remained, and would remain unaltered until the 1944 Education Act. Paton himself was deeply involved with education on a national level, appointed to the consultative committee of the Board of Education in 1907, and later that year becoming president of the Teachers' Guild of Great Britain and Ireland.

As a result of these reforms, MGS, which had already been accepting aid from the city council to fund its science teaching, became even more reliant on state funding. By 1905 the school's endowment income amounted only to £3,000 annually, almost all of it in rent from the railways. As a recognised secondary

Even when Paton arrived, the school's premises were increasingly squalid, lacking a playground, devoid of electricity and adjacent to a foul-smelling river. Electricity arrived in 1905, to dispel the foggy gloom that often surrounded the school, and the river was covered over at the expense of the railway company in 1906. It was only further criticism from the school inspectors in 1910 that finally forced the governors to consider ameliorating the situation. In 1911 a new dining hall was opened, which increased from 100 to 500 the number of boys who could sit down and eat at any one time. In 1913 the old wing was reconstructed to create three physics labs and ancillary accommodation, a plunge bath large enough for teaching boys to swim, a shooting range, new boiler house and more classrooms.

The school was still unable to fund a pension scheme or pay its staff properly, a problem they had endured at least since Walker's time. Pensions were discretionary, small and time-limited. The French master, who retired in 1903 at the age of 68 after 18 years at the school, was granted the sum of £50 a year for two years.

Sick pay was also discretionary, and paid out of a special fund, the John Harling Fund, which was used for other costs incurred by staff, such as paying substitutes to cover absences.

At least in 1908, after one or two false starts, a pension fund was started. The matter of pay was still unresolved on the outbreak of the First World War. In 1903 the governors were relying on the grants from Manchester and Salford councils to support staff salaries, and several staff were allowed to supplement their income through private tuition. Women (in 1904 there were two teaching in the prep form) were even more badly under-paid than the men. By 1911 the generally loyal teaching staff were at the end of their very long tether and despatched a petition to the governors, which noted their 'long and deeply-felt dissatisfaction with one of the conditions of our service, viz., the limit of £300 per annum as the maximum salary'. They pointed out that the limit had been in place for many years, and had been outstripped by the cost of living, noting that many lesser schools already paid superior salaries. Although a few staff earned above £300 through special allowances, for most there was little incentive beyond the age of 36, the point at which a master joining the school after graduation attained the maximum salary; while a married master 'is compelled to look outside the school for work which will enable him to supplement his income, as it is quite impossible for a married man, on the

From the top: A packed assembly at Long Millgate in the drawing hall. The hall was used intensively with different classes often taking place simultaneously. By 1910 the school was bursting at the seams with 951 boys; the plunge bath where boys learnt to swim opened in 1913 and a new dining room, large enough for 500 boys to sit down, opened in 1911.

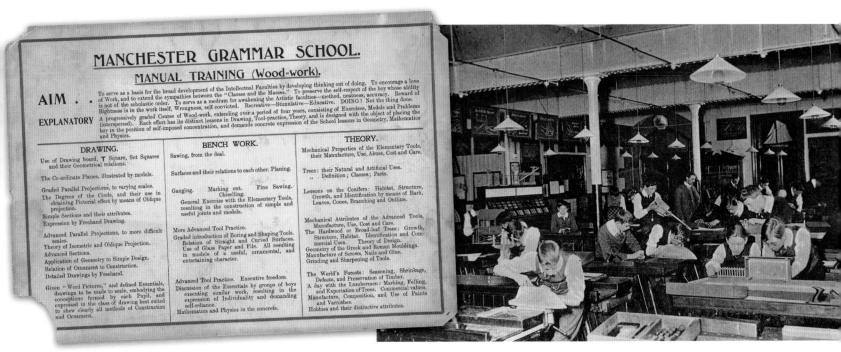

The ambitions of High Masters both before and after Paton were often hindered by the school's limited financial resources and it is a tribute to their calibre that they achieved so much. One of Paton's outstanding achievements was to make camps and expeditions an enduring part of the MGS calendar. For him, they were an important part of translating his philosophy into action. He was influenced by Arthur Leonard, the pioneer of holidays and outdoor recreation for young people in the 1890s. Leonard, a friend of Paton's father, became general secretary of the Co-operative Holidays Association, of which Paton senior was president. Beginning with expeditions to the Lake District, the Association organised its first overseas visit in 1902.

income which he derives from the School, to live decently and sociably, to educate his children as a professional man would wish to do, and at the same time make reasonable provision for his wife and family'.[112] The proposals made in response by the governors were seen as wholly inadequate and turned down flat after which the whole subject was buried, with the ever-patient staff waiting until the end of 1913 to raise the matter again. The governors felt they could do nothing more than appeal for funds from the local councils, and when their response fell short, simply conveyed the board's regret that it was impossible to improve salaries. Less than four months later, war intervened and any resolution of this pressing problem was once again postponed.

Above: The handicraft room.

Below: The receiver's office with boys manning the front counter selling books, postcards and other items. It is unlikely that the boys would have regularly staffed this post, and more probable that this is a posed photograph.

Above: Camp at Alderley Park, c.1910.

Right: MGS 'wanderbirds' setting off on the first German Trek, 1910.

Below: Grasmere camp watercolour by R. Carnforth.

The first MGS camp under Paton took place during the Whitsun holiday of 1904 in the grounds of Alderley Park, the Cheshire home of Lord Stanley, continuing a connection with the family that stretched back to the founder. Forty-seven boys attended, Paton told the governors, playing cricket and learning 'many lessons, which School cannot teach, in the fundamental economies and simplicities of life'. For many of them, too, it may well have been their first intimate acquaintance with the English countryside. This became an annual event, interrupted only by war, until the land was sold in 1939, and initiated the MGS tradition, adopted by no other school, of a long Whitsun holiday.

By 1907, 100 boys were spending a fortnight at Alderley Park under the supervision of just one master.

The success of the Alderley camp led to the first Grasmere camp, under Mr Varnish in the summer of 1904, and this, too, became an annual event.

We climbed anything from the height of a threepenny bit to 3,000 feet – shew us an absolutely unclimbable mountain, and we climbed it; and in fishing, tell us of a fish that had never yet been caught, and we caught him; show us the village cricket team captained by Mr Gibson, and we beat them; bring the whole force of the local football strength against us, and we lost! Bathing in "Dead man's pool", boating on the lake, collecting stones, serenading and torch-light processioning, eating at the tuck shop – these and other pastimes made up the life.

Paton was an often enthusiastic participant. At the 1913 camp, he 'seemed to take his pleasures strenuously; if he was not cutting bread or working at the stove, it usually proved that he

was carrying four gallons of water up an almost precipitous slope. He turned out dinners that would have done credit to the Ritz'. He also accompanied many of the day excursions organised by the field club.[113]

This rapidly established tradition coincided with Paton's love of Germany to initiate a series of overseas expeditions that lasted until 1914. Paton had always seen modern languages as the way to open a window on the world for young boys and he invited a young German teacher, Dr Bernhard Neuendorff, to spend a year teaching his native language at the school around 1905–6. Neuendorff attended the Alderley Park camp and on his return to Germany published an article in a local journal about the school and its camps. Paton was also collaborating with Arthur Leonard in arranging exchange visits between British and German schools, students and young workers. As a result, a party of German walkers, or 'wanderbirds', visited the school in the summer of 1909.

In the following year, as one boy later recorded, 'The first German trek was launched with all the panoply and fireworks that J. L. P. [Paton] could command in a Drawing Hall oration. It was my first conscious experience of spellbinding. The intention as advertised was to take a team of supermen worthy to represent the School. Every member would have to be capable of swimming a specified distance, of climbing a rope "feet off", and so on.'[114]

Paton and another member of staff, Mr Nicholson, took two parties totalling 30 boys. Led by German guides, they travelled mainly on foot, taking trains or boats where necessary, and camping in the open air whenever possible. A second expedition took place in 1911, subsidised by the school, when a party of 30 'wanderbirds' from MGS enjoyed the hospitality of staff and parents from the Musterschule in Frankfurt. At the same time MGS hosted a party of boys from Frankfurt, Paton remarking that 'These international visits were a sign of something greater … the sign of a coming common spirit'.[115] Several further exchange visits were arranged in the years prior to the First World War, the last ones in the summer of 1913.

The term 'trek' was not actually used until 1912, adopted in that year to describe the long journey made on foot by boys through northern France, when they covered 500 miles in six weeks. This was organised by Mr Hope, who ran the newly founded school Scouts, a group Paton believed would appeal to boys who disliked team sport. Four troops were formed in July 1912, with 120 boys, and scouting quickly became popular. Three months later, Baden-Powell, the movement's founder, visited the school.

The formation of the school's Officer Training Corps in 1910 created yet another opportunity for outdoor exercise, including route marches as well as camps. The school corps movement had been in existence since the 1890s but gained momentum in the aftermath of the Boer War, and the Officer Training Corps (OTCs) were formally established by the government in 1908 as part of wide-ranging military reforms. Many schools maintained

Practising first aid at a Scout jamboree, c.1914.

Paton saw the playing field as another opportunity to encourage the collaboration, co-operation and teamwork fostered by the treks and camps. He saw this as an important way of binding a day school together; the author of a short history of the school written in 1905 observed that the school did as much as possible 'to counteract natural disintegrating tendencies'.[116] Paton led by example, heading the parties of boys who volunteered to help level the additional land acquired for the playing field, the Cliff, at Lower Broughton in 1903. The Harriers, the school cross-country club, were revived one Saturday morning in 1904 when some 30 boys turned up in response to Paton's announcement that he and two other masters would be organising a run. This became a weekly event and a school team was formed under Herbert Newbould in 1905, following a course from the Cliff along the Pendleton side of the Irwell to Thirteen Arches, Molyneaux Brow, back along Drinkwater Park, through Agecroft, up the hill to Kersal Moor and down Lower Broughton Road, finishing at the bottom of the hill. In the same year sports day was reorganised to reflect Paton's belief that winning should be about the team rather than the individual. Cups and prizes were no longer awarded for individual success, although bronze medals were given out to winners, but four divisions of differing forms would compete for trophies. Handicaps were abolished and events for younger boys were introduced. The bicycle races also went, replaced by shot-putting and throwing the lacrosse ball. Paton's changes stimulated a record number of entries, with keen competition for the form trophies. Paton was eager 'to popularise manly out-of-door games'.[117]

Above: OTC camp, pre-1914.

Right: Boys from MGS and South Manchester Grammar putting their map-reading skills to the test on an Easter ramble to Middleton Dale in the Peak District, c.1910.

their own corps for decades while others, including MGS, demonstrated only fitful enthusiasm. The MGS corps began with 56 boys in 1910, rising to 124 in 1913–14, a much lower proportion of boys than at many other schools.

By 1913 there was an extensive programme of camps. As well as the usual camps at Alderley and in the Lakes, a trip was also arranged to Ireland, the 'wanderbirds' were visiting the Black Forest, an OTC camp was planned and a camp was being organised for the Hugh Oldham Lads' Club at Penmaenmawr in Wales. The Scouts were particularly active, visiting Belgium at Easter, followed by Whitsun camps at Alderley and Congleton, and there were ambitious but ultimately abortive plans for a visit to North America. A member of staff, F. A. Burton, had written handbooks for several camps, the one covering Grasmere being adopted by Westmorland Local Education Authority as a textbook for schools.

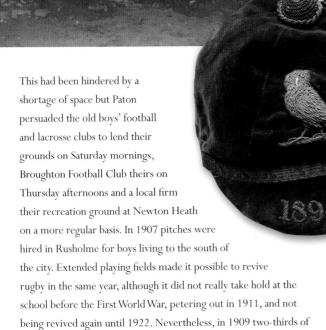

This had been hindered by a shortage of space but Paton persuaded the old boys' football and lacrosse clubs to lend their grounds on Saturday mornings, Broughton Football Club theirs on Thursday afternoons and a local firm their recreation ground at Newton Heath on a more regular basis. In 1907 pitches were hired in Rusholme for boys living to the south of the city. Extended playing fields made it possible to revive rugby in the same year, although it did not really take hold at the school before the First World War, petering out in 1911, and not being revived again until 1922. Nevertheless, in 1909 two-thirds of all boys were taking part in sport.

Part of the reason for Paton's emphasis on fresh air and exercise was a desire to build up the boys' health. This was an important priority for schools in the early 20th century, when child mortality rates were still high, diets and living conditions often poor, and antibiotics had not yet been discovered. Deaths of boys while they were at school were not uncommon. For some years Paton had asked a local practitioner, Dr Mumford, later the author of a school history, to keep an eye on the boys' health, which led to his appointment as the school's first official medical officer in 1909. Paton and Mumford worked together to assess the health of every boy against standards set by the Anthropometric Society, with Paton urging parents to encourage their sons to take more exercise and introducing a more energetic form of drill as part of the school's system of discipline. Mumford was a man of good intentions but his approach was criticised by a doctor despatched by the Board of Education to review the school's system of medical inspection in 1914, who reported that it was more attuned to Mumford's interest in statistical analysis than the needs of the individual boys. Even so, the visiting doctor concluded that Mumford 'is probably caring for their health in a simple homely way quite apart from all the paraphernalia of his cards'.[118]

Wanting to inspire the boys, Paton succeeded in bringing a number of inspirational leaders of men as guest speakers to the school. Ernest Rutherford, the outstanding physicist of his day, professor at Manchester University and Nobel Prize winner, lectured to the upper school in 1909. Later in the same year the school welcomed the polar explorer Ernest Shackleton, followed in 1910 by Robert Scott, who described the plans for his ultimately ill-fated expedition to Antarctica, for which the boys subscribed towards a sledge. Scott told them that 'it was the boys who would understand him best, and upon whom would devolve in future days the task of encouraging the spirit of adventure and enterprise'. Today his final remarks have a tragic air about them, with the school magazine reporting him as saying that it would be from October 1911 'when the real dash for the Pole would be made.

Above left: Rugby 1st XV, *c*.1909.

Above: Cricket 1st XI, *c*.1910.

Inset: An early sporting colours cap.

Below: A boy in his gym kit proudly showing the medals and cup that he has won.

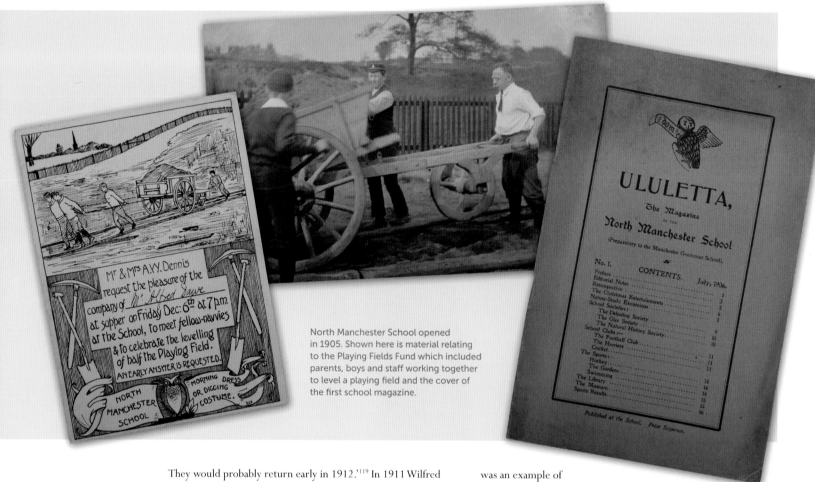

North Manchester School opened in 1905. Shown here is material relating to the Playing Fields Fund which included parents, boys and staff working together to level a playing field and the cover of the first school magazine.

They would probably return early in 1912.'[119] In 1911 Wilfred Grenfell, the medical missionary and social reformer, also spoke to the boys, many of whom must already have read his popular account of surviving on an ice floe in the open sea.

Boys were also encouraged to take an interest in the world of teeming economic activity on their doorstep, with staff arranging visits to local businesses, including chemical works, cotton factories and Pilkington's glass works. The school continued to help boys find jobs with local banks, insurance and shipping offices, commercial works and other employers, developing Glazebrook's employment registry into an employment bureau, started in 1906.

Paton's willingness to listen to good ideas from the boys was exemplified by the first mock elections held at the school in 1906. It was an exciting time in national politics, as the range of candidates illustrated: 'The free trader, the tariff reformer, the protectionist, the women's suffragist, the socialist, all stood on the same platform.' The woman's suffrage candidate was H. F. Pankhurst, the son of Emmeline Pankhurst, who herself had been born in Moss Side. One of the two socialist candidates, George Benson, recalled that the idea of a mock election had come from a group of senior boys, himself included, who had then approached Paton about it. As Benson remembered, 'He looked at us – this

was an example of the way in which he seemed to know every boy, for I do not think he ever attended our debating society – and said, "Liberal, Conservative, Socialist … this looks like a deputation, gentlemen. What can I do for you?"' Paton was enthusiastic, arranged the hustings and agreed to act as returning officer. Benson received a letter of good wishes from that pioneering socialist Keir Hardie, which is still contained in the school archive. He garnered just 34 votes but later became a Labour MP and penal reformer. In the year when Campbell-Bannerman's great reforming Liberal government took office, MGS elected two Liberal candidates. Every boy must have cast a vote, since more than 1,000 were recorded.[120]

Paton believed that parents, old boys and the wider community should be an integral part of the school's sphere. In 1905 Paton started what were termed 'friendly conferences' between parents and teachers, divided between the upper and lower schools, and they became an annual event. He wanted a stronger bond between the school and its old boys than the longstanding annual dinner. In September 1904 he appealed for old boys to found a formal association. The OMA flourished, gaining nearly 1,000 members by 1909, organising orchestral, lacrosse and football sections, a literary and social union and a Masonic lodge. In 1907 the old boys began the tradition of laying a wreath every year on the tomb of the founder in Exeter Cathedral. Today membership of the OMA is automatic for all old boys and staff and in recent years a thriving Old Mancunian online community has developed.

Paton was eager to strengthen links with Manchester and with Salford. Loyalty to the school, he told old boys in 1905, should be combined with loyalty to the city. In 1910 he told them that the school 'existed not only for themselves and for the universities, but above all to serve two civic communities'. He worked hard to strengthen links with the local education authorities, helped in those days by MGS's representation on the education committees of both Manchester and Salford. There was a regular dialogue between these authorities and the school, although financial support was often hard to prise out of them. In 1909 Paton discovered that many elementary school boys rarely entered the school entrance exam without private coaching. As a result, Paton invited an elementary school master to help set the scholarship papers, which now had to conform to the requirements of the Board of Education, and select candidates. By 1913 Paton was able to speak of an ever closer and more cordial relationship with local elementary schools.

Such links helped to increase applications for places, as did two further prep schools. The first followed a suggestion from the school inspectors in 1904, not the first time that an inspection acted as a catalyst for action. The North Manchester School opened with 65 boys in September 1905, taking over the premises of the former North Manchester Girls' High School in High Broughton. In 1908, following an approach from Cheshire County Council, MGS also took over the former Sale High School. This proved rather more controversial, revealing splits between radical nonconformists and Tory Anglicans on the governing body reminiscent of the former school boards. The dean of Manchester, James Welldon, led the opposition, claiming that if the school could afford to spend its money on subsidising external schools, it surely no longer needed funding from the local rate-payers. The plan was approved after the chairman, Edward Broadfield, assured governors of the benefit of the prep schools 'in assuring the proper and adequate preparation of junior boys before their admission to the Grammar School'.[121]

By 1910 the three prep schools contained 300 boys. It would have been impossible to accommodate them in the overcrowded and understaffed main school buildings. The school squeezed in 820 boys in 1904,[122] yet somehow managed to shoehorn 951 into the same space in 1910. As demand for places grew, Paton made

sure the entrance examination remained a stiff test of ability, even if it was tailored to meet the needs of those applying from elementary schools. Most boys in 1910 (702) were aged between 12 and 16, with 130 over 16, and 87 boys in the four sixth forms. More than a third came from Manchester, and nearly half from the rest of Lancashire. Edward Broadfield told the local evening newspaper in 1911, 'Anything like caste or class distinction is utterly unknown at the Manchester Grammar School, and we have always rejoiced that it should be a meeting place for boys of different social standing.'[123] But most boys came from middle-class backgrounds, whether the 28 per cent from professional families, the 39 per cent from wholesale and retail trading backgrounds or

Top: Boys with pillows during an Easter trip, 1914.

Above: Looking down a mine shaft on a visit to a colliery.

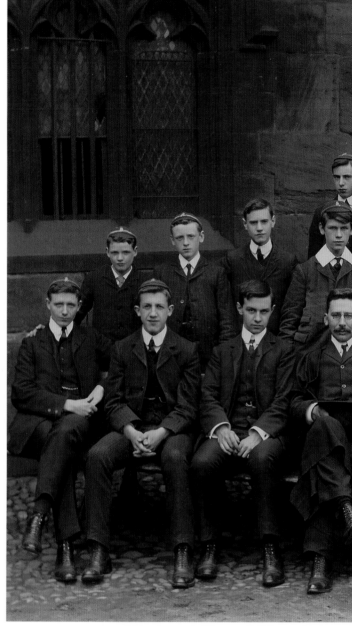

Above: The modern sixth 1905–6 with Simon Marks on the far right of the front row, and his future brother-in-law, Israel Sieff, second from the right on the back row.

Right: Form photograph, *c.*1910.

the 18 per cent whose fathers were clerks and agents. Just under 100 boys were the sons of domestic servants, artisans or labourers. Almost 400 came from elementary schools. Since 1907, in return for funding from the Board of Education, the school had agreed that not less than 15 per cent of places should be set aside every year for boys from elementary schools; in fact, the school regularly exceeded this limit, reaching 24 per cent in 1913.

There was a significant Jewish minority, for whom separate prayers were arranged for the first time in 1903, followed by the provision to learn Hebrew in 1910. As one Jewish boy who knew Paton after the war would later remark, 'The kindness which he, Paton, showed towards the children of immigrant parents, parents to whom English was not the first language, has left the Jewish community of Greater Manchester with a great love for MGS.'[124] Simon Marks, the founder of Marks & Spencer, spent four years at the school, sent by his father on the grounds that MGS admitted boys regardless of class or creed. Marks would recall in later life how the school had taught him to appreciate literature and poetry, Shakespeare, Molière, Goethe and Schiller. But he left the sixth form at the age of 15 in 1905 to round off his languages with a year in France and Germany. Marks was perhaps the most notable example of the still common practice of parents to take away their sons too early. Paton told the governors in 1907 that 'we have not yet succeeded in eradicating the current notion of the Grammar School as a finishing School'.[125]

Jews were not the only minority welcomed into the school. Indian names can be found in the school register as early as the

1880s, probably the sons of well-to-do Indian/Anglo-Indian cotton merchants. MGS made such an impact on one of them, Satish Ranjan Das, later a member of the Viceroy's Council in India, that he initiated a project for an all-India boys' public school where admission would be based on freedom from religious, racial or social prejudice. This reached fruition only after his death, with the opening of the Doon School at Dehradun in 1936, still one of India's leading residential schools today. Such boys were still coming to MGS in Paton's time. Govindyas Madarhas Jadhava, an Anglo-Indian, came to the school at 13, developing an enthusiasm for treks and scouting. After graduating from Manchester

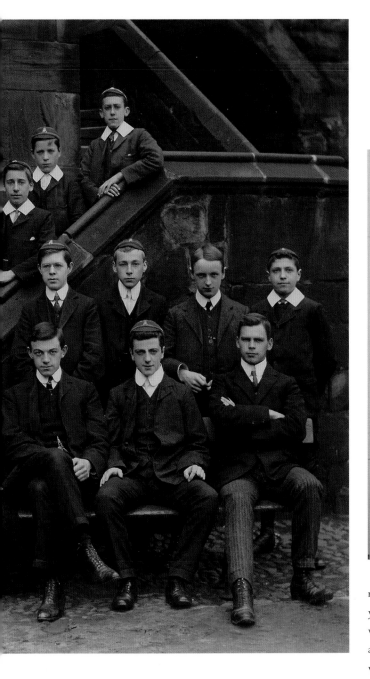

far. 'We came by 6.40 train and arrived at Warington at about 9.15, rather tired. It was such a change getting a nice bath and sleeping in a bed. I went to bed regretting that the holidays had come to an end.

16-1-14.

13 TUESDAY (13-352)
St. Hilary.

School again! Worse Luck! We had a "General Knowledge" paper in which I did fairly well. I had not done the holiday task which Mr. Mayo had set for us, consisting of about 60 sentences of Latin + Greek. So he said I should have to do them on Saturday morning as he would not have his work cut. I decided to get them done before Saturday + offer them to him. I did the first sheet of Greek; the whole lot of work taking about 4½ hrs   16-1-14.

14 WEDNESDAY (14-351)
Oxford Lent Term begins.

I asked "John Pym" to let me off the Saturday morning + offered him the first sheet. He said he thought ... ing them would interfere with my other work; ... would take

University, he returned to MGS for a time, assisting the Scouts and leading his own trek to France before returning home to India. There he worked in secondary schools in Baroda, extolling the example set by Paton and helping to establish scouting. A number of Anglo-Chinese boys also came to MGS through the links Paton forged with the Anglo-Chinese College in Tientsin (now Tianjin).

High academic standards were sustained under Paton. Although he limited form promotions to once a year, able boys could still reach the sixth form as early as 14, as W. H. Bruford, later professor of German at Durham, did in 1909. High standards were epitomised by the award of the Christ Church, Oxford,

maths scholarship to R. A. Llewellyn in 1907, the 15th time in 18 years it had been won by an MGS boy. While Oxbridge awards were still regarded by leading schools as the benchmark for academic performance, MGS boys were actively encouraged to work towards places in other universities, notably Manchester, Liverpool, Leeds and Sheffield. In 1910 the inspectors observed that 'the School continues to maintain unimpaired the high traditions and distinguished record of the past, and to develop in accordance with modern educational ideals and the local requirements', while the president of the Board of Education, Walter Runciman, singled out MGS as 'one of the greatest' of English schools, and an educational journal in the United States published an article that ranked MGS alongside Eton and Rugby.[126] In 1912 the High Master could announce that the school's successes in scholarships and exhibitions were matched among leading schools only by Winchester.

Extract from the diary of Norman Birnage (1911–16). The diary begins in January 1914 and runs until December that year. Until August, Birnage details school life. After this, he decides 'as far as possible, to try to keep an accurate record of the war'.

6 INTERRUPTIONS 1914–31

'Not Merely the Storing Up of Knowledge'

Whatever Paton's internationalism, he led MGS enthusiastically into the first days of the war. Presiding over a meeting at the university at the beginning of September, he outlined a scheme to form a corps of public school and university men to serve as privates. He even acted as recruiting officer for the recruiting station opened at the school the day after the meeting. Posters appeared outside the school entrances, the gym was used as an examining station and the drawing hall as an enquiry office, school Scouts acted as orderlies and many old boys volunteered as examining doctors. In just a few days more than 1,000 men had enlisted, a rate of recruitment the army could not cope with, bringing the exercise to an end. The first draft of 300 men was sent to join the Royal Fusiliers (City of London Regiment) on 17 September. The rest followed a week later, receiving an enthusiastic send-off, with a great crowd hearing the lord mayor address the men before they left by train for Leatherhead in Surrey.

Prefects 1914–15: 19 young men, impeccably dressed, exuding quiet confidence and looking older than their years. Seven of them were to die in the First World War, their potential unrealised. (Four of the seven had won scholarships at Oxford or Cambridge.) Of the 12 in the photograph who survived, three – J. P. Bowden, I. Tenen and A. Wilson – were to enjoy long careers as teachers at MGS. (Adapted from an article by John T. Bever (1990–2000) in *Ulula*.)

Four Pals Battalions had already been formed, and Manchester would supply the men for 15 of the 134 battalions of Kitchener's New Army. More than 5,000 officers and men from the Pals Battalions lost their lives and MGS itself would lose 526 old boys. Many boys enlisted as soon as they left school, such as A. E. Jackson of the classical sixth who also joined the new battalion attached to the Royal Fusiliers. On the right is a poignant photograph from the school archive of the 19 school prefects for 1914–15, of whom seven would die in the war, four without taking up their Oxbridge scholarships. Four masters – C. E. Fry, N. V. Holden, C. W. Merryweather and E. J. Porter – would also lose their lives.

80

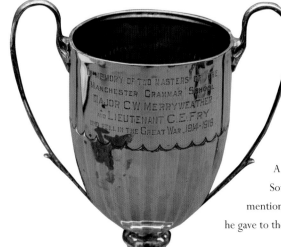

The war would cost Manchester and Salford the lives of 22,000 men; 55,000 would be wounded. The school's first casualty, reported in the school magazine in October 1914, was Second Lieutenant A. J. H. R. Widdowson of the South Lancashire Regiment. Paton mentioned him in the emotional address he gave to the OMA in 1914:

From time to time at prayers, I read letters written by Old Boys at the front – it may be one in pencil from an Old Boy in charge of one of the patrol steamers on the North Sea telling me what his life is like and the sort of job he has to do; or from an Old Mancunian who has come over from Canada and enlisted in the Belgian ranks … Still nearer does it bring us to the Old Boys, when I have to tell them at prayers that on the list of the missing – probably killed, but certainly missing – is Lieut. A. J. Widdowson (OM) of this School, and the last that has been heard of him was that at the retreat at Mons he was carrying a wounded sergeant into a cottage, and then the curtain falls and no more is known of him.[127]

Above: Commemorative cup for C. W. Merryweather and C. E. Fry, two masters who lost their lives in the First World War.

Below: MGS OTC, 1913.

Many years later one boy recalled the atmosphere of those days:

It was a curious time to be at school. The time of the murderous years, when young men were killed like flies, and it was to a small boy at school rather pathetic to know of men – they were really boys, we none of us thought of them as men – who were dead within six months or twelve months of leaving school.[128]

By early September 1914 several masters were already on active service, their pay subsidised by the governors, while the number of boys in the school's OTC had shot up to 400 and Old Mancunians were forming a company of special constables. As trade began to suffer from the impact of the war, several boys came back to school after failing to find jobs. The school opened its doors to the Evening School of Commerce, displaced from its previous premises, now turned into a hospital, with, amongst others, grocers' assistants taking tea-tasting sessions and learning how to spot adulterated coffee in the dining hall.

The pressure on those staff left behind grew inexorably. The already overfull school continued to expand, bulging with nearly 1,200 pupils by the end of the war, even though some boys were removed early by their fathers to fill gaps in their businesses as men were called up. Later, when the call-up age was changed to 18, the departure of senior boys 'very seriously weakened the Upper Forms of the School'.[129] To fill the vacancies on the teaching staff, temporary staff were recruited. The first woman teacher was Miss Davis, appointed in the autumn of 1914, and two more, Miss Hartley and Miss Sullivan, both graduates of Manchester University, would be appointed to take beginners' forms in 1916. None of this disruption seemed to disturb the school's academic performance. In 1916, for instance, 90 boys achieved their senior school certificates.

For Founders' Day that year Paton had invited his friend Cyril Alington, headmaster of his old school at Shrewsbury, and later headmaster of Eton and dean of Durham, to give the address. Alington spoke of the underlying principles of empire, notably freedom and responsibility, dismissing jingoism and militarism as having nothing at all to do with empire, and admitting that the way in which Britain's empire had expanded was open to criticism; and he exhorted the coming generation to remember that, as the *Guardian* reported, 'our aim was to make people fit for freedom, and, when they were fit, to make them free'.[130] For Paton, freedom and responsibility, and the relationship between them, was central to what

he was trying to achieve at MGS. But the stress of war was making it all too easy to forget the wider importance of these two tenets. The governors had been happy to take in Belgian refugees at the start of the war, later offered places to refugees from Serbia, and also awarded scholarships to four boys who were the sons of alien parents. But the latter decision in 1916 provoked a backlash, led once again by the dean of Manchester. In June 1917 the governors accepted the dean's proposal that during the war the school should not award foundation scholarships to the sons of parents who were enemy aliens.

Paton became increasingly disillusioned by the war. In 1915, despite the loss of his brother in the Dardanelles, he had even been prepared to send a telegram of good wishes to Admiral Jellicoe following a patriotic address to the school on Trafalgar Day by the secretary of the British and Foreign Sailors' Society. But he must have been disappointed by the views of one of his former pupils, Gilbert Waterhouse, who had taught briefly at the school before leaving to become professor of German at the University of Dublin. There he witnessed the Easter Rising, interviewing a number of the captured rebels, whom he described as 'filthy scum' and as 'a heap of carrion – the lowest of the low – and it would have benefited civilisation to shoot the lot'.[131]

Paton, who had personally invested so much in developing the potential of so many boys, must have been devastated by the terrible toll exacted on former pupils and staff. As the

number of deaths mounted, one boy would later recall how he 'had watched panel after panel added to the roll of honour'. In July 1916, at the time of Somme offensive, the school magazine recorded that 'our list of dead this month is terribly heavy, and scarcely a day passes without adding to the number'. The list that followed included the name of Willie Gomersall, once the smallest boy in the lowest form, who had shone neither in work nor sport, but who had died as a lieutenant leading his men towards enemy machine guns. There was Frank Norcross, who had won an open classical scholarship to Oxford, but joined up immediately after leaving school, gaining his commission and joining his regiment in the field on 28 July, dying in action the next day, 'one of the ablest boys we have had in the School for years'.[132]

The war also claimed the lives of those who had become friends of MGS through Paton's belief in internationalism during peacetime. Dr Bernhard Neuendorff was killed in action, Paton insisting his name was added to the school's roll of honour; while another boy, Bernhard Seib, who had made lasting friendships on his exchange visit to MGS before the war, and had refused to serve on the western front on the grounds he could not shoot dead his English friends, died instead on the eastern front.

Even before the example of the sacrifices made by so many former pupils, members of staff and friends of the school, Paton was striving to find ways in which boys still at school could show their solidarity with them.

Above left: Thomas Forshaw VC visiting North Manchester School, where he taught before the war.

Above centre: Frank Lockwood (1912–14), killed in action 1918.

Above: William Carter (1910–13), killed in action 1917.

Inset: Bronze memorial plaque awarded to Henry Rayner Claye. It was informally known as the 'dead man's penny', and was given to the next of kin of military personnel who had been killed as a result of the First World War. Claye once took temporary work as an art master at the school, and was to have had a permanent position on the staff on returning from war, but fate decreed otherwise.

Above: Plum-picking in Worcestershire, 1916.

Bottom right: The 1914–15 Star, British War Medal and the Victory Medal, informally known as 'Pip, Squeak and Wilfred', were also awarded to Henry Rayner Claye.

magazine came the exhortation, 'Now, Owlets, have you enrolled for the holidays? If not, do so at once.'[133] The Scouts were busy acting as hospital orderlies or collecting waste paper and scrap metal. A third-form boy, J. L. Fenton, organised volunteers among junior boys to work on Salford corporation's tram cars. The OTC devoted 12 hours a week to military activities. Parties of boys – as many as 200 over one weekend and averaging 100 for each shift – worked in the railway yard at Newton Heath from 10 March 1917 to 1 February 1919. They helped to unload steel (6,000 tons in 12 months), iron, timber, sawdust and coke; filled bags with sawdust for shell-cleaning and horse-bedding; and worked on the excavation of drying kilns for timber. After their first full year in the yard, the boys celebrated by inviting their foremen to tea and putting on a concert for them.

Growing food became a priority. The boys were given lectures on soil and cultivation, and carried out experiments with various types of fertiliser. They took over plots of land all around the neighbourhood and further afield, from a patch of land in Kersal given by an old boy to large gardens in Whalley Range, Victoria Park and Dickenson Road, while part of the school's recently acquired eight-acre playing fields at Rusholme was turned into an allotment and planted with potatoes, peas, beans, parsnips and lettuces. The boys sold the produce to the school at market price, giving the proceeds to war charities. They even kept a few pigs on the playing field at the Cliff. In the summer holidays harvest camps became a fixture, from fruit picking and hay making to harvesting and timber cutting. Over Whitsun 1918 boys were sent as far as Dorset to weed flax; labour was scarce, the weeds

The extent of the school's commitment to the war effort was remarkable. It began very soon after the outbreak of war when the school workshop, where manual skills had been taught, was pressed into service, making furniture for a house occupied by Belgian refugees and splints, leg-rests and bed-tables for Red Cross hospitals. (Metalwork soon ended when the school's three lathes were requisitioned.) During the first summer of the war boys found a variety of voluntary roles, working as messenger boys or in hospitals and (after completing a preliminary machine course in the school workshop) munitions factories. Two parties of 60 boys led by several staff and the school's receiver, Owen Cox, spent the summer picking fruit in the orchards of Worcestershire, while others helped to make hay at Grasmere. On their own initiative the boys gave up academic and athletics prizes, asking for the money to be given instead to the Red Cross and other charities. At Christmas boys worked for the Post Office and packed parcels of comforts to send to the front.

By 1917 all this work had been organised into a scheme of national service, with each boy given a registration form on which he had to enter the work on which he was already engaged, or which he would consider taking up. As ever, the boys shouldered a great deal of responsibility for the organisation, forming a committee that classified the information and allocated boys to various sectors. Time allocated for sport was given up in favour of national service. More than 700 of the school's 1,100 boys were actively involved most weekends, most holidays and sometimes during the week after school. In the school

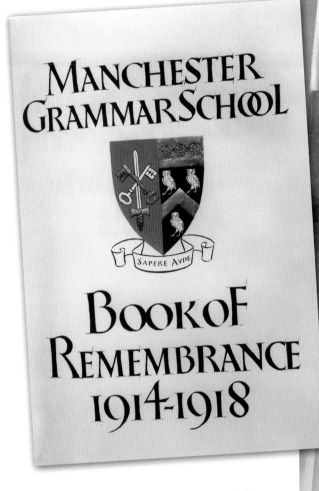

were many, southern schools did not have long Whitsun holidays and MGS boys came with camping experience. The boys scythed thistles and pulled up docks by their roots; some boys started 'to see thistles everywhere, on the road, on the walls, and even on the dinner table'.[134] But wet days gave the chance to explore the area on bicycles, and Dorset farmers had plenty of cheese, butter and bacon to share.

The most arduous work was shouldered by older boys, those aged 14 or above, and it began to take a toll on their health, combined as it was with their normal school work. In 1917 Dr Mumford warned Lord Derby, who had become secretary of state for war, that the work required of the OTC in addition to their school work was injuring their health, and regular health checks were being carried out. When meat was rationed in 1918, Paton decided to exempt boys from the more demanding athletic events. War work could prove dangerous. One boy, James Hall, lost his life after crushing his arm while working in the Newton Heath railway yard in the spring of 1918.

The influenza outbreak that struck MGS in the summer of 1918 seemed for Paton to be almost the last straw after all the other difficulties of wartime. 'There are times when what with the to and fro of staff, and the daily devouring of influenza, I feel as if we should have to shut up shop altogether. It would save a lot of trouble, wouldn't it.'[135] Over the next year the epidemic carried away at least four boys and one master. As the war ground to a close, Paton had become sick of the regressive attitudes it had generated, and the attempts to shackle liberty, writing to one old boy in September 1918 that 'I sometimes dread the coming of peace more than the continuance of war'. He also hated the spectacle of growing drunkenness, and the spread of sexually transmitted disease, lamenting that 'when you start to go downhill, everything seems specially greased to help you down fast'.[136] The return of a coalition candidate in the first mock election after the war, mirroring the results of the national election, must have further depressed Paton, who wrote to a friend of how the latter had 'set free all the reactionary forces'.[137]

The Statue of Remembrance in the Memorial Hall at Rusholme and the cover of the Book of Remembrance which is on display in the entrance to the school.

Right: Winners of the football cup and gymnastics cup, 1924.

Below: Humorous sketches poking fun at the standard of food in 'Cox's' – the school dining room. 'Drawn by our special artist with details supplied by survivors.'

One sign of a gradual return to normal was the school magazine's report that 'there are rumours that meat is to be found in School dinners'.[138] It took time to reinvigorate school life. Pleading for an urgent return of outdoor activities, the captains of games detected apathy among the boys. The OTC fell into decline and was finally disbanded in 1921 when membership had fallen to just 30 boys. But new clubs and societies, including a League of Nations Society, sprang up, the school open day made a brief comeback, and speech day, held in the Albert Hall rather than the Free Trade Hall, took place in 1919 for the first time since 1915. First XI soccer matches had been restarted in early 1918 and the swimming sports resumed in the Victoria Baths in 1920, but the revival of rugby had to wait until 1922. Even Paton seemed refreshed, the inspectors who met him in early 1920 reporting that he 'controls the School with all his former vigour and resource'.[139]

Camps and treks had been restricted during the war but were fully revived when peace returned. Overseas treks, interspersed with treks around the British Isles, were led by Hyman 'Harry' Lob, Arnold Heathcote, Harold Green and W. H. Madden. Madden founded one of MGS's most enduring features. In 1921 he inspired the Owl's Nest at Disley, a hut built on land bought and donated by Paton and equipped with basic facilities, where thousands of young boys in the decades since have had their first experience of fending for themselves away from home. It was typical of MGS

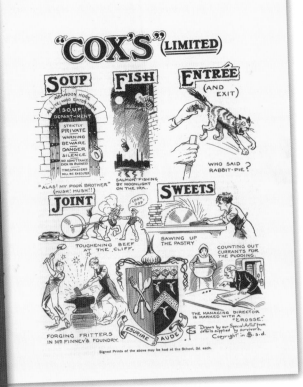

returned to the teaching staff. In 1921 Paton brought back Mrs Anderson and Mrs Elsden, who had taught at the school as unmarried women during the war. Paton's decision was unusual since it was common practice for women to give up teaching on their marriage, and indeed local authorities had the right to force them to do so. Their pay at MGS, however, was between 20 and 30 per cent lower than their male colleagues'.

In the spring of 1919 the governors had revised the salary scale for teaching staff but it was not enough to satisfy the long-suffering staff, who had put up with poor pay for so many years. In 1920 their cause was backed by the school inspectors, who once again pointed out that the school was understaffed. The governors protested that unless the school raised fees or received an increase in grants, there was simply not enough money to improve staff salaries, as the school had been losing money for the past few years. The staff agreed that in the circumstances they would drop their opposition to the previously agreed scheme. But this was the year that Viscount Burnham's committee recommended uniform salary scales for all state-school teachers. Paton seized the opportunity, began offering salaries on the Burnham scale for vacant posts, insisted this was essential for attracting new recruits, and persuaded the governors to implement the scale without delay. As a result, fees increased from £15 to £24 a year, accompanied by a system of maintenance bursaries for parents who might struggle to pay, a precursor of the scheme of fee remission that would emerge under Paton's successors. In 1921 Paton could report that the

Left: The exterior of the Owl's Nest today; a boy reading by the ping pong table, 1922.

Below: Campers on their return from the French Trek, 1921. High Master Paton is on the far right next to Govindyas Madarhas Jadhava, an old boy who returned to help with scouting and various treks after university.

that Madden encouraged the boys to take charge from the outset. The boys' committee issued a circular, stating that the camp had been established to allow boys 'to enjoy and appreciate an outdoor life; to pursue their hobbies; to grow stronger and healthier; and to observe the processes of Nature as the seasons succeed one another'. It was available for weekend and holiday parties, weekly excursions and half-term expeditions. The committee not only drew up the rules but also set the charges (7s 6d a head for a weekend stay). An account of an early weekend camp appeared in the school magazine in June 1921: 'It was late before we thought of porridge for the morning. We had the oats; we had the water; we had a double-cooker; and we even had a fire and a coal supply; but though we mixed them all together correctly enough, no porridge could we get.'[140] By the end of the year 24 camps, involving 353 boys for periods of a weekend to three weeks, had already been held at the Owl's Nest.

By early 1919 all except two masters who had survived active service had rejoined the school. For a time women actually

adoption of the scale 'has done much to stabilise the work of the staff and remedy the discontent and unrest'.[141]

The inspectors once again highlighted that the school was still badly overcrowded, with nearly 1,200 boys (73 in the sixth form) in October 1919. Their social composition and geographical dispersal had changed little since before the war. More boys were coming earlier and staying longer but a sizeable minority of up to 150 boys at any one time still entered at the ages of 14 or 15 to spend a year or two at the school, 'having as a rule come only in order to say they have been at the School'.[142] It was a practice that the governors finally decided to bring to an end, asking all parents to sign a guarantee that their sons would remain in the school until they were at least 16.

The inspection report made two major points. First, the prep schools run by MGS hindered the school's progress. Boys left to join MGS at the age of 14, entering the school midway through a course, and without having studied much if any science.

The school cap.

Depending on which side of the school they entered, some boys could leave with almost no knowledge of science whatsoever. MGS was taxed to the limit in taking these boys to the exclusion of all others. Once again Paton had already taken the initiative. With soaring demand for places after the war, he had been squeezing in as many boys as possible to give the most able the chance of a good education; and he had been prioritising applications – the handful of boarders finally disappeared, younger boys were given preference to older boys, and boys already at secondary schools were advised to stay where they were and apply for admission to the sixth form. One consequence was a further strain on school finances to support a growing number of boys given free places, now 20 per cent of the annual intake. But this was important for Paton, who could later say that the school 'had the proud distinction, among old foundations, of having kept nearer than any other to the intent and spirit of its Founder that it should primarily give to boys who had not much financial backing a chance of distinguishing themselves. The governors had not, by their increased fee, either excluded boys who came from humble homes, nor had they succeeded in attracting those undesirables who came from the homes of profiteers.'[143] The inspectors, however, noted that the school could no longer afford to support

Clockwise from top left: Art and anatomy, 1920s; J. L. Paton shaking hands with the Prince of Wales, Edward VIII, during his visit to Manchester while MGS boys parade in the background, 1921; pageant, 1923; sketching at the Long Millgate site, 1920s.

the prep schools. Moreover, they were no longer needed, and in fact had become a hindrance. This sparked a long-running debate over their future among the governors. As a result, North Manchester and South Manchester became secondary schools in 1926, their brightest boys sent to MGS as sixth formers, but all three still remained a financial burden for MGS.

Second, the inspectors again pointed out the disadvantages of the school's existing overcrowded buildings. There was an urgent need for modern science facilities, a playground and easy access to playing fields. The buildings were deteriorating as a result of minimal maintenance. The receiver, Owen Cox, who had been in post since 1888, never had an easy job. Described by one master as a man never lavish with school funds, he refused to spend money on repairs until the last possible moment. Traffic noise made many classrooms unfit for teaching. One boy later gave an evocative description of the old school.

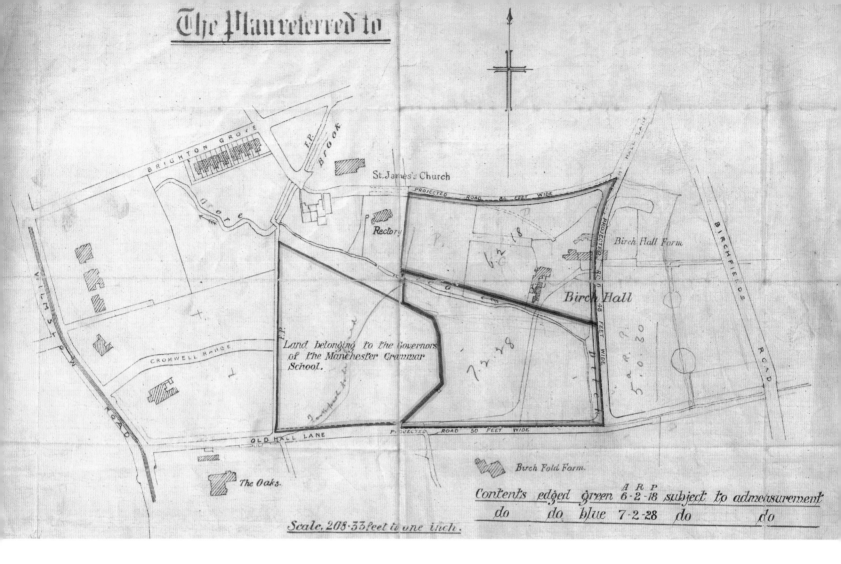

The Plan referred to

St. James's Church

Rectory

Land belonging to the Governors of the Manchester Grammar School.

Birch Hall Farm

Birch Hall

Birch Fold Farm.

BRIGHTON GROVE

WILMSLOW ROAD

CROMWELL RANGE

OLD HALL LANE

PROJECTED ROAD 36 FEET WIDE

PROJECTED ROAD 48 FEET WIDE

PROJECTED ROAD 50 FEET WIDE

BIRCHFIELDS ROAD

The Oaks.

7.2.28

6.2.0

5.0.30

Contents edged green 6·2·18 subject to admeasurement
do   do   blue 7·2·28   do   do

Scale. 208·33 feet to one inch.

Map showing the land acquired in Rusholme for the new school in the 1920s.

Everything in Millgate smudged him who touched it, and one collected grime steadily all day. Horses clanked steel-shod hooves on cobbles, carters shouted 'whoas' and other things, and lorries roared and blew off steam below one's room so that the voice of wisdom was drowned. The windows were perpetually grimed with a sort of breath of dust in which the rude drew faces or wrote the unheeded appeal, 'Please clean', and only a poor sort of light got through.

Another described his journey into school from Whalley Range, 'through Moss Side and Hulme, line upon line of black brick buildings, along Upper Jackson Street, more grimy brick, into City road, still more – wharves, warehouses, more brick, all grimy, the railway viaducts, gasworks', ending up eventually 'behind the back of the black cathedral and finally into the long dismal canyon of Long Millgate'.[144] Improved public transport now made it easy for boys to travel out of the city centre. The inspectors understood that the school had minimal capital reserves but suggested that the time had surely come when serious consideration should once again be given to relocation.

Paton strongly supported the idea and in the summer of 1920 the governors finally decided to press ahead. A suitable location had already been found in Rusholme, where additional land was promised by the city council, and by the end of 1921 an enlarged site covering 23 acres had been acquired, fronting Birchfields to the north and Old Hall Lane to the south. The governors were prescient in piecing together the larger site but at a time of national austerity and spending cuts in education they were reprimanded by the Board of Education for buying too much land. Nevertheless, all the official correspondence, whether from the governors or the Board, expressed confidence that the project would be financed by the sale of the old school buildings. As one official wrote in February 1924, 'it is practically certain that it will be found to present no difficulty'.[145] It would, however, be more than eight years before the move took place. In the meantime, the announcement of the relocation caused uproar among the old boys, and Paton and his successor would spend a lot of time reassuring them that the school's traditions and character would not only survive but be strengthened by the move.

In January 1924 Paton advised the governors that he wished to resign, 'as, after 21 years of service, he felt he did not now possess that vigour and freshness which the post demanded'.[146] The governors made repeated attempts to persuade him to stay

and oversee the move, but Paton had previous experience at UCS of the delays that could occur with such projects, and obviously felt he should devote his remaining energies to new fields. In the autumn of 1924 he sailed for Canada and in 1925 became the first president of the Memorial University College in St John's, Newfoundland, where he remained until his return to England on his retirement in 1933.

He had refused to sit for his portrait on leaving MGS, although the old boys raised funds for the bronze portrait medallion now in the school's Paton Library. He also destroyed all his personal papers to prevent any memoir being written and turned down every honour he was offered. The collection for his retirement raised the substantial sum of more than £4,000 from the old boys towards helping poor boys attend camps. Paton was still looking forward. In his farewell address, he said that 'without change there could be no progress, and when the whole world was moving forward, it was not for the pioneer school of the pioneer city to hold back'.[147] The last public examination results of his time indicated the sustained level of academic success throughout the school. The pass rate at school certificate, the equivalent of the GCSE, was more than 81 per cent, and at higher school certificate, the equivalent of the A level, more than 91 per cent.[148] After his final speech day in the summer of 1924, when the cheering was dying away, his send-off was completed when the school captain asked for more, crying out, 'And now, three greater, for the Chief!'[149]

The first advertisement placed for Paton's successor attracted only one serious candidate, forcing the governors to raise the salary offered. Their unanimous choice was Douglas Miller, rector of Aberdeen Grammar School. Aged 44, he was an amiable, shy

and kindly man, courteous and diffident, a man in a very different mould from his predecessor. Educated at Glasgow Academy and Fettes College, he had graduated in 1904 from Merton College, Oxford. He gained his blue in rugby and played international rugby for Scotland before the First World War. After teaching practice at Manchester University, and experience in several schools, including MGS, he was appointed as rector of Kelvinside Academy in 1913, where 'his breadth of outlook, his skill in combining the humanities and science in education, and his keen interest in his school marked him out as a headmaster of a high order'.[150] He took the same post at Aberdeen Grammar School in 1921, where he was a popular leader, and his decision to leave was met with the same reluctance Paton had experienced at MGS.

Squeezed between two charismatic High Masters, Paton and James, Douglas Miller has been underestimated. The very fact that he was not another Paton – how could he be? – attracted unmerited criticism from some quarters, including a number of staff members. It is arguable that he led MGS during one of the most difficult periods in its history. His time in office was divided into three phases: the long-drawn out, financially difficult relocation; its aftermath during the depression of the 1930s; and the Second World War. Miller had to handle the enormous pressures on the school that were generated by all three episodes. Yet he shared the same educational philosophy as his predecessor and successor, appreciating the sincerity and 'a hatred of shams'[151] characteristic of the boys, and wanting to see every one of them, whether the average boy or the most able, reach his potential in order to make the most of his opportunities in the wider world.

Left: Douglas Miller, High Master (1924–45).

Below: Boys studying in the 1930s.

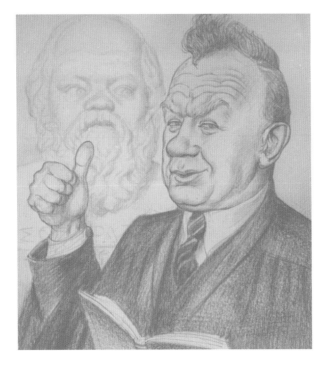

Miller had just introduced the subject in the science sixth as an alternative for study at higher school certificate level. Speight replaced the collection of stuffed animals and withered plant specimens with modern apparatus and, coming to MGS from research at Aberystwyth, treated his sixth form pupils as university students, encouraging them to think and observe for themselves.

Miller's sixth-form strategy was a resounding success. In 1930 it encompassed not only boys seeking places at university but also one form, Modern Transitus, filled with boys seeking places in commerce and industry. Almost without exception every boy remained for the full two years, following one of five recognised advanced courses. Between 1928 and 1930, 554 boys were entered for the higher school certificate and only 32 failed. In 1930, 40 of the 50 boys seeking university places were successful, 26 of them gaining Oxbridge places. But this bald figure disguised the quality of the boys: for the period covering 1928–9 and 1929–30, MGS boys had won 39 Oxbridge open scholarships, spread across classics, maths, science, modern languages and history, along with seven state and 28 municipal scholarships, still vital for so many boys to ensure they could afford to complete their degrees. Such boys were an undoubted challenge for some staff. When W. H. Mason was appointed by Miller to teach the history sixth in 1930, he found himself in front of a haughty group of very able young men, with 'a certain reputation for intransigence',[153] which taught him just how high were the school's standards. And he found himself surrounded by dauntingly intelligent masters in the common room, men like R. C. Chevalier, Twentyman and Albert Hyslop. As one boy of the

He set out his views on education to the old boys in 1928, telling them that he and his staff did not believe that intellect was the only thing that counted in life. He did not want MGS to be a school that took in only boys of outstanding intellect and ability but wanted also to admit boys of average ability with the potential to prosper at a grammar school. He built on Paton's work and strengthened the ethos of the school, later well expressed by one boy who arrived early in Miller's time, Harold Lever, another boy from Manchester's Jewish community: 'I quickly learned from the tolerant, easy-going, shrewd, scholarship-loving atmosphere of Manchester Grammar School that though being yourself might not be a very noble or exhilarating thing, it was about the best thing you could do.'[152]

One of Miller's universally agreed strengths was his judgement of character. He made some outstanding appointments to the MGS teaching staff, which helped to sustain and refresh the school at a time when the relocation was becoming bogged down in interminable delays. While he wanted to reform the curriculum to increase the options available for all boys, he was particularly interested in developing the sixth form. With more boys staying longer, numbers in the sixth form grew steadily, reaching 165 boys by 1930. The school, as ever, included some outstanding teachers, such as two of Paton's later appointments, R. M. 'Simmie' Simkins and R. T. 'Arty' Moore, who between them dominated the teaching of classics for more than 40 years. Miller wanted to appoint more specialists, and one of his first appointments was MGS's first specialist biology teacher, William Speight, in 1925.

Above: R. T. 'Arty' Moore taught classics for 40 years (1921–61).

Right: Michael Winstanley (1929–36), politician, broadcaster, physician and writer, was taught by a number of exceptionally gifted masters, many of whom served the school until retirement. He commented on MGS that 'the individualism of its boys depends upon the individualism of its staff'.

Above: MGS boys and staff setting off to visit J. L. Paton in Newfoundland, 1926.

Left: They sailed on the RMS *Nova Scotia*, a new mail ship that operated from Liverpool to Boston via St John's, Newfoundland and Halifax, Nova Scotia.

time, Michael Winstanley, later recalled of MGS, 'the individualism of its boys depends upon the individualism of its staff'.[154]

Miller took no notice of those who still criticised day schools for a lack of community spirit by comparison with boarding schools. This mistaken assessment was usually made by those who came to MGS after experience of boarding. Some years earlier, one boy joining MGS after boarding school clearly missed the point about the school, not only bemoaning what he perceived to be a lack of corporate spirit, but also wondering why an MGS boy could not be smarter, rather than 'straggling along, hands in pockets'.[155] Miller had chosen to teach in day schools, he said, because 'with the day school lay the real vital future of this country'.[156] Acknowledging the important contribution made by parents, he pointed out that boys in a day school were never isolated from ordinary daily life. He made sure that the school still came together

regularly, whether for prayers each morning, for lunch, or for activities between the end of school and late afternoon.

Miller wanted to further what he called the school's democratic tradition, and believed it was important that it remained socially diverse: 'I want to see the School, with all its traditions, take in and absorb all classes, and receive something back from all classes, and produce a really fine attitude.'[157] When the boys came to school, he wanted them to widen their horizons. Camps and treks remained an essential part of this experience. The traditional camps continued. In 1926, at the time of the general strike, Thomas Stott took his party to Grasmere in a furniture removal van, returning in an old bus that took 13 hours to get back to Manchester, suffering four punctures on the way. The Stratford-upon-Avon camp became an annual event for a while, with the tenth annual camp taking place in 1930. The treks began to multiply; in 1927, for instance, there was a Scottish trek, a Devon and Dorset trek, a Northumberland trek and an Alsace trek. Under the leadership of Harry Lob and W. H. Madden, overseas treks became more ambitious. In 1926, for instance, a party of 40 boys travelled with Madden to Newfoundland, where they enjoyed the hospitality of Paton and the Memorial College, while Lob led a trek in the Dolomites. The Alps became a popular destination, and treks to Germany were resumed. In 1929 a group of 24 boys sailed by P&O ferry from Tilbury to Morocco. In the same year US school boys joined the summer trek to the Lakes and two years later formal exchange links were established with the oldest school in the US, Boston Latin School in Massachusetts, founded in 1635.

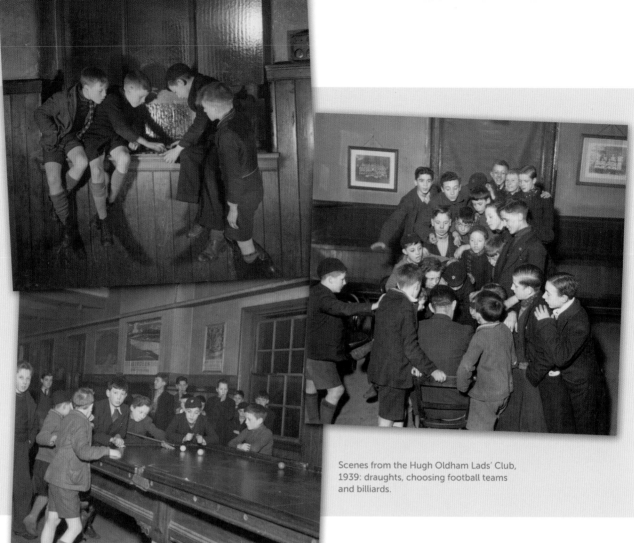

Scenes from the Hugh Oldham Lads' Club, 1939: draughts, choosing football teams and billiards.

Miller also wanted to foster the school's service ethos, which saw boys helping out at the Hugh Oldham Lads' Club, operating the magic lantern for the lectures to prisoners in Strangeways Prison, and collecting significant sums every year for charity. In 1925 a group of boys on their own initiative had invited 20 children from disadvantaged homes in Ancoats to tea at the school, which, said Miller, was 'significant of the School, and what we are living for – not merely the storing up of knowledge, but to help others who have not the same advantages that we have'.[158]

Following a critical review of *As You Like It* in 1926 by old boy Edgar Lustgarten, who wrote, 'Chief credit must go to the camp-fire which burned steadily through three acts,' attempts were made to stimulate drama and music, with plays by Shaw performed alongside concert performances of Gilbert and Sullivan, but these were subjects that were not strong in boys' schools until well after the Second World War.

There was greater success in sport. G. T. Richardson,[159] captain of the 1st XI, hit a century in 45 minutes, including 18 fours, against Merchant Taylors' School in 1925, followed by 109 against Craven Gentlemen in 1926, by which time the

school was running five first teams plus two under-14 sides, a Rusholme XI and an occasional under-16 team. The school also ran several football and lacrosse teams. MGS won the North of England junior schools lacrosse championship in 1927, repeating the feat in 1928, when the swimming team won the Urwick Cup. Rugby was extended to junior boys at Rusholme in 1929. Many school sides were divided between teams playing at Rusholme and those playing at the Cliff, where one boy, Ian Bailey, recalled many footballs ending up in the Irwell. Athletics flourished, with the school developing a particular reputation for relay running, winning the inter-schools relay race on several occasions. An annual triangular athletics meeting began in 1931. Another regular annual event was the boxing tournament.

And all this time the school was still waiting to move to its new premises in Rusholme. It was only in 1926 that the governors won approval from the Board of Education to raise a loan for the project, which both school and Board were confident would be covered by the proceeds from the sale of the old buildings. The governors optimistically believed the relocation would take place in 1928. In March 1927 the *Guardian* printed the drawing and plans of the new buildings under the title 'Our New Grammar School'. Miller had to keep reassuring the old boys that progress

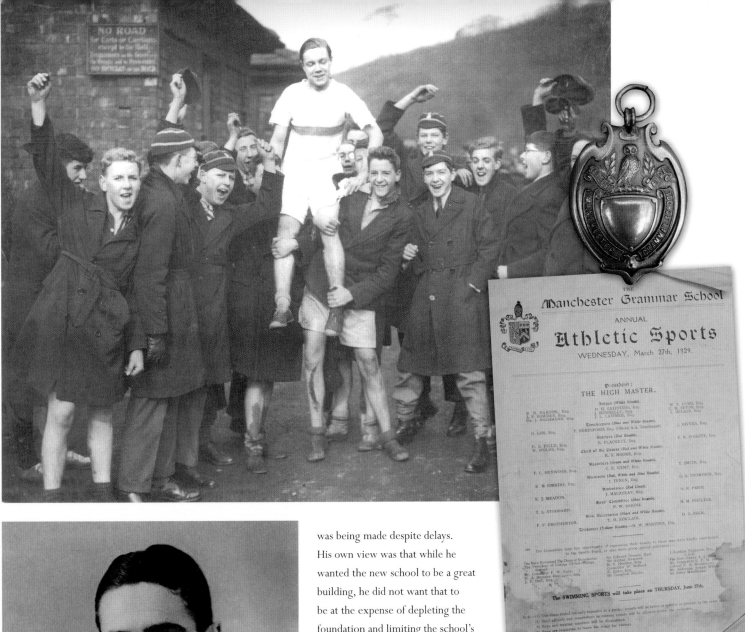

was being made despite delays.
His own view was that while he
wanted the new school to be a great
building, he did not want that to
be at the expense of depleting the
foundation and limiting the school's
independence. By 1928, as the tender
was accepted, similar concerns were
being expressed by some civil servants,
who felt unable to intervene, given the Board's
earlier approval of the project's finances. Indeed, one civil
servant concluded:

> On the general question of finance, the uncertainty as to the
> price which the old buildings will fetch no doubt imparts an
> element of doubt, but it is to my mind fantastic to imagine that
> the hard-headed businessmen who control the affairs of the school
> would embark on a scheme in which there was any risk of their
> obligations to the Bank which is advancing the capital monies not
> being met or of the future of the school being jeopardised.[160]

These doubts were, however, shared by the school's receiver,
Owen Cox, who warned the governors in 1928 that he believed

Above: James
Wooley (1928–33)
being held high
after winning the
Steeplechase at
Drinkwater Park;
Athletic Sports
programme and
medal, 1929.

Left: Douglas
Gordon Arthur
Lowe (1915–17)
was a British double
Olympic Games
champion, winning
gold medals in 1924
and 1928. On both
occasions he set
British 800 metres
records.

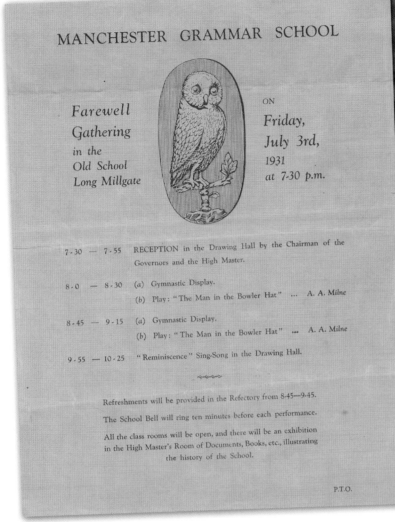

MANCHESTER GRAMMAR SCHOOL

Farewell Gathering in the Old School Long Millgate

ON Friday, July 3rd, 1931 at 7·30 p.m.

7·30 — 7·55   RECEPTION in the Drawing Hall by the Chairman of the Governors and the High Master.

8·0 — 8·30   (a) Gymnastic Display.
              (b) Play: "The Man in the Bowler Hat" ... A. A. Milne

8·45 — 9·15   (a) Gymnastic Display.
              (b) Play: "The Man in the Bowler Hat" ... A. A. Milne

9·55 — 10·25 "Reminiscence" Sing-Song in the Drawing Hall.

Refreshments will be provided in the Refectory from 8·45—9·45.

The School Bell will ring ten minutes before each performance.

All the class rooms will be open, and there will be an exhibition in the High Master's Room of Documents, Books, etc., illustrating the history of the School.

P.T.O.

Above: Programme for the 'Farewell Gathering' at Long Millgate, 1931.

Centre: The laying of the foundation stone for the new school at Old Hall Lane, 1931.

the value of the old buildings was overstated. On 1 May 1929, the foundation stone was finally laid at Rusholme by the chairman of governors, Sir Arthur Haworth. Concerns over funding had been based partly on the shaky state of the economy, so the onset of the depression in the autumn of 1929 was calamitous for the governors, who were alarmed to find that the value of their property had halved, falling short of covering costs by almost £100,000. Emergency action had to be taken, with the Board of Education granting approval for a further bank loan, and arrangements were made for a public appeal, launched early in 1931 by the bishop of Manchester in the lord mayor's parlour (as was the previous appeal in 1876), but none of these measures would alleviate the emerging financial difficulties that would plague the school throughout the 1930s. One of the most touching donations to the appeal came from one man, disabled during the war, who sent in a two-shilling postal order; 30 years previously

domestic circumstances had prevented him from taking up his scholarship and instead he had entered a cotton mill. He wrote with poignancy that, 'the dream of 30 years ago, though never realised, has never been forgotten'.[161] It was such dreams that MGS strove to make real.

Over the Christmas holidays at the end of 1930 the Owl at last left the old school for the new premises. On 3 July 1931 more than 2,500 old boys and partners attended a farewell gathering at Long Millgate. Among them was Raymond Streat.

Morning clothes were worn, and there was no attempt at order or regulation of the evening's programme. You pushed your way into the old Drawing Hall to shake hands with the High Master, Douglas Miller, and the chairman of governors, Sir Arthur Haworth. Then you pushed your way out again and jostled a path through the crowded corridors to whichever old classroom you wanted to revisit ... The steps and the corridors were dark and gloomy ... I had forgotten that when I first went there as a boy it struck me that it was a forbidding spot.[162]

The last day in Long Millgate was 24 July; the first day at Rusholme was 15 September. One boy later remembered that not

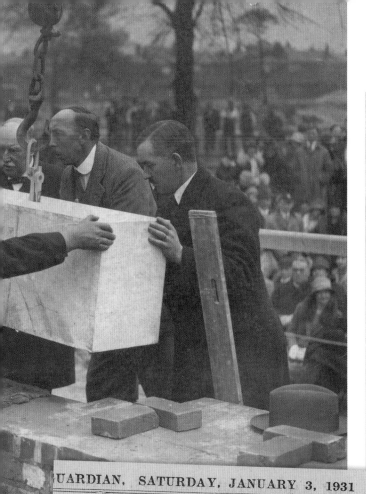

THE GRAMMAR SCHOOL OWL

Manchester Guardian Copyright.

Mr. Owen W. Cox, the Receiver of the Manchester Grammar School, watching the departure of the school's famous emblem to the new buildings in Rusholme.

one pupil sighed for Long Millgate, while another recalled quite aptly, given the circumstances, that the move was 'a glorious nebulous something, which, like final World Peace or a new car on order, seemed now nearer, now further, but never quite real'. The beginning of term in the new buildings was a very muddy affair, with loud hammerings as the final plumbing and carpentry work was completed. The opening was impressive, with staff in their robes lining the drive, as Lord Derby and a party of Manchester dignitaries made their way down, Derby insisting on shaking hands with every member of staff, which rather flummoxed Miller, who in consequence got several names mixed up. 'And the differences all this has made? Quite surprisingly, little in fundamentals, but there is much less grime, much less noise, and much more light.'[163] In this it was exactly what Miller had wanted.

The end of an era; Owen Cox, the school receiver (1888–1934) and W. H. Jepson, the school porter (1884–1934), closing the gates at Long Millgate for the final time. 'Jeppy', as well as keeping the boys in order, was also publican of the nearby Manchester Arms.

7 A DIFFICULT BEGINNING 1931–45

'A New World'

The school skirted financial disaster during the 1930s. On Christmas Eve 1931 Raymond Streat dined with J. Rankine Finlayson, another prominent Manchester businessman, who had just taken over as treasurer on the board of governors. 'Finlayson was terribly worried about the deficit on the new building. Their inability to sell the old building had landed them in a bad mess.' In January 1932 the school's overdraft stood at £200,000 and the bank was enquiring how the school would meet its monthly interest payments. At the same time the national government's drastic public spending cuts led to a reduction in grants from the Board of Education and local education authorities (as well as a cut of ten per cent in teaching salaries). The school had also failed to dispose of its three feeder schools, all of which were a financial drain. In the autumn of 1932 the school inspectors, pointing out that 'no large economy could be made in any direction', emphasised that 'the problem of finance is the most serious the School has to face, perhaps the most serious in its long history'.[164]

Opposite: 'The Main Drive and Archway at Rusholme' by Dennis Roxby Bott.

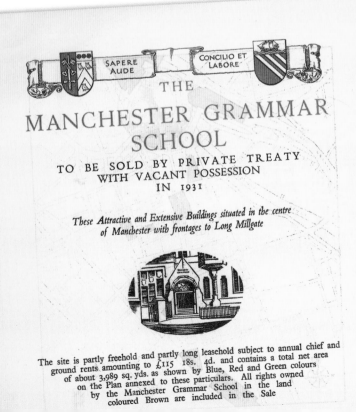

The school was burdened by debt throughout the 1930s. Although a loan was taken out in 1936 to pay off the overdraft, with the loan itself repaid over 25 years through an insurance policy, the old school buildings remained unsold in 1938. This had three consequences. First, to reduce the deficit, fees had to be increased, sanctioned by the Board of Education in early 1932. Second, the school had to admit more boys (1,162, including 375 free place holders, in 1932) than the buildings had been intended for (900). Third, the squeeze in grants meant that the school could rarely afford to appoint more staff. With so many boys, including nearly 200 in the still growing sixth form, the school coped only because every member of the 58 staff had a full teaching timetable (the High Master himself taught 12 periods every week) and by having 30 boys in most classes below the sixth form. Since his arrival Miller had replaced more than half the staff and most teaching was now done by specialists. The inspectors noted that 'the staff is very

Right: Owen Cox, W. H. Jepson and Fred Etchells in front of the new school, 1932.

Centre: Masters and pupils taking part in a chess competition, 1930s. Hyman Lob (1908–41) is smoking a pipe.

Inset: A chess medal from 1894.

strong'. Their calibre (nearly a third of them possessed first-class degrees) and their extraordinary devotion held things together.

Many staff showed a deep commitment to the boys in their charge in an age when the concept of pastoral care had scarcely been defined. While form masters remained primarily responsible for the boys' welfare, many boys also turned to other staff, particularly those, like Scout leaders, who led camps and treks. Boys were encouraged to talk through their problems with them until they were resolved. Among them was Hyman (Harry) Lob, who had joined the school from King's College, Cambridge, in 1908, and had served in the First World War. Heavily committed to treks, junior cricket and music, he loved chess and contributed scholarly articles to mathematical journals. He was known to give poorer boys their tram fares and beg team shirts for them so they could play in school matches. He also helped to console parents whose sons had died or were going through serious illness. Another was Lob's friend, H. A. 'Haffy' Field, who thought nothing of cycling from his home in Rusholme on a Saturday morning to see the parents of a boy about whom he was concerned. Bert Toft, the school's rugby coach and an old boy, once showed his solicitude

towards the boys in a very direct way. A Wall's Ice Cream man was in the habit of pulling up on his tricycle outside the school gates and encouraging young boys to buy penny ices by showing them well-thumbed pornographic photographs. One day Toft strode past the boys as they were forming a queue and promptly punched the ice-cream seller, who, once he had picked himself up, pedalled furiously away, never to be seen again.

On the other hand, some teachers took a different approach to discipline. With corporal punishment regarded as an integral part of a boy's education, MGS boys did not escape the occasional brutal beating. The cane finally disappeared from state schools in 1987, and from independent schools only in 2003, when it was banned in Northern Ireland (it had been banned in English independent schools in 1999). Eccentric forms of discipline were commonplace. At MGS, recalled J. R. Anderson, W. 'Billy' Hulme 'was quick to display his armoury of wooden spoons (one broken), a bayonet frog, a slipper and a rather tatty cane, expiated on their corrective potential at length; but during that year [taking form 2b for English in 1935–6] he only slippered one boy and that with a couple of not very impressive swipes'. Ian Bailey

remembered how Hulme's 'style of punishments and their application made life miserable for many generations of boys'.[165] Hulme's approach may have been influenced by the ordeal of his first term as a master in 1922. Many new teachers met their match when deliberately tested by the toughest forms in the school. Apparently Hulme did not escape unscathed, but at least there was no terminal damage to his career.

Miller and his staff achieved great things. By the early 1930s, less than 15 per cent of boys left the school before they were 16, and nearly three-quarters of those who did had passed their school certificate. Most forms took the certificate in four years, one

Top: Hubert Astley ('Haffy') Field (1923–63), a good friend of Hyman Lob; they were both known for their kindness to boys and dedication to the school.

Above: High jinks on a field trip, 1930s.

Left: William ('Billy') Hulme (1922–64) taught French and German and had a reputation for being a strict disciplinarian.

Top: Sol Clynes (1938–88) teaching in the early 1940s.

Above: Ernest Hollowell (1940–56) teaching art, c.1944.

Centre: A momentous day: the first assembly at Rusholme, 1931.

weaker form taking five, a pattern that lasted into the 1980s. The long-identified weaknesses of the sides remained unresolved, with too many boys on the classical side learning too little science, none at all on the modern side learning Latin, and boys on the science side having to choose between Latin and French. More options, urged the inspectors, but little would change until the 1960s.

The number of boys entering other universities, particularly Manchester, now exceeded those winning Oxbridge places. MGS boys shone at university, observed the inspectors in 1932, recording that they were 'amongst the leaders of undergraduate intellectual life',[166] a further rebuttal of the claim that the school

was nothing more than an exam factory whose products failed to sustain their progress once they had left. Geoffrey Stone never felt this to be true. 'That we took exams was quite incidental. Nobody really bothered about them.'[167] Boys were expected to take exams in their stride. High standards were sustained throughout the decade: in 1938, 90 out of 101 entrants passed the higher school certificate and boys won 23 Oxbridge scholarships, including five at Trinity, Cambridge, as well as seven at Manchester and one at St Andrew's. These were essential for many boys, as were awards from local authorities and school leaving exhibitions. As a result, far more boys left the sixth form for other destinations; as Sydney Dobson recalled, for many of them their ambition was not university but 'a thousand-a-year job'.[168]

Sydney Dobson entered the school as a foundation scholar in 1933. School blazers and trousers were available from a city-

THE MANCHESTER GRAMMAR SCHOOL MAGAZINE
OFFICIAL ORGAN OF THE OLD MANCUNIANS
ASSOCIATION
Vol. LXI   MARCH, 1933   No. 428
Annual Subscription to the O.M.A. (inclusive of this Magazine), 5/-

Above:
Photographic
Society, 1930s.

Left: Ulula, March
1933.

centre outfitter, but Sydney's family, like many others, was among those who could not afford uniform, which was a bit of a mish-mash, the only compulsory item being the school cap. MGS was a revelation for a young boy. 'For me, it was a new world.'[169] Dinner tickets were bought, with five for every four paid for. Each boy was given a folding card on which to write down his timetable. Downstairs lessons were lettered, upstairs ones numbered. In each form room, every boy had a locker and a desk. All the furniture was new and boys were expected to keep it in mint condition. In the school tuck shop, boys could buy potato cakes in the winter, which took the chill off cold hands at playtime. Chocolate bars were sold as well, but Sydney never had enough pocket money to afford them. Sixth-form boys could walk out of school at lunchtime, often buying lunch at a local fish-and-chip shop. For their meals in the refectory, boys sat at long tables, each headed by a master. A spilt glass of water earned a fine of a penny, and a spilt jug, a shilling.

Every effort was made to make the most of the new school's sporting facilities. The boys swam naked in the new baths at Rusholme, not a usual custom at boys' schools; they had worn dark cotton slips for swimming at Long Millgate that were laundered after use. The slips' disappearance at Rusholme was put down to the pressures of austerity. The playing fields came into full

Above: Swimming competition at Victoria Baths, Hathersage Road and the Novice swimming cup awarded from 1921 to 1991.

Below: Freddie Riley (1923–29), was a member of the British Olympic football squad in 1936.

Below right: Bert Toft, captain of the England rugby team, old boy, and MGS rugby coach from 1932 to 1939.

use in 1933, enabling games to be timetabled for every boy below the sixth form. In the following year, as a further refinement, Miller introduced four houses (Ainsworth, De Quincey, Lockwood and Bradford), aimed at stimulating sport among the boys, but they were never popular, as boys from the same form who had made firm friendships resented being split up. Geoffrey Stone felt houses ran contrary to the spirit of the school: 'MGS was a place for individuals, not cliques.'[170] Miller also embarked on a more ambitious fixture list, and MGS played soccer against Shrewsbury, swam against Sedbergh and ran against Rossall. In 1938 the MGS athletics team took part for the first time in the Public Schools' Championship at White City. Sporting fortunes ebbed and flowed,

but MGS proved particularly strong in football, lacrosse and rugby, the latter coached by Bert Toft. Toft had captained the school rugby team and was England's first choice as hooker between 1936 and 1939, captaining the side in 1938–9.

The range of other activities remained wide, supported by hard-working staff, some of whom showed their lighter side through an entertainment troupe called the Pedagogues. Started in 1933 by D. D. Lindsay (later headmaster of Portsmouth Grammar School) and D. G. Richards, the troupe specialised in concert performances of sketches and songs that often parodied school life.

The school's great tradition for camping and trekking remained just as strong. Geoffrey Stone recalled weekends spent at the Owl's Nest, where boys slept with rough sheepskin covers over their beds, and the shower was a water tank atop the outside shed. One change was the move from the original camp site at Alderley Park to Booths Hall, Knutsford, in 1939. Treks still had a huge impact on young boys, taking many of them out of the city into open countryside or beyond Britain's borders for the first time. Sydney Dobson, who had never been abroad, found travelling to the French Alps 'a great adventure'. The boys made their way down through France via Paris to Grenoble. 'When we reached our destination, we were dazzled by the warm

sunshine and the brightness, which was so different from the gloom we had become accustomed to in the city of Manchester.'[171] Trekking was organised into trekking days (the whole camp moving on), 'bivvies' (bivouacking overnight en route to an overnight stop), excursions (hiking up to high peaks) and free days (washing, laundering, shopping). Waterproof gear, fleeces, anoraks and proper walking boots were unheard of when Harry Lob urged boys preparing for the Dauphine trek in 1938 to 'bring as little as possible'. By this he meant a rucksack, boots, shirt, sweater, shorts and stockings, with a complete change of clothing; towel, bathing suit, soap, comb, toothbrush, deep plate, enamel mug, cutlery, light shoes and soft socks; a light mackintosh; and

'a length of flannel, about four or five inches, to go round the waist if the nights prove unduly cold'.[172] In the summer of 1935 boys travelling to Germany were hosted by members of the Hitler Youth, who in return visited MGS in the following summer. Led by Herr Liebeskind, who had been a German assistant at the school in 1934–5, they joined the Scouts at their camps in Deepdale and Borrowdale. Bemused MGS boys trailed behind them, as they marched three abreast singing the Horst Wessel song.

Summer cruises were organised throughout the 1930s. In 1933, for instance, a dozen boys once again sailed for Morocco during the long Whitsun holiday. In 1936 the Easter cruise around the Mediterranean was on board the SS *Lancastria*, which in June 1940 was sunk by the Germans off the French coast, with the loss of 6,000 lives.

MGS hosted the boys of the Hitler Youth in the same year that it welcomed the first group of Jewish boys taking refuge from Nazism. In 1936 Otto Julius Lowenstein and the two Wolf brothers, Gerhard and Peter, joined the school. Gerhard recalled the special effort made to teach them English as quickly as possible. In 1937 they were followed by R. H. Fritzsche,

Above: Scenes from the Owl's Nest, 1930s.

Below left: Camping in the Lake District, 1930s.

Above: Visit of the Hitler Youth, 1936.

who would later remark that 'I will never forget the equality of treatment and the complete absence of national prejudice I experienced at MGS'. It would have helped that the school had a long tradition of educating local Jewish boys.[173]

MGS was evacuated from Manchester just before war was declared in September 1939. The city's evacuation plan led to the removal of 72,000 children and 23,000 adults. Fewer than 900 boys applied to join the school in Blackpool, where they arrived on the day before war broke out, sent to 'a rain-sodden field and a collection of leaking bell tents'[174] on the outskirts of town before being parcelled out to billets in local boarding houses. The billeting process was not satisfactory. 'The boys were marched out in batches and dumped, like Japanese merchandise, wherever the door was half-open. Some found good homes; many did not.'[175] Some first formers found themselves sleeping in baths and a number of landladies were reputed to have offered their services to senior boys. Staff devised their own system, inspecting countless homes where offers of reception had been made, moving more than 500 boys into better billets.

MGS shared the premises of the Palatine Road Central School, alternating between mornings one week and afternoons the next. The school was far too small and there was a shortage of books, chalk and paper, but for science the boys were allowed to use the local technical college. Half-days were spent playing games, on the beaches or in Stanley Park, or filling sandbags for the defence of the Miners' Home on the seafront at Bispham. In the evenings a few boys would go dancing to the Tower Ballroom; there 15-year-old Derek Hull met his first girlfriend, smoked his first cigarette and tasted his first pint of beer.

It was all very unsatisfactory and some parents began removing their sons and sending them to other schools. Miller was worried that MGS was starting to fall apart, reporting to the governors

Above and centre:
Dolomites Trek,
1933.

Left: Sketch of
'Harry' Lob, 'Haffy'
Field and 'Billy'
Hulme planning
the trek.

that 'it was obvious that the work of the School would be seriously affected'.[176] On 22 September, Sir Arthur Haworth, the chairman of governors, accompanied by Owen Cox's successor as receiver, Tom Nutter, met the secretary of the Board of Education in London, and asked for permission to bring the school back to Manchester. The governors argued that the school was in danger of losing its character and traditions among the boarding houses of Blackpool. The school's request was granted on the grounds that

107

Documents and photos relating to the evacuation of the school to Blackpool in 1939.

MGS was located 'on the fringes of and in a sparsely populated portion of the evacuation area'. But the decision antagonised Manchester corporation, which sent a deputation to protest to the Board. With one minister, Lord Woolton, the minister of food, being an old boy and a governor, there was a suspicion that strings were being pulled. The corporation also feared that MGS's return would encourage other schools to do the same and wreck the entire evacuation scheme. The secretary of the Board refused to budge. He did, however, add that another factor had been 'the proximity of the school to the evacuation boundary, the

exceptionally high age range of the pupils, and the importance of the school and the effect of prolonged closure on the school's finances'.[177] Miller himself told the old boys, 'After all, the MGS stands for a tremendous amount not only in Manchester but throughout the country.'[178]

MGS moved back on 8 October – 'there has been no happier train load than the one which left Blackpool' – on a private train to Victoria Station, where the boys were greeted by press photographers and parents, with porters

Right: Parents, masters and boys arriving at Marton Moss, Blackpool.

Inset: 'Greetings from Blackpool' card by the art master, Frederick Garnett.

Clockwise from top left: Damage to the school building caused by a bomb coming down on the playing fields, 1940; Hyman ('Harry') Lob (1908–41), one of the school's most beloved masters, was tragically killed by a bomb at the age of 55 while on air raid patrol in Withington; ARP warden giving advice in front of the school air raid shelter, 1940.

shouting, 'Make way for the Manchester Grammar School Special!' School re-opened on 19 October, by which time basement shelters had been completed.

The school had one very near escape after its return. Manchester suffered its heaviest bombing just before Christmas 1940 when 363 people were killed and more than 1,000 injured. In the badly damaged city centre, half the old school was destroyed. At Rusholme a landmine came down on the playing fields, causing extensive but superficial damage to the buildings. Windows were blown out and doors flung open, their locks shattered. In the art room and gym, shards of glass were blown into panelling, blackboards and equipment. The school extended the holidays for another week to allow the mess to be cleared up. Many of the houses opposite the school were damaged and several had to be demolished. The same raid also destroyed the Owl's Nest at Disley.

Just days later, in January 1941, another raid killed Harry Lob and several of his fellow air-raid wardens. It was Lob's death rather than the list of old boy casualties that really brought home the war to the boys. His friend 'Haffy' Field described how Lob's 'blazing enthusiasm made everything he did turn to gold'.[179] While daytime raids continued to disrupt school life, no more damage was caused and the disturbances diminished considerably after June 1941.

MGS's feeder schools became a casualty of war. Both North and South Manchester Schools lost many of their pupils after evacuation, confirming for Miller the wisdom of MGS's decision to return to Manchester. It was a common danger for evacuated schools and some failed to survive the war. The North and South Manchester Schools never recovered after they returned to the city. Having run at a loss since the mid-1930s, they were closed at the end of the summer term in 1940, with the remaining 58 boys transferred to MGS. Miss Robins and Miss Gaskill were appointed to take the new prep classes. Later they were also joined by Miss King to teach physics, Miss Graham to teach maths and Miss Williams to teach modern languages – but women teachers were appointed only 'for the duration of the war'[180] and were forbidden to use the common room. The latter would become known formally as the 'masters' common room', reverting back to 'common room' in the 1980s as more women joined the teaching staff.

One young master, M. M. Scarr, was awarded the George Medal for bravery for moving shells out of a munitions factory after an explosion.

A determined effort was made to keep activities going despite a restricted timetable and regular interruptions to routine, and by and large this was successful. The dinner-hour piano recitals given by languages teacher Cyril McGuire were popular, attended by hundreds of boys, giving many of them their first introduction to classical music. The school baths were closed and then re-opened, but the water was always freezing. The school cook and her staff made the most of the special rations given to all schools, baking huge numbers of honey, almond, currant and Chelsea buns for sale at break times, in addition to the famous potato cakes, all at a penny each. In October 1943 a group of boys took part in a wireless programme, *Transatlantic Call*, linking up with Weequahic High School in Newark, New Jersey. Discipline remained good and academic standards never faltered. In 1943, for instance, 109 out of 116 boys were awarded higher school certificates, there were 20 Oxbridge open scholarships and three exhibitions, as well as 18 state scholarships and 35 local education authority scholarships. In the following year the school achieved a record 37 Oxbridge open scholarships.

Numbers revived after the return to Rusholme. Squeezing ever more boys into the school, Miller was able to claim by 1942 that MGS was the largest school in the country. By the end of the war the school roll stood at 1,464 boys. Miller had to report that

Top: Contributing to the war effort by hoeing cabbages at Lathom Hall in Ormskirk, 1941.

Above: Masters and boys working hard to prepare a field for planting.

Right: The Lord Mayor and other dignitaries amid the ruins of the Free Trade Hall after the Manchester Blitz, December 1940.

The pattern of MGS life during the Second World War had echoes of the First World War. To replace masters on active service (by 1942 they numbered 18), Miller found 'capable substitutes', including Herbert Newbould, who had retired from the staff shortly before the war, and Charles Tunnicliffe, the distinguished wildlife artist. Speech day was moved to the memorial hall after the bombing of the Free Trade Hall. As a result of austerity, the school cap lost its stripes, and the metal owl that used to embellish it was replaced by an embroidered version, although both were restored after the war. Harvest camps returned, a daily class was given up to allow boys to help a local farmer, collections were made for wartime charities and parcels were sent to prisoners of war. Some boys worked for the Post Office, sorting and delivering mail, and even driving vans, while others helped at the RAF Maintenance Unit at Heywood. There was no revival of the OTC but an Air Training Corps (Squadron No. 600) was formed in 1941, with 201 boys under the command of Cyril 'Dickie' Radford, who had won the Military Cross during the First World War, assisted by acting instructors Kennelly and Hulme.

Douglas Miller retired as High Master at the end of the summer term in 1945. At a reception in the lord mayor's parlour Lord Woolton proposed and the lord mayor seconded the resolution recognising Miller's contribution to the school and the city. After his farewell to the school at the first post-war speech day, held in the Palace Theatre, the school sang 'The Road to the Isles', a touching tribute that revealed true affection. Miller had steered the school safely through a series of crises, none of which were of his making, while strengthening the calibre of the teaching staff and the school's academic reputation. By the end of the war this had come at great personal cost. He deserves a higher place in the pantheon of High Masters.

'we have had regretfully to deny admission to a large number of well-qualified boys, but the space available is exhausted'.[181]

Miller's achievement was marred by tragedy. His youngest son, David, was among the first of the old boys who lost their lives in the conflict. He had trained as a merchant navy wireless operator and was lost on the *Tiberton*, sailing in the first convoy to cross the Atlantic. By 1945 the war had claimed the lives of 229 old boys.

DIRECT GRANT HEYDAY 1945–64

'It is a Good Thing to be Intelligent'

At the age of 36, Eric James was the unanimous choice of the governors to succeed Douglas Miller. With a first-class degree in chemistry from Queen's College, Oxford, followed by a doctorate awarded two years later, and 12 years' teaching at Winchester, his academic credentials were impeccable. Slightly balding, with an expressive face, he had piercing blue eyes, just like Paton, although unlike Paton, he was often seen with a pipe in his mouth, a useful prop in the conversations he enjoyed, spun from his extensive knowledge and endless fund of ideas. Full of energy and enthusiasm, his generous nature masked a degree of ruthlessness.

Opposite: The Paton Library, described by *The Illustrated London News* as a place 'of diligent study, with scholars taking a keen interest in various branches of learning'.

Below: Eric James, High Master (1945–61).

His appointment as High Master coincided with the implementation of the 1944 Education Act, which established the basis of today's secondary education system. This coincidence would elevate the status of the school beyond anything it had yet achieved. The Act regularised and revised the direct grant regulations, giving scope for half of all places in any one direct-grant school to be offered as free places, the proviso being that any boy taking up a free place had to pass what became known as the 11-plus examination. The latter determined whether a boy passed from primary school to grammar school or to the newly created secondary modern schools. For MGS, which became one of fewer than 200 direct-grant schools, it resulted in a continuous stream of able boys attending the school at the expense of the state and the local education authorities on a scale never matched before or since. As the new High Master told the governors in 1946, the new rules made 'the school still more accessible to the poor boy, and it is gratifying that there is every evidence that the school is now completely open to any boy of sufficient merit'.[182]

The school's academic success would lead to yet another revival of the accusation made regularly ever since the days of Frederick Walker that MGS was no more than an exam factory. Since James was one of the most adept of High Masters in raising the public profile of the school, it was an accusation that constantly came his way. It was even made among some of his own staff. Sol Clynes, an outstanding teacher of science, whose service to MGS

spanned six decades, believed that James 'rather overstressed our academic achievements, and our public image became somewhat tarnished'.[183]

James certainly believed in an elite that had achieved its position through ability and whose needs could be met only through highly selective schooling. Yet from almost the very first day he became High Master, he emphasised that academic excellence should never obscure the fact that MGS was always about much more. There were some who suspected he was not altogether sincere. One member of staff who thought highly of him as a person would accuse him of taking 'refuge in the comparatively superficial' and of being 'that rare thing – a selfless careerist'.[184] Outsiders – and some insiders – resented James's overt elitism, which extended beyond education. He hated commercial television, for instance, believing it would corrode cultural values, as boys dashed home not to read but 'to listen to something quite awful'.[185] He did once consent to a boy appearing on a commercial television programme about youth, much to the boy's amazement, but only on condition that the school was not named, which was rather undermined by the boy's school tie and blazer.

On the other hand, James himself came from a humble background, giving him empathy for the boys who came knocking on the door of MGS. The son of a commercial traveller, who imbued in his son a love of literature, James had been unable to afford to fulfil his original ambition to become a doctor, which instead led him into teaching. At Winchester his belief in a broad education was evident from the way that, as his obituary recorded, he 'maintained and extended the tradition that the scientist should be a man of wide interests in philosophy, literature and the arts'.[186] He believed strongly in equality of opportunity, and by conviction was a Fabian socialist, which surprised some who thought they

knew him well. He would later tell the local newspaper that the essence of a great city school comprised 'a regard for ability that transcends any concern with social class, a respect for the integrity of scholarship, a readiness to adopt methods and curriculum to a changing climate of thought, and a recognition that legitimate independence is not incompatible with a place within the State system'.[187] One of his criticisms of the new idea of comprehensive education being widely discussed after the war was that in narrowing the curriculum, and omitting minority subjects, it was in danger of eliminating equality of opportunity for the brightest children. In contrast, he felt that grammar schools offered the nation a pool of first-rate intellects to lead the development of an expanding post-war state and its industry.

So, speaking to the old boys soon after his arrival, James insisted the pursuit of academic records was inimical to him, and said he knew academic achievement at MGS had not come at the expense of the boys' wider education. He told them he had reached a clear view of the school's strengths even before his appointment, and while intellectual achievement was one of them, so too was an ethos of public and social service, and a sense of democracy, in that it was possible for able boys from any class of society, regardless of income, to come to the school and mix with their peers. Two years later he told the same audience, 'We have to create an education that shall be at once genuinely democratic and at the same time shall not sacrifice its standards one jot, and shall retain a proper grip on the traditions of the past.' And on another occasion he was proud to say, 'We get boys from every class of society, and they work and play together because they are the same kind of boy, whatever their fathers' income may be … I pray God we may never be surprised that the boy from the bricklayer's family may, nevertheless, be good at French prose. The character of the place may be found in the high academic standard … These intelligent boys form the element of our strength in the School. The School exists for the education of the most intelligent boys, and it is a good thing to be intelligent'.[188] Yet he also understood that the school's success in sending boys to university was not the school's 'whole task', but nevertheless helped to 'get some light on the success with which we are discharging other portions, that of sending boys of merit and of character into every other department of public life and occupation'.[189] As a colleague later recalled, 'He took as much trouble, and often more, to get the "C" stream boy into the right niche in the University or Training College as he did to get the "A" stream boy into the right College at Oxbridge'.[190] The former head of Salford Technical College valued the links with MGS that came through James and the boys he sent there. The accusation

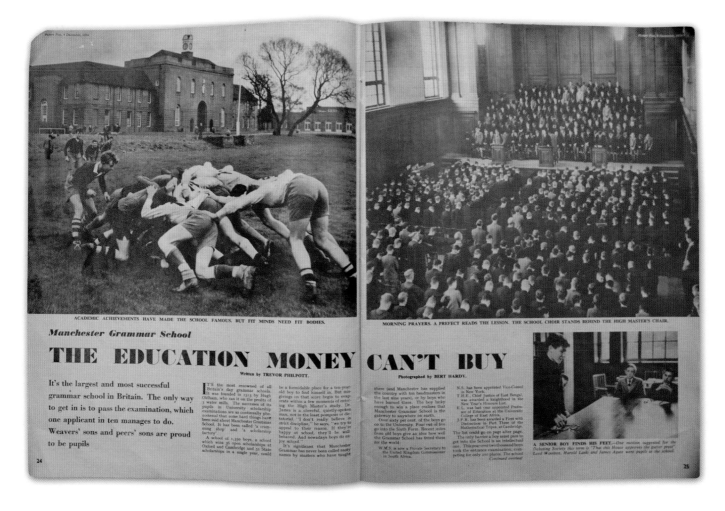

ACADEMIC ACHIEVEMENTS HAVE MADE THE SCHOOL FAMOUS, BUT FIT MINDS NEED FIT BODIES.

MORNING PRAYERS. A PREFECT READS THE LESSON. THE SCHOOL CHOIR STANDS BEHIND THE HIGH MASTER'S CHAIR.

Manchester Grammar School

THE EDUCATION MONEY CAN'T BUY

Written by TREVOR PHILPOTT.   Photographed by BERT HARDY.

It's the largest and most successful grammar school in Britain. The only way to get in is to pass the examination, which one applicant in ten manages to do. Weavers' sons and peers' sons are proud to be pupils

A SENIOR BOY FINDS HIS FEET.

that James considered those other than the most able to be intellectually subnormal was not just cruel and unfair, it was also wrong. He had the highest expectations of every boy, although for some, such expectations proved too demanding. As one of his pupils later recalled, 'Eric James would stop at no lengths for "his" boys, but in return, with a kind of innocence, he expected adherence to his precepts. A boy was automatically assumed to be self-motivated, ambitious in the best sense, and, by the Sixth Form, to have shaped some direction to that purpose. Not every boy responded, or had developed so far at that age, and Eric James was not unequivocally popular with all.'[191]

Although in a large school the High Master could seem remote, James deliberately decided to continue his predecessor's practice, and teach, making a huge impression on many of the boys who came into contact with him. Ernest Fox, who had joined the school during the war, remembered how the arrival of a new High Master brought 'a perceptible change of atmosphere'. Michael Lee, who entered the school in 1948, remembered James's occasional lessons in organic chemistry to the sixth form as 'a tour de force' and was open-mouthed at the impact of his wide-ranging lectures

on philosophy. Reaching the sixth form, Alan Garner found James to be 'a man of total intellectual honesty, a relentless brain and will, which were the product of continuous reassessment of belief and thought, who held that the highest, and for him, only, pursuit

Above: Article published in the *Picture Post,* December 1954. 'Weavers' sons and peers' sons are proud to be pupils.'

Left: The clock tower given to the school by Owen Cox, the school's receiver (1888–1934). The initials OCR appear on the clockface.

115

was the development of individual potential to its fullest, in the cause of excellence and the service of humanity'. Fox, uncertain whether to pursue teaching after Oxford, rang James for advice, and was astonished to find 'he knew everything about me'.[192]

James inspired as many staff as pupils. He inherited an outstanding body of teachers, largely put together by his predecessor, a calibre he sustained through his own good judgement. Like so many of his predecessors, he expected many of those he appointed to learn from their time at the school, and, moving on to higher posts, take with them something of MGS. Ernest Fox was among them, later becoming head of a school in Devon, and found teaching at MGS under James an exhilarating experience. Another master, O. R. Corbett, wrote, 'By merely being around the place, he brought a vigour to the school which amounted in the course of time to a kind of revolution,'[193] while E. R. Taylor recalled how James had injected a new sense of camaraderie and unity into the common room. Influenced by his headmaster at Winchester, Spencer Leeson, James saw the High Master's role as *primus inter pares*, as colleagues later remembered. 'Things were done, not because it had been decreed that they should be done, but because one knew that the Chief would like them to be done. Responsibility was delegated freely, with trust and confidence.'[194] He made efforts to get to know his staff and always encouraged them in their work. Many of the staff he appointed not only admired him, they saw him as a friend and adviser.

James welcomed the surge of applicants created by the 1944 Education Act, particularly since this would allow the sixth form to grow, a challenge James relished, feeling that 'this school has a great responsibility to fulfil'.[195] In 1946, when MGS abolished interviews and began admitting boys entirely on the results of a tougher entrance exam, there were nearly seven applicants for every place. This figure rose steadily, even after the reduction in entry streams from nine to seven, and reached a peak of ten applicants per place in 1955. After finally closing its own remaining feeder schools, MGS made strong links with other feeder schools, and James initiated the first conference with primary school heads in 1950. By that year nearly half of all boys entering the school paid no fees, thanks to a combination of the direct-grant scheme, the fees paid by several local education authorities for boys from their own areas, and MGS's own scholarships, which numbered in excess of 50. Most of the rest benefited from the school's fee remission scheme. Boys came from as wide a catchment area as ever, although more than three-quarters were from Cheshire, Lancashire and Manchester.

James was happy to meet parents but at a time when parental contact with school was limited and most heads regarded parents as a necessary nuisance, he tended to conduct parents' evenings in what could appear to be an off-hand manner. Geoff Fox, brother of Ernest, heard from his father how he had responded to James's habit of reacting to questions from the floor by striding back and forth, gown swishing from side to side, across the dais in the memorial hall. Mr Fox, a self-made businessman, rose to ask his question before pausing halfway through, prompting the High Master to urge him, 'Yes, please do carry on!' 'I will do when you stop walking up and down and look at me,' responded Mr Fox, continuing as James turned to meet his gaze. 'Why is it that my two boys work longer hours than I do – and I work a long day?' James simply insisted that was the price to be paid if they wanted their sons to gain places at a good university.[196]

Student numbers remained around 1,400, nearly half as many again as the intended capacity of the school buildings. Large classes had become a permanent fixture. By the late 1950s over 40 per cent of boys were sixth formers, more than double the number in 1945. In 1951 over 80 per cent of boys sitting their school certificate returned to join the sixth form. This growth created a major challenge for James and his staff, as it had for his predecessor, since the school lacked the resources to fund either the bricks and mortar or all the additional staff needed to establish an ideal sixth-form curriculum. As previous historians of the school noted, 'the School did not fully succeed [in the mid-1950s] in catering for the very varied and unusual capabilities of the boys entering it'.[197]

One consequence was that, as an inspection report hinted at in 1951, the curriculum appeared to be focused too narrowly on the pursuit of examination results. MGS, which the inspectors labelled as 'one of the most famous schools in the country,'[198] excelled as ever in winning awards at Oxbridge and other universities as well as prestigious state scholarships. The proportion of sixth-form leavers going to university rose constantly, from 55 per cent in 1952 to 80 per cent in 1961, as aspirations changed and more places became available. In that year MGS had won more Oxbridge places than any other school for the sixth year in a row, although there was a feeling among some sixth formers heading for university that MGS regarded true success as nothing less than an open award at Oxbridge. Pressure also came from the young age at which some boys entered the sixth form, thanks to accelerated learning, often before their 15th birthday. One boy later summed up MGS as nothing more than 'a shrivelling crammer too geared to tables of examination results'.[199] With hindsight some reflected that their immaturity, coupled with academic pressure, produced below-par results at A level.[200] On the other hand, there were boys who, while acknowledging the relentless pace of learning, coped well and never had any sense of cramming.

Drinking milk during morning break, and boys besieging the tuck shop for rationed sweets, 1950.

James himself reduced to one the number of forms following a five- rather than four-year course to O level. He was conscious of the need to educate every boy in the school:

The danger that, in a school of this kind, we may concentrate on the brilliant child and lack a proper concern for those who are not by our standards outstanding, is one of which my colleagues and I are keenly aware. It is perhaps impossible to remove from the public mind the belief that this school is good only for the very able boy, but I should like the governors, at any rate, to be aware that we make every effort to meet the needs of the boy who quite properly may not want a university career or be intellectually fitted for one.

How far this percolated down to the lowest stream is a moot point, with one of their form masters, an Old Mancunian himself, detecting a strong sense of disaffection stemming from their perception that they had very evidently been 'labelled' as weaker than their peers. But James was sincere in his views, which found further expression through his membership of the Crowther Committee, which investigated how best to expand educational opportunities for senior pupils attending secondary modern schools. The ensuing Crowther Report of 1959 recommended that the interests of all children, regardless of their ability, should not be neglected; that all pupils with the ability should be given the opportunity to sit O levels; that the sixth-form curriculum should be reformed and extended; and that a school's record should not be judged on the basis of its examination results. Needless to say, the report was largely ignored. James was also aware of the concept of what nowadays would be termed 'added value', and the benefits of continuously monitoring boys' progress, reporting in 1957 that 'from the age of ten or eleven we are diagnosing and fostering abilities which are still showing ten years later, often in competition with boys from much more favourable backgrounds'.[201]

Even though it hampered his ambitions, James believed the challenge of managing with limited resources was worth it. As he told the governors in 1951, 'There are some of us who think that the price paid … by the great independent schools for their amenities of staffing and equipment – the price of excluding any but the comparatively wealthy – is too high, and that all our limitations and economies are more than repaid by our complete accessibility.'[202] Yet his constant ambition for the school was to be able 'to liberalise our teaching without sacrificing standards'.[203] One boy recalled how he had concluded his philosophy lecture to one group of sixth-form biologists by saying, 'You must not be narrow technocrats but familiar with philosophy, music and literature. Only then will you be able to serve your country as men of the New Enlightenment.'[204] Progress came only slowly. To further the aims of the school, James had to rely heavily for many years on existing staff and those new appointments he was able to afford. On the other hand, he never attempted to do away with the major obstacle to a broader curriculum, the school's traditional system of sides, which disadvantaged boys by limiting the number of options and encouraging early specialisation. Throughout the 1950s, for instance, boys on the classical side were still taught very little science, while one boy, Michael Leach, remembered how many boys on the modern side never had a single lesson in biology after nature study in the first year. His group was not taught art after the second year and music was never timetabled. Things began to change only late in James's tenure. In 1956, for instance, geography was introduced at A level, and in 1959 the money was finally found to appoint a director of music, David Cawthra. This was an inspired move, since music would remain a Cinderella

Feature on MGS in *The Illustrated London News*, 1959.

504—THE ILLUSTRATED LONDON NEWS—October 24, 1959

ORATORS IN THE MAKING: THE DEBATING AND LITERARY SOCIETY DISCUSSING MATTERS OF MOMENT IN THE J. L. PATON LIBRARY.

METALLURGISTS IN THE MAKING: MR. M. POOLE TAKING A CLASS IN METAL WORK IN THE SCHOOL FORGE. THE QUALITY OF WORK PRODUCED IS HIGH.

Continued.] the fees of the fee-payers are graded according to the parental income. Thus the school is accessible to any boy, whatever his economic background, and admission is determined only by academic ability. As a result the school combines an unusually wide social range with a high academic standard. Here one can find the sons of mill-workers and company directors, bus-drivers and professors, working and playing together, united

OCTOBER 24, 1959—THE ILLUSTRATED LONDON NEWS—565

TE TO AN EXPERIMENT: LIFE AT THE MANCHESTER GRAMMAR SCHOOL.

YOUNG CRAFTSMEN OF THE SECOND YEAR AT WORK IN THE WOODWORK SHOP MAKING CHAIRS FOR THE SCHOOL.

IN THE HIGH MASTER'S STUDY: LORD JAMES OF RUSHOLME TALKING WITH (L. TO R.) J. LONEY, N. GOODEY AND J. CHAMPION.

(Left.)
PRACTISING A DIFFICULT ART: BOYS WORKING ON A CUT-OUT PAPER MOSAIC UNDER THE SUPERVISION OF MR. DAVID PRICE, THE ART MASTER.

(Right.)
A SPLASHING AND FLURRY OF ARMS—AND A GOAL! A TRIUMPHANT MOMENT DURING A WATER POLO MATCH IN THE SCHOOL SWIMMING BATHS.

MIC STRUCTURE: THE VIth FORM DIVISION III SCIENCE CLASS LISTENING ATTENTIVELY TO MR. STONE.

THE SCIENCE VIth AT WORK IN THE PHYSICS LABORATORY. INDIVIDUAL EXPERIMENTAL WORK IS OFTEN OF A MINOR RESEARCH NATURE.

A SCENE IN THE LABORATORY IN THE SCIENCE BLOCK. ABOUT TWO-THIRDS OF THE 500 SIXTH-FORMERS WILL BECOME SCIENTISTS, DOCTORS OR ENGINEERS.

interests and abilities. Nearly all boys stay for a sixth-ee-quarters go on to a university. As one would expect alised area, there is now a strong science side and two-xth-formers in the school are future scientists, doctors or st recent addition to the school is a very fine sixth-form a was made possible by a grant from the Industrial Fund.

At the same time, arts studies remain very strong, and the classical sixth takes pride in the fact that its numbers have remained remarkably steady over the years. But if the Manchester Grammar School is usually associated with a high standard of scholarship, other activities flourish there. It has, for example, produced Blues for cricket, soccer, lacrosse, tennis, athletics and cross-country, and had two of its old boys in the last Olympic team.

A special feature of the school is the emphasis which it puts on Scouting and camping. Even apart from the four Scout troops, 300 or 400 other boys annually spend part of their holidays in a number of camps at home or abroad, the most ambitious of which are two "treks" through the Western Highlands and the Alps on which the boys rely entirely on the tents and equipment that they themselves carry. As [Continued overleaf.

Photographs specially taken for " The Illustrated London News " by Chris Ware, Keystone Press Agency Ltd.

subject in many boys' schools well into the 1970s. Thanks to
Cawthra, music at MGS finally emerged from the doldrums. He
formed a choral society and initiated instrumental tuition, which
at Christmas 1960 led to the first combined choral and orchestral
performance, of the cantata 'Wachet auf', while a year later the
orchestra attempted a complete symphony, Schubert's 3rd, for
the first time. It was only now that James began to introduce some
flexibility into the curriculum, delaying until the sixth form a
boy's decision on whether to opt for the arts or the sciences, and
enabling most sixth formers studying science to spend a third of
their time on other subjects.

During the 1950s one of the school's most pressing challenges
was to meet the needs of the increasing number of boys wishing to
study advanced science. They were by far the largest single group
in the sixth form. In 1955 the old rectory in the grounds was
converted into a biology department, releasing more space for
chemistry and physics. This was only possible because the changing

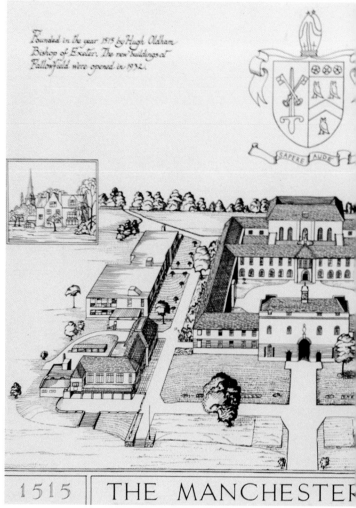

Sketch of various
members of staff
including High
Master James
(centre) and Ernest
Hollowell (top
centre).

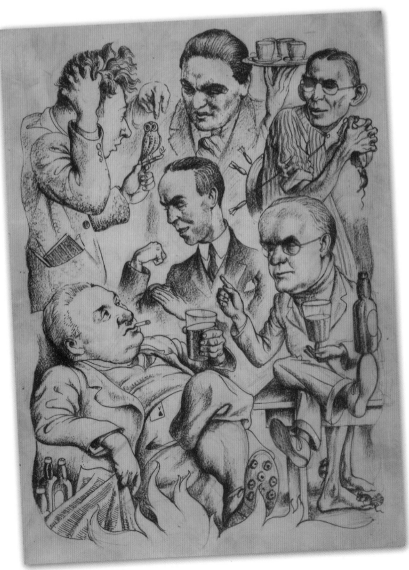

rooms, previously located in the old rectory, were being moved
into the brand new pavilion erected as a war memorial. Opened by
Lord Woolton, the chairman of governors, on 14 July 1956, it was
completed thanks to a generous bequest from an Old Mancunian,
Robert Flintoff, who had been at the school in the 1880s.

MGS was also among the many schools that benefited from the
generosity of the Industrial Fund for the Advancement of Scientific
Education in Schools. In the 1950s, as in the 1890s, science was
subject to considerable encouragement from businessmen and
politicians, and the Fund, in the formation of which James was
influential, and which was sponsored by industry to help fund
major improvements in school science facilities, was one of
the most impressive results. At MGS the Fund paid for nearly
two-thirds of the new science block, opened in 1958 by the
distinguished research scientist Sir Willis Jackson. Yet within
two years the new building was overcrowded. Thanks partly
to the Industrial Fund but mainly to the generosity of two old
boys, Simon Marks and Israel Sieff, the block was extended,

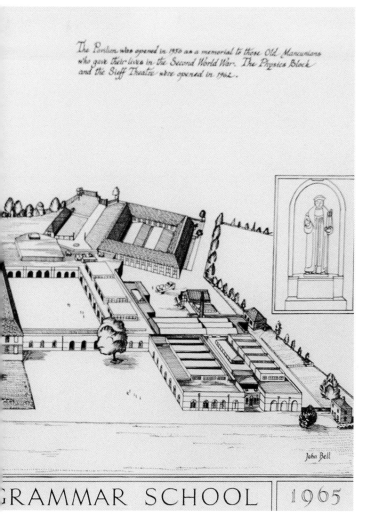

The Pavilion was opened in 1950 as a memorial to those Old Mancunians who gave their lives in the Second World War. The Physics Block and the Sieff Theatre were opened in 1962.

John Bell

GRAMMAR SCHOOL 1965

to return from the war. Much teaching was still being done valiantly by those persuaded not to retire or brought out of retirement, resulting in a temporary downward blip in school certificate results. The change was striking as younger men with new ideas joined the staff. Michael Ainsworth recalled how teachers like Kearney, a former sergeant-major, and Tyzack, a former major, 'jumped all over us and shook all the sloth out of us'.[206]

James did a good job. In 1951 the inspectors were impressed, picking out several masters for particular praise. By then there were 70 staff,[207] almost all men, squashed into the tiny common room, largely hidden from sight by a fog of cigarette smoke. Perhaps Brian Giles, appointed in 1951, was typical, if anyone could be typical of a band of such individual men. One of his pupils, Michael Leach, remembered how Giles, like other newcomers, many of whom came from the forces,

Above: The cricket pavilion, erected as a memorial to those who died in the Second World War, opened in 1956.

Centre: Plan of the school, 1965, donated by art master and head of art John Bell (1951–81).

Below: The masters' common room, 1954. The common room was, until relatively recently, solely for the use and enjoyment of masters. Even the High Master required an invitation to enter this exclusive environment. Nowadays, all staff are welcome to take breaks in the common room.

complete with lecture theatre, in 1962. The new facilities would be accompanied by new teaching techniques, thanks to the involvement of the Nuffield Foundation. In addition, Roger Stone, the second master at the time, would also be seconded to lead the Nuffield Physics Enterprise in the North West.

The new science block, however, was the limit of any new development. The lack of money was obvious in the boggy state of the playing fields. In the late 1950s Alan Welsby, later head of PE, recalled that it was 'no wonder … that plantain, ducks and herring gulls much preferred our site … At times, after a sudden downpour, the whole area resembled a lake.'[205] It was only in the 1980s, after persistent pressure from staff, that a rolling programme of much-needed improvements was agreed, including the complete re-draining of the fields.

The burden truly remained on the shoulders of staff, as James acknowledged, and the school's circumstances made it critical to maintain and improve their calibre. It was a lesson he had learned the hard way, coming to the school just before young men started

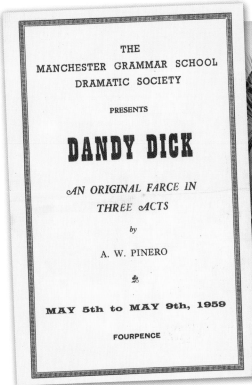

THE
MANCHESTER GRAMMAR SCHOOL
DRAMATIC SOCIETY

PRESENTS

DANDY DICK

*AN ORIGINAL FARCE IN
THREE ACTS*

by

A. W. PINERO

MAY 5th to MAY 9th, 1959

FOURPENCE

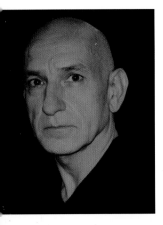

brought 'a refreshing informality and humour' as well as high standards of scholarship and discipline. He recalled Giles urging one uncommunicative boy, 'Why not attempt to contribute a little instead of sitting there like a fakir, hard-arsed on a bag of nails?'[208] Ian Bailey, who had been a boy at the school, returned after distinguished war service to teach in 1949, and never really left until his death in 2007, becoming a well-loved institution. In 1949 James also appointed the lively Bert Parnaby who laid the foundations for post-war drama at MGS. For the first time many boys found drama exciting and attractive. In 1954 Parnaby scored a great success with a staging of Goldoni's *The Servant of Two Masters*, followed up with Wilder's *Our Town* in 1956. He would later team up with Brian Phythian, appointed in 1959; those who fell under their spell included Robert Powell, Ben Kingsley and Nicholas Hytner. Phythian was conscious of the mantle of tradition being passed from one generation of staff to another, of inheriting a sense of purpose, sustained by the continuity of those long-serving members of staff in a transient community, the past informing the present.

There was a determination that the MGS tradition should be seen as very different, much more distinctive, from the traditions of other schools. In 1954 a spoof in the school magazine, entitled 'The Founders' Game', describing a ludicrous game, was obviously intended to poke fun at the traditions of more hallowed schools and the virtues they were supposed to represent. But the article also spoke volumes about the chippiness or contrariness characteristic of MGS. As one pupil, John Horsfield, who later

MANCHESTER GRAMMAR SCHOOL

The Pedagogues

CAST:

F. WINTERBOTTOM   C. E. McGUIRE
O. R. CORBETT   H. RAISTRICK
G. W. CROWTHER   T. B. EDWARDS
J. B. PARNABY   F. R. WATSON

MARCH 29th, 30th, 31st, April 1st and 2nd, 1960

Thy company, which erst was irksome to me, I will endure
(As You Like It)

taught at the school, recalled, 'We were never looking over our shoulders at other schools either as boys or staff. That may have been something about Manchester: "This is what we do." It was not a sense of back-handed pride; it was just the way things were.' It was a characteristic treasured by James who believed that 'the heretic may ultimately be the best citizen'.[209]

As new men came, so old men went. Among them was F. L. Heywood, the head of the mathematical side. Retiring in 1954 after 37 years, he had been form master for the maths sixth for 17 years, having succeeded the brilliant R. C. 'Shandy' Chevalier in 1937. During Heywood's last eight years the maths sixth had won 74 Oxbridge awards. Ernest Hollowell, who had been art master since 1940, having first taught at North Manchester School, retired in 1956. Responsible for a subject largely ignored and under-resourced, he nevertheless retained an infectious enthusiasm for it, encouraging at least one boy to open his eyes to the built environment around him in his successful attempt to become a professional architect. C. G. 'Dickie' Radford retired in the same year after teaching geography for 36 years. He had valiantly striven to keep music alive but had also run the school soccer team and led the Alderley camp. C. E. 'Mac' McGuire, who retired after 34 years in 1960, had taught mainly languages, but as an accomplished pianist had supported Radford in his bid to maintain some semblance of musical activity. In 1958 three distinguished masters left after long service: Albert Hyslop, second master since 1945, Jack Rivers, who had taught German, and Isidore Tenen, a

pupil of Paton's, a member of the classics department since 1923, a gentle and sympathetic man, who found time between teaching, editing the school magazine and running swimming to produce a series of history textbooks. John Lingard, a much admired trek leader, a great raconteur and an outstanding linguist, died suddenly in the summer of the same year at the age of only 48. In 1961 two more school institutions retired. R. F. I. Bunn had been senior history master since 1933, and had promoted a wider vision of the subject, encompassing art and science, music and literature,

Above left: The Pedagogues, one of a series of hugely entertaining revues performed by members of staff, 1960.

Below: John Ogdon (1947–53).

Above: Isidore ('Ike') Tenen (1923–58), classics master and old boy, with students on a field trip.

Above right: John Lingard (1934–58) teaching French to 1C, 1950.

Right: R. F. I. ('Bob') Bunn (1933–61), history master, showing the school charter to a sixth form class.

to his attentive sixth-form audience. R. T. 'Arty' Moore was an outstanding classicist but had also been deeply involved in school scouting since joining MGS in 1921.

Looking back in 1959, James reckoned that 48 masters had left the staff since 1948, of whom 12 had retired, three had died, three had left for research posts and 13 had left for headships. Among the latter group was Roger Young, later Sir Roger, who left in 1958 to become a distinguished and long-serving head of George Watson's College in Edinburgh. Another was the languid

chemistry master David Williams, himself a pupil of James, who spent 12 years at the school before leaving in 1962 for the first of two successful headships. A year later Denis Rendall, the first full-time head of geography, appointed in 1959, did the same. By the early 1960s the staff had been transformed, with more than two-thirds under the age of 35, and more than half appointed during the previous five years.

All these men, young and old, rarely had difficulty in maintaining discipline. Corporal punishment was sparingly applied, although there were still instances when it was used excessively. Several boys in particular felt traumatised by their maltreatment during swimming lessons, struck by gym shoes as they ran naked around the pool, or thrown into the deep end unable to swim and left to be rescued by their more able peers. It was, recalled Ernest Fox, a terrifying experience for small boys. It would have been little comfort to the victims to know that such practices were common in many boys' school in the 1950s.

It was the self-knowledge of the boys that they were among the most able in the country that was often a more effective means of discipline than any gym slipper. This could have adverse consequences. Geoff Fox would later reflect that the fear of being made to appear foolish in front of his peers led him to learn some subjects parrot-fashion, because he felt unable to ask questions of anything he did not understand. 'I always felt that I must achieve to the highest standard that I could, that I would somehow be letting someone, or some notional ideal, down.'[210]

On the other hand, bullying seems to have been almost entirely absent, a tribute to the culture of tolerance in such a large school, and most boys found discipline fair and humane. That was not to say that MGS boys were perfectly behaved little angels. Eric James summed up the situation succinctly: 'the behaviour of our boys sometimes leaves something to be desired. On the other hand, it must be remembered that this is a very libertarian school, and the fact that it is run with comparatively little punishment of any kind, and with practically no corporal punishment at all, does indicate that by and large the boys are thoroughly sound'.[211]

Camps and treks remained at the heart of the school's activities, a window on to the world outside the classroom. Scouting remained very strong; the school had four large troops, all of them involved in camps and other assorted activities. In 1956 it was calculated that nearly a third of MGS boys took part in scouting. As one boy, Brian Taylor, recalled, 'These were great days of walking in the fresh air and sunshine, some of the happiest days of your life.'[212] Maurice Watkins, later a Queen's Scout and troop leader, found that scouting gave him, as a shy and uncertain young boy, confidence, independence and initiative. He was one of the more than 70 boys in Scout Troop I, led by Mr Simkins himself. Unlike the other troops, Troop I met not in school on a Friday evening but in Pendlebury on Saturday afternoons and evenings. Troop I also did things rather

differently from other troops. At the troop's two annual summer camps there was no patrol cooking, for example, but instead boys took it in turns within their patrols to cook twice a fortnight, which allowed everyone more free time. The troop was also envied for having comfortable lavatory seats at camp, rather than the boys perching perilously over a pit; for Maurice Watkins, 'it

Above: Snowball fight.

Below: Scout Troop II at Borrowdale Camp, 1947.

was camping luxury'. Troop II was led by David Copley from 1945 until 1962, with annual camps in diverse and far-flung locations, and boasted eight patrols in 1961. Troop III, under Arnold Ashbrook from 1951 to 1964, was well known for the gang shows it produced. Troop IV was led by 'Mac' Ricketts and Alan Morgan.

The first post-war trek took place in the Scottish Highlands at Whitsun 1946, the only year in which a camp was not held at Grasmere.[213] In 1947 John Lingard resumed overseas treks, taking a party to France. These adventures still retained the power to transform. Stephen Murphy, a fellow master, accompanied Lingard on that first post-war overseas expedition. They had been lost and suddenly came across a magnificent view of Mont Blanc. 'It was, I think, in all my years of teaching, the most exciting thing that ever happened to me, to stand on that ridge and watch these boys, none of them having ever set foot out of Britain before, climb that last step and look out over to the wonder and the glory of the Alps.'[214] Camps to Germany began again in 1950 with a summer visit to Osterode, and in 1953 the first winter sports trip took place, when a group of boys spent Christmas and New Year skiing, skating and luging in Switzerland.

Arthur Kahn, who joined the staff in 1955 and later became head of science, was a keen supporter of treks, and later recorded just how different things were at the time. Anoraks were 'new-fangled' and cagoules unheard of, yellow cycle capes always failed to keep the wearers dry, and rucksacks were ex-army, steel-framed and heavy; cooking was done not over camping gas but over open fires, the meals usually stews made from

Camp at Rathdrum in County Wicklow, Ireland, 1961.

locally sourced fresh meat and vegetables, produced in a huge primitive pressure cooker, fondly called 'the Bomb', weighing 20 lb and carried by two boys from site to site slung between two poles. A new initiative right at the end of James's time was the mountaineering club, formed by eight experienced staff climbers, which took boys on climbs across the UK and overseas. While there had never been a major accident on a trek since they had started, an MGS Mountain Safety Committee was also set up to promote safety standards to all boys.

The Lads' Club had outlived its usefulness by the late 1950s. As living standards improved membership declined, interest fell away, and it closed in 1958. Instead the boys spontaneously

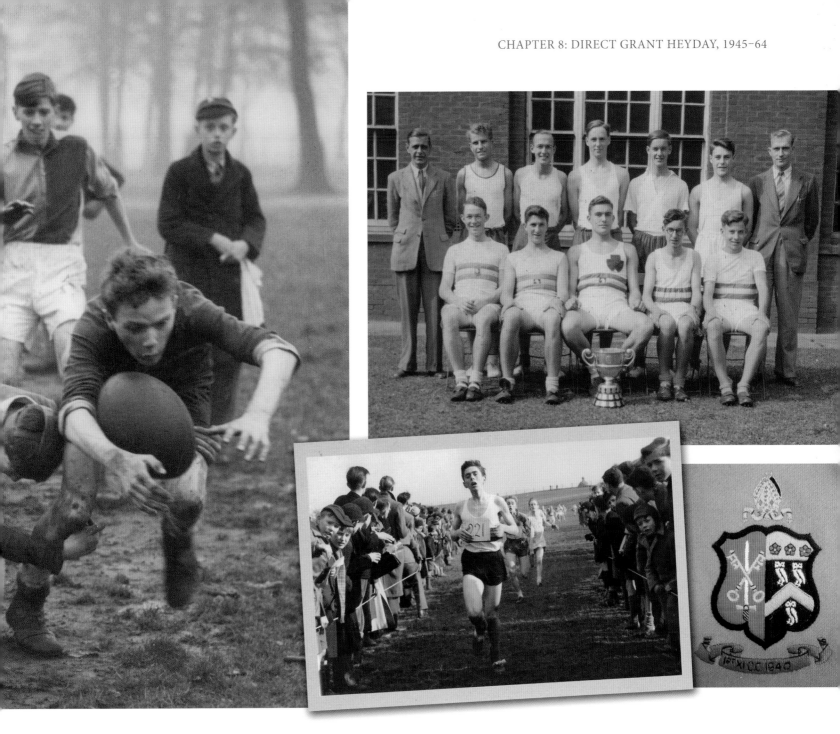

organised a collection for the World Refugee Appeal that raised £1,800, beginning an annual charity collection that continues to this day.

In 1946 one of James's first decisions had been to abandon Miller's house system and bring back inter-form competition for sport, which proved very popular. Very quickly the school returned to running several teams of different ages in cricket, football, rugby and lacrosse. Cricket flourished, enjoying more consistent success than ever before. Gordon McKinna, who had joined the school during the war, was an outstanding medium-pace inswing bowler, who later gained his Oxford Blue and played for the RAF. The school twice defeated the MCC, and during the

summer tour of 1956 T. M. Richardson scored a century against Eton. Rugby, too, had its highlights, with the first 15 unbeaten in 1950–1. In 1951 the school also won the English Schools' Athletics Championship for the second time in three years. Badminton flourished, new hard tennis courts were opened, and the cross-country course moved to the school grounds. All this, for James, was further ammunition to fire at those who accused MGS of being an academic crammer: 'A school recruited on the basis of intellectual ability is not deficient in either keenness or prowess in games.'[215] But sport was still run by teaching staff, as it was in most schools, forms had games only once a fortnight, and they were no longer timetabled.

Centre: Rugby match, 1950.

Top: Winners of the London Athletics Club Public Schools' Trophy, 1949.

Above left: Cross-country running with the winner, Paddy Montague, setting the pace, c.1956.

Above: 1st XI Cricket Club blazer badge.

Above: Founders' Day – boys outside Manchester Cathedral.

Above right: Peter Mason, newly appointed High Master, with J. H. King, chairman of governors and Lord James, who left MGS at the end of 1961 to take up the position of vice-chancellor of the University of York.

As the head of a school that probably sent a higher proportion of its sixth form to university than any other linked with the state, James found himself appointed to the University Grants Committee in 1949, which had become responsible for the post-war planning and expansion of the university sector. He chaired the Headmasters' Conference in 1953–5 and also sat on the Central Advisory Council for Education and the Standing Commission on Museums and Galleries. His stature in the world of education was recognised when he was knighted in 1956 (the same year that the chairman of governors, Lord Woolton, became an earl) and again in 1959 when he became a life peer. He was one of the first serving headmasters to be knighted and the first to become a baron. On the day the papers announced his peerage, the boy playing the organ in assembly chose the hymn 'Praise the Lord, ye Heavens adore him!' to the tune 'Austria', indicative of the general respect with which the boys regarded the Chief. By then, with all his many external commitments, James was a rare presence in school. In addition, he spent part of the summer term in 1957 on a lecture tour of US universities and colleges, and in 1961 part of the winter term lecturing in Nigeria. He also welcomed many overseas visitors to MGS during the 1950s, from the US, Canada, Ghana, Nigeria, Uganda, Japan, Thailand, Iran and Australia.

James was the right man to appoint as vice-chancellor for the new University of York, which under his guiding influence became one of the best of the new universities. He took his leave of MGS, to which he had devoted 16 years of his life, at the end of 1961. The governors recorded how 'he had succeeded in raising [the school's] stature, its morale and its academic achievement to new pinnacles, whilst at the same time recruiting and building up a staff of which any school could be proud'.[216] The Old Mancunians showed their gratitude by giving James and his wife Cordelia, who had played an important supporting role, a painting by the distinguished Manchester artist L. S. Lowry.

James's successor was Peter Mason. Only five years younger than his predecessor, he had spent 13 years as headmaster of Aldenham School before coming to MGS. The son of schoolteachers, he had won a scholarship to King Edward's School, Birmingham, then read classics at Christ's College, Cambridge, where he graduated with a double first. His teaching career was interrupted by distinguished war service in the Intelligence Corps. Speaking fluent French and German, he was later posted to 'a department of the Foreign Office'.[217] From 1943 he was attached to the Special Intelligence Service and liaised with de Gaulle's staff in London until the Normandy landings, a role requiring tact and sensitivity. Immediately after the landings he was parachuted into France to establish contact with the French resistance. After a spell in charge of the sixth form at Rugby, he was appointed head of Aldenham at the age of 35. He was a keen sportsman and outdoor enthusiast, enjoying squash and tennis, fishing and sailing, mountain-walking and skiing. A tall, handsome but shy man, he was a more daunting personality than James and also a less visible presence, but one that nevertheless proved to be all-pervasive. One member of staff recalled that Mason 'floated through the corridors of MGS like an Ice King', while another, John Horsfield, later described his new High Master as 'an unfathomable and enigmatic figure'.[218] Horsfield observed that Mason 'could be very understanding and helpful in individual cases but his persona was such that he often gave the impression he could not be bothered to remember who you were'.

For Mason, education was 'the full development of individual talents in the context of society' and he believed that the 'full development of the personality includes the development not only of the mind and the body, but of those emotional and artistic responses which are likely to provide no less clear keys to the meaning of truth than the purely logical processes'.[219] This had much in common with the views of James but, unlike his predecessor, Mason found it difficult to judge MGS on its own merits rather than by comparison with the boarding schools in which he had spent his teaching career. Hence his mistake on arriving at the school in believing it lacked a sense of community, which he declared he wished to rectify. While he had many attributes, and did much to secure the future of the school, MGS boys were often a mystery to him and he to them.

His more immediate concern was to prevent over-specialisation, and in 1963 one of his earliest moves, probably the most influential of his tenure academically, was to remove the division between the classical and modern sides. This aroused considerable indignation among some staff, who regarded the sides as an almost untouchable tradition, but Mason was right, and the action he took long overdue. Every boy would now follow a common course up to O level, with Latin taught to each pupil for two years, the number of subjects limited to four or five to avoid undue pressure while achieving the minimum required for university entrance. At the same time, for their first two years boys were divided into forms alphabetically and grouped in maths sets according to ability, enabling the elimination of streamed forms and the stigma experienced by boys in the lowest stream. In the middle school the choice of a third language determined a boy's form. Within the sixth form Mason developed further the seeds of cross-fertilisation sown by James, leading to all arts students studying some science or maths, and all science students studying languages, history or the fine arts. As did his predecessors, so Mason too believed that the purpose of the school 'was not to produce winners of Oxbridge scholarships but men who could go into the world and make wise choices in society on a basis of knowledge and also some understanding of the limitations of human nature as well as its potentialities'.[220]

In a climate of expanding university education, with grants available for rising numbers of students, he recognised that the school no longer needed to distribute its scarce resources in leaving scholarships and exhibitions. He would, he said, rather have as much cash as possible to do something with the buildings. He outlined his plans to the governors in the summer of 1962, expressing the wish to see better facilities for the sixth form, music and art, and an improved library. He suggested that money could be raised by an appeal, launched to coincide with the school's 450th anniversary in 1965, an idea the governors preferred over the alternative of borrowing money for future repayment from fees.

But the issue that would dominate Mason's time as High Master was the fight to save the grammar schools from becoming part of

the comprehensive education system. The idea had been around for some time, with the London County Council creating five experimental comprehensive schools in 1946, Anglesey becoming the first local education authority to become wholly comprehensive in 1952, and the first purpose-built comprehensive school opening at Kidbrooke in London in 1954. Eric James had spoken against the idea during the 1950s but it was the adoption of comprehensive education as party policy by Labour, and the possibility in the early 1960s that the party would defeat the Conservative government, that began to raise the temperature of the debate. By 1964 Peter Mason was already well into his aggressive campaign against comprehensive schooling: 'We are being smothered with comprehensiveness, with its anti-selective, anti-segregational gospel.' And it was Mason who suggested for the first time that an alternative future beckoned for MGS: 'We shall do our best to co-operate with the State system. If we cannot co-operate, we shall have to exist on our own and we must be physically prepared.'[221] In April that year plans were approved for the new sixth form building; six months later, Mason's worst fear was confirmed when the general election returned the Labour Party to power.

Stewart Platts and a junior boy in front of the statue of Hugh Oldham at the Telfer Road entrance to the school. The statue was moved into the quad in 2014.

129

9 TOWARDS INDEPENDENCE 1964–76

'Top of the Hit Parade'

Peter Mason believed that the pressure to abolish the direct grant was a sign of the times, when, as he wrote in the school history published in 1965, 'there is much criticism of established institutions'. With much still to be done to improve equality of opportunity, he failed to understand why radicals, however sincere, wished to impose an unproven system that would destroy 'some of the special excellencies which distinguish the older schools'. At a time when the debate over the future of education was becoming more intense, and when local education authorities had already been instructed to discuss with their direct grant schools how best they could take part in any local comprehensive scheme, Mason concluded the final chapter of the history with a spirited defence of the existing system: 'The direct grant system has demonstrated the advantages of a partnership between school and university on the one hand and the State on the other. This can extend to all what would otherwise be a special privilege of the rich, while maintaining the independence of the educator to maintain that individuality and diversity of emphasis which a free society needs more than flat equality.'[222]

Mason was a political animal and did his utmost to convince those in positions of influence of the values of a direct grant school like MGS. In 1965 the guest at speech day was Anthony Crosland, the Labour secretary of state for education, whose father had been an MGS boy. Crosland made no mention in his speech of educational reorganisation but no doubt Mason took the opportunity to bend his guest's ear, as he would have done the next year when the speaker was Sir John Newsom, chairman of the Public Schools Commission. He also began harnessing support from parents through the MGS Society, formed in 1966, which was asked among other things to raise funds to support various school activities.

The late 1960s was an unsettling period for direct grant schools, uncertain of their future; there were many discussions with local education authorities over their future within the state system and whether or not the authorities would continue to fund free places.

MGS drew boys from many different local education authorities, and in the period prior to confirmation of abolition, which would not come until 1974, their responses differed. By the early 1970s several of them, including Oldham, Salford, Manchester and Stockport, had ceased to fund boys going to MGS.

Despite the frequent discussions between the school and local education authorities, there was never any doubt that MGS would choose complete independence if the direct grant was abolished. Mason had no doubt that as a totally fee-paying school an economic fee could be charged, demand for places sustained and academic standards maintained. There was a touch of ambivalence in remarks he made about the school's future intake. 'A good home may help a boy of sound ability to go further and do better than an abler boy from a disadvantaged home. This of course must not make us for a moment forget what the school has been able to do

Peter Mason, High Master (1962–78).

130

for the disadvantaged. It would be more than sad to lose the social comprehensiveness which has been our special pride'. But he was convinced that, should change come, 'over the course of years … the difference between independent and comprehensive schools would operate in our favour'.[223]

In 1970 the governing body, led by Raymond Baldwin, who became chairman in 1967, decided unanimously to opt for full independence if necessary. At the meeting Mason expressed his preference for some form of graded fees in place of the existing system. The return of a Conservative government in June 1970 he saw as giving direct grant schools only a temporary respite that they needed to use to their advantage. Mason certainly made effective use of this time. He had already played an influential role on the Headmasters' Conference Direct Grant Joint Committee, which had been campaigning to retain the status quo, but he was now beginning to formulate an alternative vision. He was unhappy that free places were handed out indiscriminately to boys appearing highest in the examination lists, regardless of whether their parents could afford to pay fees or not. He began to advocate a generous scheme of fee remission that subsidised the parent rather than the school, and had the financial advantage that schools would henceforth have to set realistic fees. In July 1970 he suggested this might be on the basis of 'a Government pool which would be used to pay for aided places based on the

income of parents in the same way as places at university'.[224] Mason had the ear of the new Conservative education secretary, Margaret Thatcher, and by the time he made these remarks a small working party comprised of representatives from the direct grant schools, including Mason, and the Department of Education had already been set up. The ultimate result would be the Assisted Places Scheme, introduced by Thatcher's government in 1980. In the meantime Mason became insistent that should MGS become independent it should no longer offer free places, but assisted places, which would stretch the same funds twice as far.

On the return of a Labour government, the governors reaffirmed their decision in favour of independence in January 1975, with the dean of Manchester and a Manchester city councillor voting against.

Predicting at a time of rampant inflation that annual fees for new entrants would be £500 (the actual figure was £675) from September 1976, compared with existing fees of £351 a year, the board also emphasised that every effort would be made to help at least some boys from poorer homes. In April 1975 plans were announced for the third appeal in ten years, this time to raise money for scholarships. In a school with little money the role of treasurer on the governing body had always been an important one, and was often filled by governors who later went on to become chairman, such as Arthur Haworth, John King

450th anniversary appeal, 1965.

and Raymond Baldwin. So too was the post of receiver, valiantly filled in the earlier part of the century by Owen Cox, and then from 1934 until his death in 1958 by Tom Nutter. His successor, John 'Mac' McCorquodale, who held the post until his retirement in 1975, was a shrewd administrator and financial manager, delivering a sound financial basis for the school as it approached independence.

The funds raised by the appeal were held by the MGS Trust, formed for the purpose during an earlier appeal in 1966, following a donation in memory of Lord Marks. At Mason's suggestion the governors also added five per cent to any agreed fee increase for boys entering from September 1976 to go towards the remission of fees for poorer boys. Based on the fees charged, and the average remission, the school calculated it could help 35 boys in the first year. With assistance from some local education authorities, the proportion of new boys given help would rise to 25 per cent. This, however, was a long way from the school's position in 1965, when nearly two-thirds of boys were completely exempt from fees.

There were expressions of unease as the school journeyed towards independence. Some staff were uncomfortable with the idea, and so were some boys. While the boys' newspaper, *The Mancunian*, first produced in 1966, condemned the push for comprehensive education as 'dogmatic and ill-conceived', comments from other boys suggested some of them were unhappy at the political stance taken by the governors and the High Master. Mason's interview in the *Times Educational Supplement*, in which

he likened MGS to a public school, drew adverse comments, while one sixth former complained that the arguments against comprehensive education were becoming mixed up with direct criticism of the Labour Party. Another sixth former, Keith Hurst, wrote in the summer of 1970 that 'an independent MGS implies that the conditions for entry into the school would no longer be superior academic ability but rather the ability to pay the necessary fees … This would obliterate one of the institution's most cherished recommendations: that it offers its services to boys of every social class according to intelligence and not prosperity.'[225]

The 1960s was a decade when young people began to assert their independence, leading to disruption at a number of universities and a series of protests on issues ranging from nuclear disarmament to Vietnam. By 1969 the voting age had been lowered to 18, preceding a similar change in the age of majority in 1971. But unrest was rarely found in schools, and, in any case, MGS boys already had an awkward streak and tended to turn up their noses at the rare attempts made to foment revolution. As one master recalled, 'there was a great tradition of rebellion at the

Above: All smiles as HRH Queen Elizabeth II arrives at the school flanked by High Master Mason, on the left, and J. H. King, chairman of governors, on the right, at the beginning of her visit in 1965 to mark the school's 450th anniversary.

Centre: A boy demonstrating how a lathe works. Workshop was detailed simply as 'Shop' in the timetable. In 1971, it became CDT.

school but such boys were tolerated because of what they brought to the school'.[226] A school branch of the Union of Secondary School Students was formed, but the school magazine reported that 'militancy at MGS is, it seems, in its infancy and the Union's activities to date – a few somewhat disappointing demonstrations – have received publicity rather out of proportion to its size. One result of this was a complaint from one Old Mancunian about the School as a hotbed of Communism.'[227] In 1972 the High Master reported that pickets, presumably university students, had twice been seen at the school gates attempting to incite the boys to rebel. Mason observed drily that 'it appeared to date that boys in the School were not impressed by these attempts at subversion'.[228]

On the other hand, Adrian Dobson, who came to the school in 1962, remembered staff were challenged by the greater questioning of authority that came from the boys, although he recalled that often it was the school and the High Master that chose to pick fights with the boys, usually over the length of hair (Mason decreed no boy's hair must touch his collar), and which they usually lost. As Peter Foulkes, the school captain in 1968, observed at the time, 'courtesy and good manners are not exactly the outstanding feature of MGS life – one is tempted to say that below sixth-form level they are in fact non-existent'.[229] While the many new staff joining the school came with new ideas and new approaches, and generally employed a discipline that was both

gentle and effective, it was clearly difficult for some older staff to change the way they treated older boys. One, Paul Rose, had his punishment for speaking during Jewish prayers confirmed by his sixth-form master, only to be reprieved by the more sympathetic master in charge of supervising punishment schools. In the upper sixth Adrian Dobson was two weeks away from leaving school when the High Master hauled him into his office because he had spotted hair on his upper lip and told him either to shave or leave. Mason professed to understand the changes that were taking place – he knew, he told the old boys in 1967, that the young were less inclined to take things on trust, and expected to be given reasons for what they were asked to do – yet there were times when he clearly failed to connect with the boys.

Sex education was taught to boys in the first two years, complemented in 1967 by sex-education films shown to the sixth

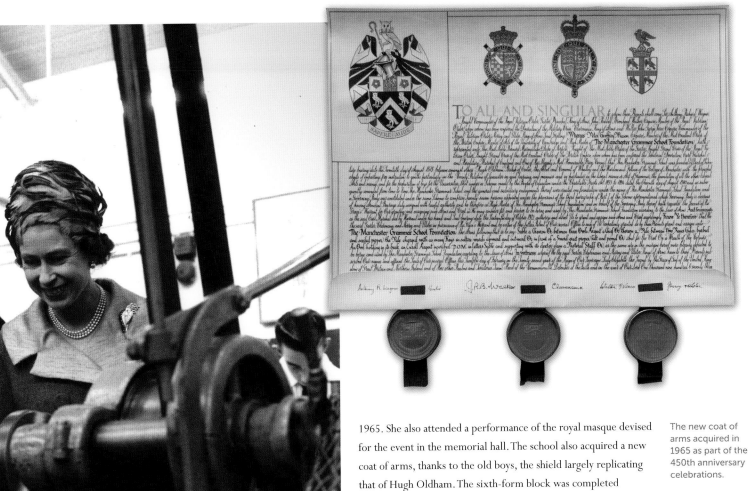

The new coat of arms acquired in 1965 as part of the 450th anniversary celebrations.

1965. She also attended a performance of the royal masque devised for the event in the memorial hall. The school also acquired a new coat of arms, thanks to the old boys, the shield largely replicating that of Hugh Oldham. The sixth-form block was completed in 1967, by which time a rolling programme of classroom refurbishment was also under way. In 1968 a second appeal to raise half a million pounds was boosted by a generous donation from Marks & Spencer, while the boys raised £9,000 from sponsored walks. A long overdue new common room (the old one, intended for just over 50 staff, had to accommodate more than 90) was completed in 1972. Three years later squash courts, more hard tennis courts and a music school had also been added, the latter paid for partly by the £21,000 raised from the sale by the school of Arthur Devis's painting of Dr John Clayton and his Salford school. Rising inflation reduced the value of the money raised, which led to the launch of a third appeal in 1974.

The music school reflected the huge musical progress made by the school under David Cawthra, which continued under his successor, Richard Sinton, appointed from Eton in 1965, who held the reins as music director until his retirement in 1993. Over that time Sinton, with the help of a number of assistant staff, pursued an adventurous programme, including performances of many major classical and modern choral works. A showman and entertainer, he did not believe in over-rehearsing, a popular ploy among music directors, creating nervous tension among

form, although as the student newspaper put it, 'discussions on sex and moral problems tend to be spontaneous here'. Ken Robbie, who joined the school in 1964, recalled that the times mostly made their mark on boys in terms of fashion, but they also engaged in heated political debate: 'The spirit of the times was reflected in the kinds of arguments we had as boys.' Boys did smoke, and there were occasional problems with drugs, while plenty of free time for private study in the sixth form led some boys to form an informal lunchtime drinking society, frequenting in particular 'a big old Victorian Manchester boozer' on Dickinson Road, and a smaller one closer by off the Wilmslow Road.[230]

The school launched an appeal during MGS's 450th anniversary in 1965. Fittingly it was marked by a visit from the Queen, who laid the foundation stone for the new sixth-form block, one of the first projects funded by the appeal, on 16 March

OWLS OF MIRTH

An Entirely Original Entertainment

by members of the Common Room

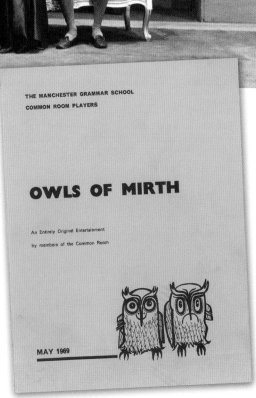

MAY 1969

Clockwise from top left: Richard Sinton (1965–93), director of music, conducting; Nicholas (1967–74) and Richard Hytner (1971–8) were involved in many productions during their time at MGS. Featured photographs show Nick Hytner as Baron Bolligrew (holding shotgun) in *The Thwarting of Baron Bolligrew* (1970) and Richard Hytner in *The Miser* (1978).

performers that usually produced outstanding results on the night. There were a few occasions when the magic failed to work, notably when chorus and orchestra ground to a halt (twice) during the middle movement of Stravinsky's Symphony of Psalms. One of Sinton's first major concerts was a combined event with other school choirs in the cathedral early in 1966, the first time for many years that music-making at MGS had reached beyond the school walls. Within school, informal concerts became a regular event. In aid of the appeal, a week-long music festival was held in March 1969, with a performance by pupils at the Whitworth Art Gallery, a new opera composed by Malcolm Williamson, later master of the Queen's music, a recital by two old boys, Raymond Cohen and Anthony Goldstone, and a final concert in the memorial hall. Special choirs had been formed since the mid-1960s on an ad hoc basis, notably for Barbirolli's recording of Mahler's Third Symphony with the Hallé, followed by several concert performances, including an appearance at the Proms. But it was only after a performance of Britten's War Requiem with the same orchestra in 1973 that a permanent special choir was established, which flourished until 1993. In 1974 music made a breakthrough when the subject was raised to the status of a major department.

Drama too was catching up, thanks to the persistence and inspiration of masters like Robin Griffin, John Shuttleworth and

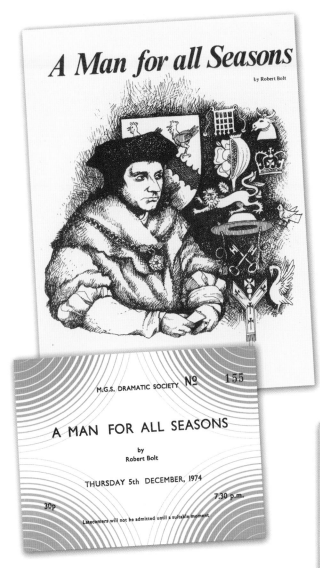

society, war games society and folk and blues club. The railway society possessed its own model railway in the basement of the chemistry department, with the boys organising their own outings to destinations like York, Leeds and Crewe. The geography society, under John Cook, gave Ken Robbie 'the most astonishing experience of potholing in the Derbyshire Dales'.[231] A voluntary service group, later renamed Community Action, was formed in 1961, forging links with a local school for disabled children, as well as local primary schools and centres for the elderly.

Sport still suffered from the poor state of the playing fields and one major team sport, lacrosse, fell out of favour. The lacrosse team was running out of opponents as the game declined in popularity, and the last school match took place on 22 March 1975. It would be nearly 30 years before the game was revived once more. Football, rugby and cricket remained the main team sports. In addition, there was basketball, hockey and volleyball, while individual sports ranged from squash and tennis to swimming. Intermittently the school produced individual champions, such as Goodman and Appleton, who swept up several major boys' tennis titles in the early 1970s.

Left: In 1974, *A Man for All Seasons* by Robert Bolt (1938–41), playwright and two-time Oscar-winning screenwriter, was staged.

Below: Football 1st XI, 1964; Tennis 1st VI, 1968.

David Wilde. The late 1960s and early 1970s were notable for the emergence of a number of fledgling actors, often performing in plays by old boys. The drama performed for the 450th anniversary was *Hobson's Choice* written by old boy Harold Brighouse in 1915, while at Christmas 1974 the choice was *A Man for All Seasons* by Robert Bolt, another old boy. Bolt had previously judged a school poetry competition in 1969, first prize going to Francis Barker. In 1971 a production of *The Government Inspector* featured Stephen Pimlott, Nicholas Hytner and Martin Sixsmith. Girls first took to the stage in 1970 when eight of them from Manchester High School took part in *Romeo and Juliet*. (One Manchester High School girl, Joan Mathieson, had even joined the modern sixth to study maths for a time in 1967.)

Societies proliferated, waxing and waning according to boys' enthusiasms, and counting among them at one time or another an angling club, model flying club, inland waterways

Above: Scouts at Coleraine, 1967.

Above right: Scottish Trek: MGS boys at Kyle of Lochalsh station, 1960s.

Camps and expeditions were almost countless. The Owl's Nest was refurbished in 1968. A blip in the popularity of overseas treks in the late 1960s and early 1970s proved to be temporary. By then trekkers had abandoned open fires, and light gas stoves made it possible for the boys in each tent to do their own cooking. As valley campsites became more difficult to find and trekkers spent longer in the mountains, they began carrying food for several days at a time. With the advent of high-level camping, 'bivvies' came to mean overnight camps where boys slept under the stars in sleeping bags.

The organisation of expeditions to Russia, Iceland and Iran (twice) in 1967–72 was part of a trend to send boys to what were then remote countries in an age before cheap air travel. This was the time of the Cold War, so a visit to the USSR behind the Iron Curtain must have created a frisson or two among those who went. The country would prove a popular destination for MGS boys both before and after the Berlin Wall came down. In the 1970s regular exchanges were arranged with the Phillips Academy, Andover, Massachusetts, St Albans School, Washington, DC and L'École Alsacienne, Paris, reviving the internationalist outlook fostered by Paton and Miller. On one occasion MGS toured a revival of Goldoni's *The Servant of Two Masters*, produced by David Wilde, and starring Nicholas Hytner and David Walton; they received standing ovations for their performances at the Phillips Academy and St Albans School.

The school open day was revived, albeit on a triennial basis, in 1965, part of changes that saw Mason sweep away the traditional speech day in favour of an internal prize-giving ceremony, although Founders' Day was left untouched.

Peter Mason's curricular reforms only enhanced the school's academic record. He was particularly pleased at the improvement in O-level results, for which boys rarely took more than five subjects. Adrian Dobson, for example, was typical in sitting only English, French, German, Latin, maths and joint physics with chemistry, the latter intended for boys not wishing to study advanced science. Boys were warned not to be too clever, one English master citing to his form the example of a boy who had taken the essay title 'Art in the Home', and gone on to describe the exploits of one Arthur in an old people's home. By the early 1970s the O level pass rate was constantly 90 per cent or more, while at A level 76 per cent of boys achieved grades A–C in 1972.[232] Changes in the middle school had flowed through into the sixth form, creating more diversity, with the addition of new A level subjects, such as economic history and Russian. Ken Robbie, for instance, found the optional subjects, such as art history, Greek democracy and world affairs, as valuable a learning experience as those studied for examination.

There were the usual outstanding Oxbridge results, with 44 open awards in 1965, and 41 open awards and 34 places in 1975. Some boys who distinguished themselves at other universities sometimes felt aggrieved with what seemed an obsession with Oxbridge. But on the basis of these achievements it was unsurprising that the school still attracted many applicants. In 1967, for example, there were 1,100 applications for 200 places, and they remained at this level into the early 1970s. It was only as the abolition of the direct grant loomed that applications dipped, reaching 700 in 1976, although a third of the successful entrants

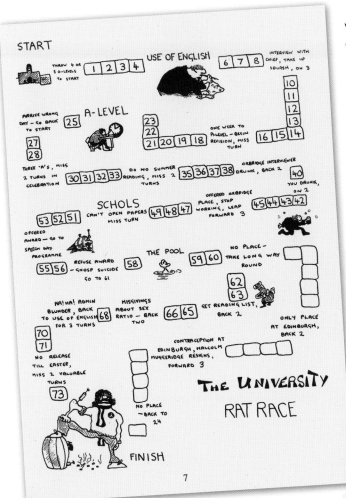

wealthier family, and how he would never take home letters about overseas trips in the belief, rightly or wrongly, that his family could not afford to pay for them.

There was still a degree of concern among some staff that MGS could also be a place, as one put it, 'where if pupils couldn't swim fast enough they sank. For many, their school experience must have been a pretty bleak and depressing one during that period'.[234] Some staff felt that the teaching was too much dominated by Oxbridge; the accelerated four-year O-level course for most boys was intended to enable them to spend three years preparing for Oxbridge entrance exams in the sixth form. Some boys were still pushed through the system too quickly, and staff were aware that a number of them did not enjoy the experience. In retrospect some boys felt that a fast stream denied them better results at O level and A level. In the sixth form, the very evident division of boys into 'sheep and goats', as Ian Thorpe put it, with only the most able entered for Oxbridge, in effect denied everyone else the seven-year education that might have seen them gain better A-level results. David Walton, who left to study law at Sheffield in 1974, observed that 'there was an expectation that Oxbridge was the destination you were heading for. Some people felt very strongly that if you did not go to Oxbridge, you were not regarded very highly; I never felt that, but that was the expectation.'[235]

Left: A humorous view of the long road through school to university. Taken from *Ulula*, 1967.

Below: Language lab, 1970s.

were still supported by school bursaries or free or assisted places from several local authorities. As a result MGS was able to sustain the calibre of its intake. As one teacher recalled on joining the staff in 1974, MGS was 'an academic hothouse of extraordinary merit', full of boys with lively, questioning minds.[233]

Many of these boys still came from less advantaged backgrounds. Ian Thorpe's parents were a semi-skilled textile machinery worker and a textile finisher living in a council house in Rochdale. His mother, who was at home when Ian first started at MGS in 1962 as a 'sprog', as first-year boys were called, returned to work as a dinner lady to help pay for part of the fees not covered by the grant. Russell Withington entered MGS in 1972 from a working-class family without any previous experience either of grammar school or university, picked out with a small group of other boys and girls at his primary school as candidates for entrance to schools like MGS. Some of these boys were very aware of their backgrounds. One recalled how a master had deliberately tried to eliminate his accent, how he made the conscious decision not to visit the home of a friend from a much

Mason was particularly conscious of the two forms following a slower five-year course. He wrote that 'one of the charges sometimes made against large schools is that boys who find their way into the lower streams receive less attention than the rest and are discouraged from reaching their true potential. We have been making a number of adjustments recently to meet this kind of problem though, of course, the range of ability at MGS is much less wide than in other schools.'[236] Yet as far as the pastoral side of the school was concerned, the only change to Glazebrook's system based on form masters was the appointment of a master in charge of the lower school. On the other hand, countless boys can testify to the help they received from their form masters. Ian Thorpe, for instance, remembered Roy Cooke, his form master in 1B, later headmaster of Bablake School, who 'was a terrific bloke and a big part in helping me to settle down'. Although Thorpe recalled that quite a few of his peers felt that in a large school like MGS they were 'insignificant, that in classes of 32 they were often no more than a line in the register to many staff', many of the new teachers appointed by Mason in the 1960s were much more sympathetic to younger boys, wanting to get to know them, to understand them, leading to better relationships and less misbehaviour.[237]

Many boys shared the views of Adrian Dobson, who left the school in 1970, that 'we had no doubts about the competence of our teachers'. They relished the dynamism of Mason's new appointments, such as Peter Downes, who taught French as a living language in a new and exciting way. They also delighted in the quirky individualism of established masters like Bert Parnaby, and the inspirational teaching from men like Dennis Witcombe and John Horsfield, who both taught history, or Neville Critchley, who taught Latin. So attuned were boys to the capability of those who taught them that they set upon the faintest signs of weakness shown by any new teachers, mercilessly baiting them, leading

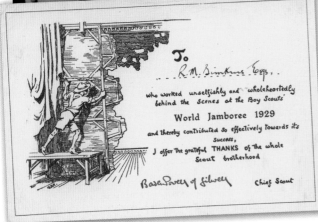

Far left: Rupert ('Simmie') Simkins (1921–66), head of the classical side and Scout leader for over 44 years. He is remembered fondly for his caring nature and commitment to the school and its boys.

Left: Charles 'Cuthbert' Seton (1921–66), a 'scintillating and truly inspiring' teacher of history.

MGS was fortunate that so many of its High Masters, including Peter Mason, but also James, Miller and Paton before him, had the gift of making excellent staff appointments. Each of them presided over the substantial renewal of staff, yet each transition left the school stronger. Under James and Mason part of the reason for the high turnover was because there were few opportunities for promotion, which was why James liked appointing able young men whom he knew would move on to higher things. The change under Mason was striking. In 1956, 30 per cent of staff had 25 or more years of service; in 1967 that proportion was just seven per cent. Between 1958 and 1968, 21 masters retired with an aggregate of 811 years of service, while in the space of six years between 1962 and 1968 Mason appointed 60 new members of staff, almost all of them male. There were very few women, and often they were appointed to temporary posts, such as the 'two ladies' Mason engaged as temporary modern languages teachers in 1969.[239]

As ever, among those who retired were some outstanding long-serving masters. The urbane W. Heppell Mason, head of English, who retired in 1965, was known as 'George' by his colleagues, after the then well-known George Mason grocery chain, and as 'Pansy' by the boys for his dapper appearance. Incisive and expressive, clear and analytical, he had joined the staff in 1930, and was an impressive master of his subject. R. M. Simkins, head of the classical side, a scholarly teacher, retired in

in one or two cases to their departure. One fourth form with a reputation for being bright but difficult destroyed a new science teacher, who confessed at the end of the year that he was leaving so he could learn how to teach. Another form tormented a young New Zealand teaching assistant, inching their desks slowly forward during the course of the lesson until he was almost pinned against the blackboard, or synchronising falling off their chairs, ruining the young man's teaching career. In the sixth form the teaching could be 'scarily good'. Arthur Shutt would lecture the third-year sixth in perfect German, many boys struggling to keep up. Ian Thorpe remembered the outstanding English teaching of men like Peter Jefferson and Brian Phythian: 'The quality of the teaching was amazing and I was willing to work.' David Walton realised on reaching university just how good his sixth-form teaching had been by comparison.[238]

Drama suddenly became exciting and attractive when taught by the energetic young actor James Bertram ('Bert') Parnaby (1949–65). Among those boys who fell under his spell were Robert Powell, Ben Kingsley and Nicholas Hytner. Parnaby's later film credits included *Prick Up Your Ears* (1987), *Daemon* (1985) and *The Dressmaker* (1988).

1966. He had taken charge of the classical sixth on his appointment in 1921 and was always known by his classicists as 'Simicidas'. Other boys knew him as 'Simmie'. Deeply involved with scouting, he had led Scout Troop 1 for 44 years, ran more than 100 camps, and was awarded the Silver Acorn for his distinguished service to scouting. Conservative in his ways, he was a great eccentric, owning a wireless radio only to hear the pips to ensure his watch kept accurate time. He was a scholar for whom scholarship was less important than people, and he held a deep concern for boys as individuals. 'His life was school, scholarship, scouting.'[240] Cuthbert Seton, who had served for 37 years, also retired in 1966. Regarded by many of those he taught as a finer teacher of medieval history than many Oxbridge lecturers, he was described by one former pupil as 'scintillating and truly inspiring'.[241] Bert Parnaby, who had done so much for school drama, also left in 1966. In the following year MGS said goodbye after 42 years to Ronnie Plackett, the forthright, pithy, thorough and efficient senior chemistry master. In 1968 another link with MGS history disappeared with the retirement of John Maugham, the last member of staff to have taught at Long Millgate, and a distinguished head of maths.

While Mason appointed many teachers with outstanding qualifications, they stepped into MGS with a sense of awe. The Common Room, discovered John Shoard, who joined to teach history in 1970, was 'quite a powerhouse', while Jeremy Ward, appointed to the same department in 1974, found 'going into the staff room was like going into a university common room'. Heads of department were powerful personalities, yet they interfered very little with the teaching of their colleagues. For most teachers, in an era when there was still great flexibility over what to teach and how to teach, their classroom was still their kingdom. They all believed MGS was 'top of the hit parade' and they were determined to keep it that way.[242]

Above: The Common Room with High Master Peter Mason, 1970.

Left: Adrian Dobson (1980–present) and Jeremy Ward (1974–97).

10 CHALLENGING TIMES 1976–94

'Free to Experiment'

Like many former direct grant schools, MGS found independence challenging. Peter Mason, with his previous experience as an independent head, had always been enthusiastic. 'The existence of an independent sector, free to experiment and to foster variety of choice is in the long run one of the best guarantees of freedom in a democratic society.' Most staff accepted the change with resignation as 'a sad necessity'. Those politically uncomfortable with the transition recognised that the character of the school could be guaranteed in no other way. Many Old Mancunians, fiercely protective of the traditions of their old school, kept a watching brief on the school's development.[243]

Opposite: Front page of *The New Mancunian*, 1986.

Below: Peter Mason and prefects, 1976–77.

Yet the school was not casting off past traditions. Historically, the post-war apogee of the direct grant system, and the benefits of a free or almost free education for two-thirds of the boys at MGS, was but a brief interlude. There had been fee-payers at the school for centuries, including the majority of boys from Walker until

James. Under Dill in 1883, for instance, just 16 per cent of boys had free places, while under Paton in 1915 the proportion was 30 per cent. But these examples illustrated the other side of the coin, that for an equally long time foundation scholars or boys otherwise awarded free places had been an integral part of the school, embedded in the school's genetic make-up, whose absence could only diminish the school's stature. It was this aspect of MGS that was treasured so highly by so many, including the High Master and the governors, who had the prescience to plan ahead to provide some future financial provision for such boys.

While overall numbers remained around 1,400, there was a definite dip in the demand for places during the first decade of independence. The number of applicants fell from around 1,000 to as low as 541 for approximately 200 places. In the first year of independence the parents of a third of applicants sought financial assistance and the High Master confessed that some bright boys were lost to the school because parents could not afford the fees. Even so, Peter Mason was able to tell governors in 1977 that the first intake after independence 'had proved to be quite as able as their predecessors'. And MGS was able to offer financial help to

THE NEW MANCUNIAN

THE MANCHESTER GRAMMAR SCHOOL NEWSPAPER
Wednesday 5th November 1986 No 263

30p

ABOLITION 'AN ACT OF VANDALISM'

by Colin Shenton

At this year's Labour Party Conference a resolution was passed which promised that independent schools will be abolished 'within the lifetime of a parliament'. If Labour wins the next General Election, this could actually happen before the end of 1992. Colin Shenton spoke with the High Master to find out more.

The threat of abolition has existed for quite a number of years now, independent education is a feature of most election campaigns, and it was as a result of this that the Independent Schools Information Service (ISIS) was established. Such is its success and the importance attached to choice in education that ISIS now boasts 20,000 members.

As the next election draws ever nearer, most likely late in 1987, the question of Labour's determination to carry out its proposals is a pressing one. They have not tried it before, though this hardly means that they will not act if they win another election. Moreover, the conference resolution is not binding

The High Master, J G Parker - 'relaxed, forthright, capable'.

on the Labour leadership and may not actually form part of its manifesto. But, the possibility still exists and so cannot be ignored.

There is no way that leaving the threat alone will make it go away and for this reason ISIS arranged a number of local meetings earlier this month in Bury, Altrincham and Cheadle Hulme. I attended the one at Culcheth Hall School in Altrincham as did 300 others, including the High Master and the Surmaster Mr Laycock. At the meeting, chaired by Sir Fergus Montgomery, the MP for Altrincham and Sale, a representative from ISIS, Mr Peter Bingle, outlined the arguments involved and called the proposed abolition 'an act of vandalism'.

In his speech Mr Bingle drew attention to the fact that abolition may not be Labour's only proposal. Indeed Mr Radice, the Labour MP responsible for putting the motion before the conference, seems a little hesitant when pressed on the matter of a complete closedown. (He was himself educated at a fee-paying school).

Alternatives to abolition are numerous: the Assisted Places Scheme (that helps 200 boys at MGS) could be abolished; VAT could be added to fees, and not necessarily at 15 per cent, 50 per cent or 60 per cent is possible; the boarding schools allowance for parents working abroad could be cut down or scrapped; the charitable status awarded all independent schools could also

be ended.

Such points show clearly that even if abolition is not implemented such measures as taxation on fees would inevitably mean a sharp increase in the cost of independent education making schools like MGS socially more exclusive and could lower academic standards.

ISIS has three broad aims: to preserve the freedom of choice of education other than state schools; to preserve the freedom of schools to exist in order to serve the educational needs of the community; to preserve the freedom of individuals to spend their taxed income as they see fit under the law.

Peter Bingle continued his argument drawing attention to the fact that 500,000 children attend independent schools. This is roughly 5 per cent of the total and yet 25 per cent of university undergraduates went to fee paying schools. Moreover, parents who choose independent education pay for it from income that has already been taxed to pay for the state-run schools and are in fact subsidising the education of the children.

cont'd on next page

INSIDE

David Maland, High Master (1978–85).

36 per cent of boys offered places in 1976, assisted by continuing funding from a number of local authorities. The governors heard that the school bursaries had been awarded to boys from a wide range of backgrounds, including the sons of chartered engineers and teachers, mattress makers and bricklayers. The High Master hoped that such help 'would go a long way to maintaining the social mixture within the School'.[244]

In 1978 Peter Mason retired as High Master. As well as revitalising the curriculum and investing in the fabric of the school, his foresight in building up funds for bursaries had helped to prepare the school for independence without sacrificing its tradition of educating the brightest boys, regardless of their financial circumstances. He was succeeded by David Maland. Educated at Kingswood, Maland had graduated in history at Wadham College, Oxford. He had wanted to enter the law but, like Eric James, found it was a path he could not afford. The law's loss was teaching's gain. Appointed to his first headship in his early 30s, he transformed Cardiff High School in the space of three years from an old-fashioned institution wedded to corporal punishment into a much more humane place of education. In 1969 he moved to Denstone College, one of the Woodard schools. As well as raising funds for new buildings, he also oversaw the admission of day boys and girls into what had been a traditional boarding school. His confident management of change must have appealed to the MGS governors. Maland was also a talented

teacher, becoming one of the few High Masters to teach a full-time examination timetable. With a quicksilver mind, and an easy and self-deprecating manner, he wore his authority lightly and had the gift of teasing good ideas out of his colleagues.

As it turned out, David Maland's tenure would be short, just seven years, before he took up an unforeseen opportunity to achieve his ambition to become a lawyer. But in that brief period he helped to ease MGS further into independence and also began to modernise important areas of the school.

He welcomed the Assisted Places Scheme, the brainchild of Peter Mason, introduced in 1980, as a crucial element in sustaining MGS's support for able boys from less affluent backgrounds. It was vital because the last vestiges of financial aid from local authorities were ebbing away. MGS applied to take up places equivalent to a quarter of the school's annual intake. Of the 40 boys admitted in 1981, half had their entire fees remitted. Most were from modest backgrounds, with 18 coming from single-parent families,

although one of the criticisms of the scheme was that the range of social backgrounds it covered was not as wide as had been hoped.

Maland also recognised that his predecessor's work in reforming the curriculum remained incomplete. Although sixth-form options had been widened, the accelerated O-level course was still in place, as it was in many other similar schools. Limiting most boys to taking just a handful of subjects, the course was described by one boy as rather like 'a sausage machine'.[245] The opportunity for change came in 1984 when Oxford and Cambridge replaced their entrance examinations with offers based on predicted A-level results, like every other university. As a consequence, the third-year sixth form vanished, enabling Maland to phase out the accelerated stream, with all boys moving to a standard five-year O-level course. At the same time a more balanced curriculum was devised. Thanks to more investment, art and music became examination subjects and new subjects, such as biology, were introduced. It also became possible for the first time for boys to be examined in O-level history and geography. Instead of five O-level subjects, most boys were soon taking ten.

There was one quirk in these changes. Boys made a final decision on which subjects they would sit at O level only at the beginning of their fifth year. The rationale for this was that it would give them the chance to study a wide range of options before making a decision, and place them in a better position to choose their A-level subjects. Some boys found this placed them under unnecessary pressure. They resented waiting so long before making choices, as well as the often arbitrary way decisions were made. For a minority of boys, what they saw as the inflexibility of the new system created considerable disaffection. Others saw things differently. One member of staff observed that Maland's 'inspiration cut the Gordian knot between early specialisation on the one hand and insufficient coverage of the whole range of O-level subjects on the other'. The local paper put it rather more vividly, taking its remarks from the description often used by Maland himself. 'The

Clockwise from top left: Keith Booth (1965–96), Malcolm Ricketts (1949–83) and Graham Curtis (1972–2010) in the common room, 1983; Philip Hill (1944–83). After being employed as a teacher of classics since 1944, Hill became the head of department in 1972. He was also involved in junior football at the beginning of his career and was the school librarian for many years; Alan Morgan (1948–87) was the head of general science, a distinguished coach of field athletics, and a keen scout leader.

boys have had their noses lifted from their books a little to enable them to pick a few flowers by the wayside'.[246]

Maland found little need to change A-level teaching. He himself relished the chance to teach history alongside a group of outstanding colleagues. For many boys, sixth-form teaching was inspirational. One recalled how set books for English A level were not studied until the second year, allowing boys to cover a much wider field of literature. Another remembered that 'it was like being taught by academics … I felt I got a higher standard of teaching in history and politics in the sixth form than I did at university'.[247]

The intellectual stimulus of their colleagues enthralled many who came to teach at MGS. One newcomer later observed how 'a chemist explained electricity to me while we were unloading tents in the Lake District; a mathematician gave me a whistle-stop tour of Russian literature as we climbed Eagle Crag'. 'The strength of the school,' he continued, 'is undoubtedly the breadth and depth of The Common Room.'[248] Several stalwarts said farewell to the school after long years of service. Sol Clynes, who left in 1981, first came to MGS in 1938 as a student chemistry teacher, later becoming head of science. Arthur Shutt retired as head of German in 1983 after 37 years on the staff. Philip Hill, who retired in 1983, had joined in 1944, becoming head of classics. Maurice Watkins, who had been taught by Hill during the 1950s, recalled how he was always immaculately dressed and could sometimes be seen practising his ballroom-dance steps as he whistled his way across the classroom floor. Mac Ricketts, who preceded Hill as head of classics and retired in 1982, had been keenly involved with the Scouts, along with Alan Morgan, later head of general science, who retired in 1983. Ricketts had also been surmaster, a term revived by Peter Mason when he had created two deputy head posts. Such examples of devoted service were becoming less common as staff moved schools more frequently, but David Maland also recognised that many good staff were leaving too soon because there were few chances of promotion. Improvements were introduced that made it possible for teachers to remain in post without feeling compelled to move elsewhere. And while most teaching staff were still men, more women were beginning to join the staff.

Perhaps surprisingly, given his record at previous schools, David Maland only tinkered with the school's elementary system of pastoral care. The only significant change he made was to create a head of middle school, appointing Richard Turk to the post in 1983. He had been impressed by the encouragement and support given by the head of lower school, Peter Laycock, to the form tutors, who still shouldered most of the pastoral responsibility. The majority of them did an excellent job. One boy described his own form tutor, Keith Booth, as 'thoroughly lovely and caring'. But there were some who found it difficult to separate pastoral care from their academic responsibilities. Stuart Leeming, who joined the school in 1982, noted how 'boys were expected to thrive on the basis of their cleverness. A majority did, but a significant minority did not.' This led to some disaffection, exacerbated by a belief among some staff that the only solution was for boys to work even harder. Nor was the situation helped by the old-fashioned discipline still employed by some masters, with board rubbers flying across classrooms and desk lids dropped on fingers. As a result, there was near-riotous behaviour among the forms based along the upper corridors in the school. This was

PASTORAL CARE

4

Organisation

MGS is large and this could suggest that it is impersonal. However, great care is taken to ensure that boys are given individual attention from their first day in school and all boys are looked after by Form Tutors who get to know their boys well. Each Form Tutor is one of the subject teachers of the form and monitors the development and welfare of his or her boys in all aspects of school life.

First and Second Forms consist of no more than 30 boys. This number decreases gradually via Middle School forms of about 25 to around 12 at Sixth Form level. In the Lower and Middle School some subjects are taught in half-form groups.

There are four senior members of staff directly concerned with pastoral care:
Head of Lower School   Rodger Alderson
Head of Middle School   Stephen Davidson
Head of Arts Sixth   Jeremy Ward
Head of Science Sixth   John Willson
The High Master has three deputies who share with him the ultimate responsibility for all boys in the School.

Parents have ready access to their son's Form Tutor and to the appropriate senior members of staff.

Reports & Monitoring

Parents receive regular written reports. These reports emphasise achievement and give a detailed assessment of performance in all the important aspects of each subject. Regular contact with parents is also maintained by means of Parents' Evenings each year when parents can meet their son's Form Tutor and those subject teachers whom they wish to see.

Boys' performance is monitored at the end of the first half-term in each year up to the Fifth Form. This involves an overall grading and possibly a comment from each subject teacher to the Form Tutor. This enables him or her to discuss individual progress in detail. The parents are not involved at this stage unless there is cause for concern, and we find that this process allows us to detect and resolve potential problems. We encourage self-assessment by the boys, helping them to share any concerns with either the subject teacher or their Form Tutor.

Health care

There is a part-time School Doctor and a full-time Nursing Sister with responsibility for day-to-day health care. They also contribute to health education in the School.

The Surgery is essentially a first-aid post, but the staff also provide treatment for ongoing conditions and opportunities for boys to discuss problems confidentially.

Prefects

Boys are encouraged from an early stage to accept responsibility and, ultimately, to play a significant part in the life of the School by running societies, captaining teams and becoming prefects.

All Year Six boys are given the chance to be deputy prefects. The later selection of full prefects, senior prefects and the School Officers (School Captain and two Vice-Captains) is in part determined by their performance at this probationary stage. Boys themselves take part in the selection of prefects and officers.

Each First and Second Form is allocated at least two form prefects, who will have volunteered for this extra duty. The form prefects work closely with the Form Tutor, particularly in helping new boys to settle in to the School.

overcome only in 1992, when separate form rooms were abolished under Maland's successor, as part of a major relocation of departments throughout the school, resulting instead in boys moving from department to department.

Mischief mixed with ability once proved literally explosive. One boy, a gifted chemist, from a rather anarchic form, often coming into school with fingers burned by experiments at home, devised an explosive mixture intended to make a lot of noise but little damage, and placed it in the toilets underneath the High Master's study. At first it failed to go off but when one boy was sent down to relight the fuse, the mixture promptly exploded with an enormous bang, shattering one of the toilets.[249]

For many boys, it was not a member of the teaching staff they turned to when in need, but the long-serving and familiar figure of the head porter, Wilf Robb. Wilf joined MGS in 1947 and spent 40 years with the school. He was often seen shuffling around the corridors, puffing on his pipe, cup of tea in hand. He not only knew many of the boys but had also known many of their fathers.

Peter Laycock (1967–2004). During his time at MGS, he worked in various positions including: teacher of biology, senior biology master, head of lower school, surmaster and second master. Many boys and teachers owed much to his sound advice and wise counsel.

Above: Ian Bailey inspecting a boy's work in CDT, 1988.

Above right: Surveying the scene, Grasmere Camp, c.1990.

Right: Thunderboxes – the most memorable part of life at camp. Taken by John Dilworth, 1969.

At Christmas, boys would line up outside his door, bringing him bottles from their fathers as gifts. He also had a dry sense of humour. In 1977 Robert Powell starred in the drama series *Jesus of Nazareth*, and on local television Wilf was asked whether boys and staff had been aware of Powell's talent at school. Sucking on his pipe, Wilf paused for a moment, then replied, 'They were agog – agog with indifference!'

Standards of drama remained high, with plays regularly staged throughout the year by a list of talented producers drawn from the common room. One reason for such quality was probably the realisation by producers that their colleagues would be forthright in their criticism. Occasionally, however, it was the choice of play, rather than the impression made by the actors, that aroused prejudice. One example was the production of *St Joan* in 1977, the review of which in the school magazine betrayed English teacher George Myers' firm dislike of everything George Bernard Shaw had ever written.

The MGS tradition for camps, treks and other outdoor expeditions only grew stronger, as exemplified by a piece in the school magazine in 1978.

Campers have camped, trekkers have trekked and walkers have walked. Those with a taste for skiing have skied; those who like digging have dug; and those with simply the urge to travel have sampled the delights of some of the major cities of Europe, from Paris to Moscow and from Rome to Budapest. Last summer (1977) Grasmerians spent their annual ten days under canvas in the Lake District, indulging their taste for spectacular scenery and the outdoor life. They were back again this year. The Archaeological Society Dig took place in its now familiar Monmouth setting, where for two weeks ambitious diggers sought eagerly for rare finds with varying hopes of success. More recently, ... treks, Scout camps and French exchanges have catered for a variety of interests. Foreign Trek broke new ground over recent summers by visiting the Pyrenees; in July Mr Cumberland led a Geographical Expedition to North Uist and Harris in the Outer Hebrides; while yet further afield a party of some 40-odd boys and staff visited Russia. On this occasion the group travelled by coach the whole way to and from England, and this enabled visits to be made to several cities (Prague, Krakow, Budapest)...

In sport one of the outstanding performances came from a young cricketer called Michael Atherton. First selected for the 1st XI

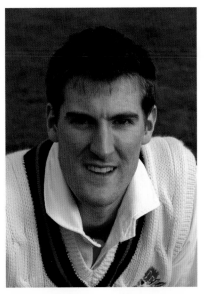

Clockwise from top left: Mike Atherton (1979–86); Mark Chilton (1988–95); rugby; boys in junior library with Eileen Bostock; water polo in the pool.

at the age of 12, he set a record of five centuries in one season in 1984, and was still playing for MGS when he became England U19 captain. He would appear in 115 test matches for England, captaining the side for five years, and scoring 16 test centuries.

Sport gained enormously when the playing fields were properly drained for the first time in the early 1980s. This was one of a series of improvements made to the school fabric in the first

years after independence. The central corridor had been 'civilised', and the 'cages', where boys had dumped their belongings for years, had been replaced with a bookshop and junior library. The swimming pool was also refurbished and the biology department extended. The major scheme was the modernisation of the chemistry block, begun under David Maland, after whom the block was named in 1986, and completed under his successor, at a cost of £1.5 million.

David Maland left MGS in 1984, his place taken from September 1985 by Geoffrey Parker. Like Peter Mason, Parker was a graduate of Christ's College, Cambridge, where he had studied history under J. H. Plumb. A lively teacher, always encouraging his pupils to think for themselves, he had been head of history at Tonbridge School in Kent, where he was well regarded for the

Right: Geoffrey Parker, High Master (1985–94).

Below right: Sir Michael Atiyah OM, FRS, FRSE, FAA (1945–47), the renowned mathematician, opened the geography department in 1993.

sensitive way he managed his departmental colleagues. In 1975, after nine years at Tonbridge, he was appointed headmaster of Queen Elizabeth's Grammar School (QEGS), Wakefield. Like MGS, QEGS was a direct grant school, and Parker had overseen its move to independence with great success. In Parker the MGS governors saw just the person who could offer the school a period of consolidation. A tall, handsome, bespectacled man, he was also an imposing presence in public. Willing to delegate, happy to trust his staff, a great pacifier of discontent, he was generally regarded at MGS as 'a really decent man, an honourable and very kind man, a gentle giant'.[250]

Parker proved to be more than a consolidator. The expanded curriculum was crying out for matching facilities, and these began to take shape under his leadership. Under the title, 'Commitment to Excellence', MGS launched its first major appeal for two decades in 1991. One of its aims was to raise £3 million towards a £6 million improvement programme. One of the most generous benefactors was Marks & Spencer. The benefits of the appeal gradually became evident over the next few years. A new geography department was housed in an extra floor added to the physics block, opened by Sir Michael Atiyah in 1993. This allowed much-needed new art rooms to be created in the former geography classrooms. Opened in September 1994, they were named the Parker Art Halls. There was a centre for English and drama. The IT centre was renovated and the sixth-form centre was converted for modern languages and politics. The latter was opened by Peter Mason as the Mason Building in 1995. Finally, an indoor sports centre was begun, completed under Parker's successor, and opened by Mike Atherton, by then the England cricket captain, in 1997. (The building was destroyed by a severe storm in the winter

of 2014.) Some of these additions reflected the rising status of subjects like art, drama and geography, as well as the increasing importance of computing, pioneered by Neil Sheldon and Alan Pickwick and still taught as a separate subject. John Bell, the art master since 1956, and his successor David Stockwell argued that art should be extended to as many boys as possible, and had found receptive listeners in David Maland and Geoffrey Parker.

The appeal also raised further funds for more bursaries. Although MGS had reached its full quota of 280 boys on assisted places by 1987, there was always a cloud of political uncertainty over the scheme, which was constantly opposed by the Labour Party. In addition, the scheme suffered from the same disadvantage as the direct grant, in that fees were determined by the government. As a result, by the early 1990s MGS was funding the gap of five per cent between actual fees and assisted-place fees.

Academic results remained outstanding. In 1989, for example, 97 per cent of boys achieved A–E grades at A level, half with A grades, while 97 per cent achieved grades A–C at GCSE, two-thirds with A grades.[251] A significant number continued to win places at Oxbridge, with a peak of 75 in 1985. But Geoffrey Parker and his colleagues still had to contend with an outdated view of MGS as an academic sweatshop. An article by the influential education editor of the *Daily Telegraph*, John Clare, caused a particular stir, as he described a school trying to shake off this image, a school 'wearing

the air of a self-confident, no-nonsense, slightly down-at-heel northern grammar school', characterised by 'a generally frenetic air that sometimes approaches pandemonium'.[252]

MGS parted company with several more long-serving teachers. Arthur Kahn's sudden death at school in 1989 deprived MGS of an outstanding head of science. A member of staff since 1955, Kahn had won a national reputation in science teaching. He believed strongly that able pupils should be taught physics, chemistry and biology and despised double-award schemes. He lamented the fact that a lack of rigorous intellectual teaching put able students off science. But he also believed in a rounded education that embraced extra-curricular activities. He was deeply involved in trekking and

Centre: The foundation stone of the Mason building was laid by HRH Queen Elizabeth II in 1965 during her visit to the school for the 450th anniversary. It was originally the sixth form block, and is now home to modern foreign languages.

Above: The geography department was added to the Marks Building (physics) in 1993.

Left: Boy using a terminal connected to the Systime computer in the pavilion. It shows the first computerisation of the Paton Library catalogue and loans system. The programs for the MGS library system were written by senior boys under the direction of Alan Pickwick (1975–2013).

Top: Philip Schofield (1954–92), surmaster and outstanding head of maths.

Above: Alan Welsby (1957–93), head of PE, and Richard Sinton (1965–93), director of music, shortly before retirement.

in 1982, recalled. 'They would walk past you as if you did not exist. You did not go into the common room on your own – it was the holy of holies and you had to be escorted by your head of section, do your work, not talk to anybody (and nobody talked to you) and leave. The line was never crossed.' Like Wilf, Harry became well known to many boys, and he too fell in love with the school, remaining past retirement as the school gatekeeper. Another long-serving member of the administrative staff was Ernest Fuller, the assistant receiver, polite and courteous, who retired after 40 years in 1988. In 1993 Mrs Skirrow, who had managed the school kitchens for 29 years, also retired. Relationships with support staff began to improve as older staff left and younger staff joined.

It was also under Geoffrey Parker that further advances were made in pastoral care. A discussion on how best to educate boys about AIDS led to the introduction of the school's first personal, social and health education programme. Called Life Skills, it was led by Gerry Peat, and initially limited to the sixth form. By the late 1980s Stuart Leeming was running the programme and became involved in sharing best practice with a consortium of independent schools. While a number of senior staff were sceptical, and there was resistance from some form tutors to expanding the scheme across the school, Geoffrey Parker was wholly sympathetic. In the early 1990s the scheme was extended to the fifth form. The next breakthrough, however, would have to wait until 1998, when the first year-group tutor, Jim Mangnall, was appointed to look after final-year GCSE students.

For many boys, their activities outside the classroom remained just as important as anything that went on inside. The Owl's Nest was still popular. One boy loved its cheerful simplicity, and the opportunity it gave young boys away from home for the first time to be 'wildly exuberant': 'I always felt the Owl's Nest was a rite of passage.' Moving on to the camps in the Lake District, he began to widen his friendships beyond his form and football team. For a boy from north Manchester, all this was a revelation. 'I remember the sense of freedom that came out of that. It felt like an endless summer. I had never attended anything like that before.'[253]

Expeditions were ranging further overseas. Russia was popular for many years, largely thanks to the teaching of Russian under Ian Leverton. The majority of boys on every trip could speak the language. Until 1986 they tended to travel by rail. In 1985, for instance, the journey took them to the Soviet Union by way of Salzburg, Vienna, Munich, Budapest and Prague. As well as Moscow and what was then still called Leningrad, these expeditions also featured less well-known parts of the USSR, including Tbilisi, Bukhara and Samarkand.

camping, and took charge of sound and lighting in the theatre. Brian Moore, a scholarly, witty classics teacher, stepped down through ill-health in 1989 and died later the same year. Philip Schofield, who retired as surmaster in 1992, having been head of maths, was part of the pantheon of outstanding MGS maths masters. Another was David Jennings, who retired four years later. In 1993 MGS said goodbye to Alan Welsby, head of PE, and Richard Sinton, director of music, who had both made great contributions in their respective fields. Welsby had also been a fine international rugby referee between 1975 and 1985.

Schools cannot function without teachers, nor can they carry on without support staff, whose contribution is often easy to overlook. In fact, with occasional exceptions like Wilf Robb, they had seemed for many years largely invisible within MGS. It was not unusual for some teaching staff to ignore their non-teaching colleagues, as Harry Bardsley, who joined as a porter and cleaner

In 1989 a group of boys visited India, under Keith Neal, head of biology, with an itinerary of schools, hospitals and factories. Neal also began links with one of Uganda's leading boarding schools, Busoga College, Mwiri. This started as a result of the collections the boys had made to raise money for clean-water projects in Uganda. Exchanges of staff took place and some senior boys even spent part of their year between school and university teaching at the college. In 1996 the school would launch a two-year project collecting old computers to send to the college.

One country that made a return appearance for the first time since the 1930s was Morocco, the destination of the foreign trek in 1992. By then the record of the legendary Harry Lob in leading the most treks (19) was under threat from Allan Witton, who completed 15. Another stalwart was John Willson, who took part in 17 Scottish treks and 12 foreign treks between 1973 and 2004.

Scouting, for so long one of the strengths of MGS's many and varied extra-curricular activities, was becoming less popular. It was becoming more difficult to persuade staff to become Scout

The Owl's Nest continues to be enjoyed by generations of MGS boys. Seen here are shots from the late 1980s and early 1990s.

Above: Boys raised money to install pumps to provide clean drinking water (pictured) to villages in Uganda in the 1990s as part of MGS's involvement with the Busoga Water Trust.

Above right: The school sent computers to Busoga College, Mwiri in Uganda. Shown here is a pupil, Bernard Wanyama, explaining a project to Roger Hand and Keith Neal from MGS.

Far right: Alec Stewart, John Crawley (1982–89), Mike Atherton (1979–86) and High Master Geoffrey Parker at the cricket reunion dinner in the early 1990s.

leaders and the enthusiasm of many boys also began to wane during the 1980s, while others preferred to commit themselves to their local troops. Keith Booth, who had been such a driving force in school scouting for many years, retired in 1996. Like many of his colleagues, his interests ranged far and wide. An outstanding linguist, he had once taken a class of boys through Spanish O level in one and a half terms from scratch. He was also involved in cross-country, school camps and overseas trips. In the early 1990s both surviving Scout troops actually folded but in 1994 Troop 1 was revived under Richard Marshall and Tim Pattison.

Under David Moss MGS became an outstanding cricketing school. During this period it produced three other fine cricketers, brothers Mark and John Crawley, and Gary Yates. Mark Crawley became the youngest member of an MGS 1st XI to score a century, making 135 against Leeds Grammar School, while Yates made a record-breaking 207 on the 1st XI's Durham tour in 1986 (beaten by Lee Marland's 208 not out against William Hulme's Grammar School in 1993). All three would play county cricket while John Crawley also appeared 37 times for England between 1994 and 2003. In 1989 MGS had the distinction of providing the captains for both Oxford (Mark Crawley) and Cambridge (Mike Atherton) in the varsity match. Three years later the MGS cricket team made its first overseas tour, to Barbados, during the Christmas holidays. While cricket was the outstanding sport of this period, there were many other successes, notably in cross-country, soccer and swimming, while numerous boys achieved representative honours at regional and national level. As the school magazine put it, 'sporting achievements are many and varied'.[254]

Drama highlights included three of James Gibb's Shakespearian productions: *Hamlet* in 1985, when Simon Petty in the leading role was praised for delivering the soliloquies with 'superb lightness of control'; *Twelfth Night* in 1988, when Bryn Bowden's performance of Malvolio was described as 'the jewel in the crown'; and *Romeo and Juliet* in 1990, when Mercutio was played brilliantly by Alex Sutherland. MGS also took *Twelfth Night* to the University Laboratory High School in Chicago in 1988. In 1991, when two recently departed pupils, Tim Scragg and Chris Addison, put on a Rattigan double-hander, the school magazine observed that 'it is a widely held belief amongst the MGS acting fraternity that the only difference between student and staff directors is that the former produce much superior drama'. In 1992 a full-time head of drama

Left: Charlie and the Chocolate Factory, 1989.

Below left: MGS orchestra rehearsing with the Stadt Jülich orchestra for a joint concert, 1987.

Below: Alice in Wonderland, 1993.

was appointed for the first time. Music under Richard Sinton and his successor Andrew Dean continued to flourish, with a plethora of choirs, bands and instrumental ensembles, performing concerts throughout the year, while MGS musicians made the first of many overseas tours in 1986, taking a small choir to Germany. In all these activities it was now commonplace to co-operate with local girls' schools.[255]

'We Can Make a Difference'

Every High Master since the time of Frederick Walker had been determined that MGS should offer to the most able boys, regardless of their background, an excellent education that might help transform their lives. In this respect the direct grant had been an outstanding success. How this aim might be achieved without the direct grant had exercised the minds of High Masters from Eric James onwards. Peter Mason's brainchild, the Assisted Places Scheme, proved to be short-lived. The doubts about its survival under a Labour government were well-founded. The scheme's abolition was amongst the new government's earliest announcements. State funding had gone for good. As a result, 1997 was a significant year in the history of MGS. There was only one way the school could continue to make places available at reduced fees for boys from poorer homes. It would have to raise the money itself. Creating an independent bursary fund of a size that would truly make a difference became a major objective of every successive High Master.

Right: Martin Stephen, High Master (1994– 2004).

Opposite: Boys walking the famously long driveway to school.

For Martin Stephen, who succeeded Geoffrey Parker as High Master in 1994, the end of assisted places seemed only too clear. Before coming to MGS Stephen had been head of another former direct grant school, the Perse School, Cambridge, since 1987. Educated at Uppingham School and a graduate in English and history of Leeds University, he had taught in several independent schools, including Sedbergh School, where he had been second master.

He was passionate about sustaining the MGS tradition, later reflecting that on becoming High Master, 'I had come home spiritually'.[256] Engaging, lively and outspoken, he was often seen walking around MGS with his Labradors, Humph and Hal. It was said that he 'came in like a whirlwind and set a totally new standard for the commitment expected from a High Master; he was everywhere and he did everything'.[257] Like Eric James, he was persuasive in promoting MGS in public. While this could

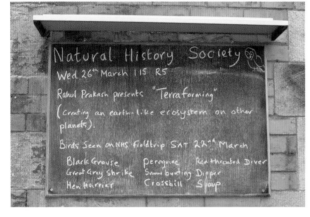

Above: Sixth formers with Tony Blair, leader of the Labour Party, 1996.

Right: Natural History Society noticeboard at the Rectory.

sometimes be in controversial terms, it was invaluable in his campaign to build up the bursary fund.

Stephen also wanted to revitalise links between MGS and the wider community. He lamented the breaking of the link between the state and MGS, and strongly believed it was not in the interests of either the independent or state sectors to grow apart. For MGS, this was particularly important, since half of all boys still came from state primary schools. But ties with state schools had become weaker, and direct contact with most primary schools had disappeared. What Stephen really wanted to see, as he noted in an article written some years later, was 'a revised system that retains the very best of the grammar school tradition, but does so in a manner that combines social justice with good educational practice'.[258]

There had been a steady change in catchment area since independence. Fewer boys came from north Manchester and more from south Manchester. The governors insisted on principle in keeping fees relatively low, and it was unsurprising that this tended to attract applications from more affluent families. MGS

could never offer as many bursaries as it wanted to boys from less well-off backgrounds because funds were limited, adding urgency to the need to raise more money. And there was also a large group in the middle of these two poles, a group for so long a stalwart element of the school, that missed out. None of this affected the cosmopolitan nature of the school, which grew even stronger. While the Jewish community remained well represented, so too did the Asian community, together accounting for 40 per cent of boys, and pupils still spoke highly of the school's positive attitudes to many diverse cultures and beliefs.

This stemmed from the school's education of each boy as a whole person, confirmed in 1996 by the first inspection for 40 years. As one governor observed, the report had remarked on 'the breadth of education and experience on offer at the school; they had emphasised the quality of inter-personal relationships within the school; and had confirmed that it is not an academic forcing house'.[259] An MGS boy in the late 1990s had no cause to find himself bored at school. He could find an activity that catered for almost any interest. The school's out-of-class activities were thriving. Societies covered everything from politics, law and philosophy to pottery, bridge and astronomy. Music and drama flourished. There were innumerable concerts and the drama society gave several productions every year. Boys took plays to

HRH The Prince of Wales, patron of the MGS foundation bursary appeal, meeting staff and pupils during his visit to the school in 1999.

the Edinburgh Fringe, and a lower school drama club had been started. Boys trekked in the Austrian Alps, skied in France, played cricket in South Africa and visited the Belgian battlefields. They exchanged places with their peers at the Wilstätter Gymnasium in Nürnberg and the Collège St-Louis de Gonzague in Paris. A trail-blazing joint expedition to China with Withington Girls' School took place in 1998, visiting Beijing and Wuhan (Manchester's twin city), with pupils hosted by Chinese families. The Community Action Group under Ian Orrell, the group's driving force since the 1970s, had established close links with the parish of St Paul's, Salford, where David Wyatt, the vicar, was an old boy. The group also had connections with a special school, the Birches, and in the mid-1990s raised £10,000 from an attempt, organised by Orrell and Geoff Chandler, to climb all 282 Munros in one weekend. As for sport, as well as the main team games and firmly established activities such as cross-country, athletics and swimming, water polo and squash had also become popular.

It was this all-round education that MGS wanted to offer more boys. The governors and the High Master were as one in agreeing that the only alternative to the abolition of assisted places was to endow more bursaries. The foundation bursaries appeal was launched in 1998. It aimed to raise £10 million. The task of achieving this was given to Ian Thorpe as appeal director.

At the launch, Martin Stephen summed up with passion the MGS tradition: 'We do not solve the problems of the world. Yet we can take a child and give that child a life that otherwise he would not have dreamt of. We can break that awful cycle of urban deprivation, that closed loop, that self-fulfilling and self-perpetuating prophecy. We can make a difference. We have been doing so for 500 years. We want to carry on doing so for the next 500.'[260] The Prince of Wales agreed to act as patron of the appeal, helping to stimulate donations. He visited the school on 15 April 1999 and hosted a reception at his home, Highgrove, for major donors and potential donors as well as representatives from other organisations connected with the school.

Above: Maurice Watkins (1952–60), chairman of the bursary appeal and current chairman of the governors, who, to the delight of many boys (and grown-ups), introduced Sir Alex Ferguson to MGS.

Right: Victorious Manchester United bring the 2013 Barclays Premier League Trophy to the school, greeted by enthusiastic junior boys.

Bottom right: Ma Zhengang, the Chinese Ambassador to the UK, Kenneth Robbie (1964–71) and Ian Thorpe (1977–present), MGS's first director of development, at the Old Mancunian London Dinner, 1999.

In a city with two of the country's leading football teams, MGS boys were perhaps more excited by the fact that Sir Alex Ferguson had been persuaded to become a vice-president of the appeal. This came about thanks to one old boy, Maurice Watkins, a leading Manchester solicitor and chairman of the bursary appeal. As a director of Manchester United, he had been part of the panel that appointed Sir Alex as manager in 1986. Watkins, who also took an active part in fund-raising, had previously arranged for Sir Alex to present the prizes to middle school boys. Head porter Harry Bardsley remembered the day well. 'I've never seen one man create such chaos in the school. The school was absolutely buzzing!' The presentation was intended to begin at nine-fifteen in the memorial hall and by eight-thirty the hall was full, with boys fighting each other for aisle seats. But, with other boys hanging out of windows waiting for him, Sir Alex did not turn up. Telephoning his personal assistant, Martin Stephen was told something had come up and Sir Alex would be unable to attend. The High Master was flabbergasted, telling the assistant that he would be torn apart if he had to give the news to a hall full of football-mad teenage boys. He was, he confessed, 'a bit cross'. With the help of Maurice Watkins, who personally contacted Ferguson, the crisis was resolved and the visit was rescheduled for noon. Sir Alex proved perfectly charming, made a short speech and received a standing ovation. He became a good friend of the school, and the draw of watching Manchester United from the directors' box, kindly made possible by Maurice Watkins, was used to persuade a number of wealthy parents to make donations, often with a persuasive Ferguson putting his arms around the parents' shoulders and telling them he himself had donated, so they should too. Sir Alex's association with the school continued when he later agreed to become a patron of the quincentenary bursary appeal.

One of Ian Thorpe's strengths as appeal director was that he had been a direct grant boy. He knew the value of an MGS education

for boys from less affluent backgrounds, and could connect with the many potential donors who themselves had benefited from such an education. The appeal also gained from the participation of Ian Bailey, who had become a much-loved MGS institution. Almost his entire life, man and boy, he had been connected with the school. As a tribute to him recorded after his death in 2007, 'for Ian, MGS was very much more than a school'. After his retirement from the teaching staff he had taken up a role as roving ambassador for the school, in particular developing closer links with old boys. He too was passionate about social diversity at MGS and would leave his estate to the bursary fund. Thorpe and Bailey became an invaluable double act in support of the campaign, wholeheartedly backed not just by the High Master but also by teaching and support staff. The MGS Common Room would become one of the major donors to the appeal. The old boys responded to the appeal with enthusiasm. They would have been impressed by the message from the High Master at the beginning of the new millennium, a message that could

Foundation bursary appeal

progress report summer 1999

This progress report comes to you a year after the Foundation Bursary Appeal was officially launched in June 1998. It has been a busy, exciting and inspiring year. HRH The Prince of Wales, Patron of the Appeal, visited MGS on April 15th and eloquently voiced his support for our aim to ensure that MGS remains accessible to all boys who meet our entrance criteria, regardless of their families' ability to pay fees.

Since the Appeal was launched just twelve months ago, the total of gifts and pledges has reached £4.9 million.

MGS

well have been written by his illustrious predecessor Eric James and illustrated the continuity of tradition sustained by successive High Masters. 'We are fighting at MGS for the cause of true meritocracy, for admission to the school on the basis of ability, rather than race, colour, creed or social and economic standing. We are also fighting for excellence, for standards and for young people.'[261] By the time the appeal ended, on Founders' Day, 2004, in the year when the last boys on assisted places left the school, the remarkable sum of more than £10 million had been raised. MGS had been more successful in raising funds for bursaries than any other independent school in England. Through the MGS Trust, which held the funds, the school was able to give financial help to more than 200 boys. To sustain fundraising for bursaries into the future, Ian Thorpe became MGS's first director of development, holding the post until 2010 and establishing firm foundations for the development office.

The bursary scheme was undoubtedly Martin Stephen's most important achievement. Exactly what it meant came home to him one evening in Oxford after he had spoken at the Union. He was pursued by a young man in a hoodie, calling out 'High Master! High Master!' He turned out to be one of the first boys supported by a school bursary. He had gone on to Oxford, graduated with a first class degree and was about to further his studies at Harvard. He simply wanted to say thank you. Martin Stephen always believed that as 'a steward of a great institution' each High Master had to ask what he might leave behind to strengthen the school; this touching incident showed him that the bursary scheme had certainly done that.

The appeal also helped MGS to extend the school's reach beyond the school gates. It not only showed the outside world a true picture of the school, it also connected MGS to the city in which it had its roots. As Martin Stephen later reflected, 'privilege must pay itself back. MGS had to be of greater value to people in the wider community.'[262] This led to the implementation of several ideas.

First, the High Master wanted to improve relationships with feeder schools in the independent and state sectors. Prep schools still had the false impression that MGS was just 'an academic sweatshop', while primary schools regarded MGS as 'elitist' and rarely regarded applications as a priority.[263] By the middle of 1998 representatives from local primary schools were coming to MGS to hear about the foundation bursary scheme and have the many myths about the school dispelled.

Second, MGS linked up with Ducie High School (now Manchester Academy) in nearby Moss Side. The heads of both schools recognised the mutual benefit in co-operating to raise expectations among boys at Ducie who had come from the same primary schools that were sending boys to MGS. Martin Stephen became a member of Ducie's governing body. A mentoring scheme was set up, with senior MGS boys making regular visits to the high school, meeting pupils, discussing homework and encouraging them to apply for university. For high school pupils with an aptitude for mathematics, an MGS maths teacher held weekly masterclasses. In connection with the charity SHINE, Neil Sheldon masterminded, led and organised the resources for teaching maths to talented local primary school pupils at MGS on Saturday mornings. Boys from MGS's Community Action group were also helping pupils at a local primary school twice a week.

Third, MGS took part in an Oxbridge access scheme, funded by the Sutton Trust. Many members of The Common Room provided after-school tuition in a range of subjects for more than 50 pupils from local colleges. Pupils were encouraged by college tutors to discuss the prospect of applying to Oxbridge and attend summer schools at both universities.

Above left: By 2014 the bursary fund had a value of £21 million. The first appeal was launched by High Master Martin Stephen to 'return the school to its original ethos of enabling any child to gain entry regardless of economic background. In my Utopia, entry to independent schools would be needs-blind.'

Left: Neil Sheldon (1970–2013). An outstanding mathematician, teacher and administrator, he served MGS in numerous capacities: head of maths, surmaster, second master and computer guru. For many years he produced the timetable – a masterpiece of intelligent design.

Singing in the Carol service at St Ann's Church and boys performing in the Christmas concert in the memorial hall, 2011.

Martin Stephen further liberalised the MGS curriculum. For the first time boys were given the option of taking alternatives to Latin and Greek from their third year onwards, and in the sixth form a standard of four A levels was set, while retaining as much as possible of the general studies programme. The widening of the GCSE course, and the introduction of more choice, went a long way towards eliminating a major source of discontent among some boys. Hand in hand with this came the extension of year-group tutors, piloted so well by Jim Mangnall, throughout the lower and middle schools. Their effectiveness in identifying boys with difficulties, and taking remedial action to solve their problems, was evident from a steady improvement in discipline as well as in GCSE results. In tandem with this, the school introduced its first learning support programme to help boys with deeper long-term academic challenges. Examination results remained outstanding by any standard, with 88 per cent of boys achieving grades A–B at A level and 83 per cent grades A*–A at GCSE in 2004.

The management and governance of the school were becoming more professional. Under Christopher Kenyon, who was chairman of governors for ten years from 1998, the governing body shrank in size, with members serving shorter terms. While the appointment of members with business skills was encouraged, the governing body valued the continuing participation of members with educational expertise as well as those who could take a broader view. More women were appointed as a matter of course, although they had been appointed occasionally as governors for many years.

The first woman to become a senior member of the management team was Gillian Batchelor, appointed bursar (the term 'receiver' was dropped) in 1999. Finance, as ever, was of critical importance, hence the massive campaign to raise bursary funds. All these funds were held by the MGS Trust, a decision on their allocation being made every year by a joint committee of governors and trustees, with advice from the High Master and bursar. A proportion of the increase in fees was applied to refurbishment and maintenance while major capital projects relied on specific fundraising.

For most schools, notable national sporting awards or representative honours would be worthy of mention, but at MGS, with so many talented boys, to do so, no matter their undoubted accomplishment, would become needlessly repetitive. One achievement that stood out in the early 2000s was Imran Azam's 266 not out for the U13s against King Edward's, Lytham, smashing the previous school record set by Lee Marland.

Musical highlights under Andrew Dean, who departed in 2002, were also numerous. For a performance of *The Dream of*

Gerontius he created the Manchester Youth Orchestra, which gathered together on a Friday, rehearsed through the weekend, and performed on the Sunday night. In the autumn of 2001 James MacMillan became composer in residence, which led to a major music festival organised around MGS, Withington Girls' School, the Royal Northern College of Music and the BBC Philharmonic. Here was another practical demonstration of MGS extending its reach into the city.

Martin Stephen probably appointed more women to the teaching staff than all his predecessors put together. In parallel with improvements to pastoral care, this made the school a kinder, warmer and less daunting institution. As newcomers arrived, the school said farewell to teachers who had devoted the best part of their lives to MGS. Peter Laycock retired in 2004 after 37 years, culminating in his position as second master. Martin Stephen said that 'working with him for ten years has been the best experience of my professional life'.[264] He was succeeded as second master by Neil Sheldon while Stuart Leeming was appointed surmaster. Nigel Reynolds finally left in 2002. He had tried to leave in 1989 but his fourth form, horrified, signed a petition persuading him to stay. A stimulating history teacher, he was, said the tribute in the school magazine, second to none in his contribution outside the classroom,

as sports coach, camp leader, founder of the battlefield trips and drama producer. In 2003–4 Bill Hardiman, head of history, David Hutton, head of modern languages, and Chris Laithwaite, head of geography, all retired with more than 30 years of service to the school. The most notable departure in 2004 was that of Martin Stephen himself. Like Frederick Walker, he moved from one highmastership to another, from MGS to St Paul's.

His successor was Christopher Ray. Educated at Rochdale Grammar School, and graduating from University College, London, followed by further study at Cambridge and Oxford, his first teaching post was at Marlborough College. In 2001 he became headmaster of the John Lyon School in north London. A man of firm convictions, with a great capacity for hard work, constantly questioning the status quo, his educational philosophy was centred firmly on the pupil. He believed that a complete education for young people combined pastoral care, academic excellence and what he insisted on calling co-curricular opportunities, and depended for its success on the absolute commitment of staff.

His immediate challenge was tackling the impact of a projected drop in the birth rate on future admissions. This was further complicated by growing competition from local state schools, notably Altrincham Grammar School, which had already prompted a revolution in the school's attitude towards positive marketing.

The favoured option was to develop an integrated junior school alongside the senior school. This was one step forward from the feeder schools developed many years before under Paton and Miller. The governors had already discussed the idea. It also became

Left: Christopher Ray, High Master (1994–2013).

Below: The common room, 2014.

Linda Hamilton, the first Head of the Junior Section, in front of Bexwyke Lodge which opened in 2008.

clear that a junior school would help to overcome the tendency for boys to be coached before they sat the entrance exam for the senior school. Considerations of cost ruled out setting up a school for 3–11-year-olds. Instead, MGS adapted the model successfully followed by Wolverhampton Grammar School, which admitted small numbers of pupils into Year 6 with guaranteed admission into the senior school. At MGS boys aged nine and ten were admitted with a similar guarantee. Land between the senior school and the sports hall was allocated for innovative new buildings, an energetic head of junior school, Linda Hamilton, was appointed, and Stuart Leeming was asked to manage the project. Christopher Ray insisted that the curriculum for the new school should be exciting, challenging and innovative. It provided scope to meet the needs of individual boys by offering a range of options within any one subject. So, for instance, within experimental science boys might choose from robotics, psychology, chemistry and forensics, among other subjects. Staff from junior and senior schools worked together to offer boys the chance to study subjects such as classical Greek, German, Portuguese, and Italian language and culture.

Opened in September 2008 by Christopher Kenyon, who had shown a close interest in the project, the junior school began with 100 boys. Bexwyke Lodge, named after one of MGS's first benefactors, is a superior log cabin, light, spacious, warm and environmentally sustainable. The junior school soon expanded, welcoming boys from the age of seven onwards from September 2011. Boys were admitted not by examination but following rigorous assessment, a method that proved so beneficial that

it influenced changes to the entry requirements for the senior school. In 2010 an inspection concluded that 'Manchester Grammar School Junior School is highly successful because of its commitment to achieving its vision, ensuring that it contributes strongly to the whole school's overall aim to stand alongside the very best schools in the UK'.[265]

The junior school also helped to extend MGS's relationship with the outside world, welcoming boys from other schools to join in various activities. Christopher Ray agreed with his predecessor that such work was one of the best ways of furthering the school's founding ethos. For instance, boys from Years 7–8 toured a production of *A Midsummer Night's Dream* around local primary schools.

One exciting project originated through Tom Bloxham, founder of Urban Splash, the urban regeneration company then working on reviving the New Islington area of Manchester. He approached MGS, where his sons had been educated, with the idea of setting up a free school in New Islington. He also persuaded Manchester City Council to become a partner in the scheme, reuniting the school and the city administration for the first time in many years. The fourth partner was the Department of Education. The project was once again overseen by Stuart Leeming, as chief executive of the New Islington Free School, while Maurice

Watkins, who succeeded Christopher Kenyon as chairman of the MGS governors in 2008, also chaired the free school governing body. With final approval from the government, the school opened in the autumn of 2013.

Ray continued the pattern of his predecessors in expanding the curriculum. More choice was given to boys studying GCSEs, with the addition of subjects such as Mandarin Chinese, drama, economics and electronics, at last allowing boys free rein to choose those subjects for which they showed an aptitude. From 2009 the International GCSE syllabus was adopted for most subjects. These changes brought further improvements in results, although not as much as the High Master would have wished. In the previous year the International Baccalaureate was offered as an alternative to A level, but its lack of general acceptance among UK universities made many sixth formers reluctant to take it up.

Another reason for improving results at 16 was because MGS had become 'a more obviously caring place than it was';[266] 'it feels a gentler school today … it is a very happy place'.[267] The task of running the middle school, with 650 boys, was the sole responsibility of the head of middle school in 2004. It was an impossible job made much easier by the subsequent appointment of a deputy, an assistant head and later heads and deputy heads of year. Similar changes were made to the lower school, and an

improved personal, social and health education programme was extended throughout the school. Steps were taken to end any distinction between academic and pastoral responsibilities in the classroom by creating a pastoral and welfare committee, bringing together academic staff, pastoral staff and boys. A school council also gave a forum for boys to express their opinions. As a result of all these measures, behaviour improved significantly, and so did standards of work, helped by a commendation scheme that gave staff the chance to praise boys for their achievements.

At MGS, as in many other boys' schools, the appointment of many more women teachers helped to create a more sympathetic environment. Christopher Ray built on Martin Stephen's record, and by 2013 there was an almost equal split between men and women on the teaching staff. Ray was also determined to eliminate the last barriers between teaching and support staff to create a

Junior school exterior; boys in lesson; eating lunch in the refectory.

167

Above: The Stuart Dale Memorial Trophy match has become an annual fixture. All proceeds go to Macmillan Cancer Support.

Above right: Old boys, Jake and Kyle and Steven Bentwood with the Old Mancunians Football Trophy. The Old Mancunian Football Tournament is played immediately before the Stuart Dale Trophy match.

Below: Harry Bardsley (1982–present). Harry is a much-loved figure whose friendly presence as the school gatekeeper is appreciated by boys and staff alike. He is always ready to offer a kind word to those who pass by him as they enter or leave the school; Rod Martin (1977–2009), teacher and head of politics. Rod passed away the year that he was to retire. Richard Kelly, the current head of politics, described Rod's teaching as 'rigorous scholarship ... fused with conversational tone'.

greater sense of unity across the school. Non-teaching staff were at last allowed to take their breaks in the common room, and the High Master made a point of attending presentations to retiring support staff.

The length of service of some members of the support staff exceeds that of most teaching staff. Jim Leathley, for instance, began as a junior lab technician in the physics department in 1966, while three other science technicians have comparable service: Peter Williams recently retired after 45 years; as of 2014, Paul Holt has been with the school for 45 years and Alex Graham for 42 years. As for the roll-call of teaching staff with 30 or more years of service who said farewell during this period the list of names is testament to the outstanding commitment of so many to the school both inside and outside the classroom.

One well-respected member of the support staff was Stuart Dale. He had joined the school as the sports pavilion porter in 1986. Like Wilf before him, he was an influential figure, whose

role transcended that of his job. Many boys of more recent times turned to him for advice and reassurance. Following his untimely death in 2005, as a mark of the respect and affection in which he was held, a charity all-star soccer match was held. The Stuart Dale Memorial Trophy match has become an annual fixture.

Of long-serving staff, Ian Leverton, who had introduced Russian to the school, retired in 2006 after 38 years. The school also lost Rod Martin, the school's founding head of politics, another outstanding teacher, who died suddenly in 2009 after 32 years on the staff. In the same year Nick Munday, who joined to teach classics in 1979 and left as surmaster, departed to train for the Anglican ministry. In 2010 Graham Curtis retired; he had joined to teach chemistry in 1972, left in 1984, and returned in 1989 to become head of department and, later, head of science.

A caring form tutor, he had an encyclopaedic knowledge of his pupils. Notable retirements in 2011 included Steve Crowther after 33 years teaching mathematics, John Cantrell, head of history, and Harry Bardsley, both after 29 years. Bardsley, however, carried on his links with MGS in his part-time role as gatekeeper. In 2012 Rodger Alderson and Richard Bradford retired after 38 and 32 years respectively on the staff. In 2013 Alan Pickwick retired after 38 years at the school. He had been instrumental in the development of computing, for administration as well as teaching. He also had an intimate knowledge of the school's infrastructure, from its telephone system and the library cataloguing system to the Old Mancunians' database and even the extent of the drains and ducts running through the buildings. In the same year the indefatigable John Shoard, an uncompromising scholar, brilliant history teacher, veteran leader of history society trips and keen squash coach, finally gave up teaching history after a remarkable 43 years with the school. His students named their departmental journal *The Shoardian* in his honour.

In 2007 the scope of school activities increased with the introduction of an activities week towards the end of every summer term, when the school becomes almost deserted. Although enthusiasm for scouting had declined, there was a surge of interest in camping and trekking. The school had celebrated a centenary of foreign trekking in 2004 with a journey over Chamonix, Aiguilles Rouges, Mont Buet, Mer de Glace and Aiguille du Midi in the French Alps. Desert treks, begun in 2000 under Eric Cittanova, became part of the trekking calendar.

A new field centre was opened at South Stainmore in 2009. The purchase of the Old Schoolhouse was made possible thanks to the generosity of Old Mancunian John Young and his wife Elizabeth. John Young was delighted to be able to support the school's long tradition of outdoor pursuits. He recalled that he had been 'fairly cerebral as a boy and not at all sporty, but I camped at Borrowdale and Grasmere and later went on the Scottish Trek. From those beginnings mountaineering subsequently became a key part of my adult life.' The Owl's Nest remained a rite of passage for young boys, and the Lake District camps helped them to form new relationships and discover more about themselves.

The Duke of Edinburgh award scheme was introduced for the first time in 2006, extending the range of outdoor opportunities available for boys, and encouraging more of them to take up the camps and treks. The scheme proved very popular. Matthew Bolton was the first boy to gain a Gold Award, in 2009, followed by 14 others in 2010 and a further 35 in 2011–12, while Andy Frain achieved the honour of becoming a Queen's Scout in 2011.

All these outdoor activities were sustained in the face of growing regulation, and the role of Eric Cittanova as educational visits co-ordinator was crucial. The school became much more professional in its management of these activities, with MGS staff undertaking training and qualifications, assisted by external expertise.

There were, as ever, countless trips at home and abroad, to such far-flung places as St Petersburg, New York, Gallipoli, Troy, Iceland, Canada, Cuba and Peru. The introduction of a two-week half-term break at Michaelmas from 2005 enabled even more trips to take place. In 2010 links were renewed with Wuhan through an exchange agreement with Wuhan Foreign Languages School.

Top: Desert trek, 2012. Twice a year, boys and staff complete a two-week trek in the Sahara.

Above: Middle school boys engaging in team-building exercises near South Stainmore, 2013.

Romeo and Juliet was staged by The Northern Youth Theatre in the quad in 2003. The NYT was founded at MGS and aimed to give students of any background a chance to be involved with acting. Pictured are MGS boys Gavin James as Tybalt and James Wallace as Mercutio.

Right: Sir Nicholas Hytner giving a lecture to boys at the school about the National Theatre Production of *Hamlet*, 2010.

Boys had 135 clubs and societies to choose from. The Community Action Group covered tasks such as organising a charity football tournament and working at a local residential home. Roger Hand maintained the school's connection with Uganda, arranging a visit to Busoga College in 2007, and establishing a relationship with a second Ugandan school, Nawaikoke College, where MGS pledged funds to enable boys to erect three basic science laboratories. A new annual lecture, the Hugh Oldham Lecture, was inaugurated. The first was delivered by Professor Sir Martin Rees, the second by old boy Michael Wood, attended by staff and pupils from MGS and other local schools. Other speakers have included Richard Dawkins and Robert Winston. Similar lectures were initiated for the lower school, middle school and junior school. In 2011 speech day, revived after an absence of more than 40 years, was held in the Bridgewater Hall.

The Northern Youth Theatre

ROMEO & JULIET

9th - 13th September 2003
MGS Quadrangle

More boys were making music, as part of instrumental groups as well as individually. Thanks to sponsorship from the London section of the Old Mancunians, a composition prize was instituted, which included a performance of the winning work at St John's, Smith Square, London. Composition became an integral part of the music curriculum. One talented young composer, Azlee Babar, had his runner-up piece for the *Guardian* Young Composers Competition played on Radio 3 in 2010. Links with the school's local orchestra, the Hallé, flourished.

As for drama, a major step forward had come following the generous donation to the bursary appeal by Old Mancunian Alan Garner of the rights to his play *Holly from the Bongs*. The play was performed by the school at the launch of the appeal in Manchester's Library Theatre. This experience highlighted

the need to upgrade the school's own facilities and in 2006 the governors agreed that the school theatre should be rebuilt. A special appeal was launched, supported by Nicholas Hytner, another distinguished old boy. He donated the proceeds from the Manchester preview of his hit film of Alan Bennett's drama *The History Boys,* which was followed by a question-and-answer session with Hytner, Bennett and cast members. Hytner made the donation in memory of an inspirational English teacher, Brian Phythian, and saw the project as a vindication of his commitment to drama and as reassurance of the priority the school was giving to drama. The Cryne family was a major donor to the appeal. The new theatre, with modern seating, an orchestra pit, fly tower and adjacent drama studios, was opened in 2009.

Above: Playing cricket on the school field.

Right: PE class in the gym, *c.*1999.

More than 700 boys were competing in one or more sports teams or on an individual basis. John Potts, who succeeded Alan Welsby as head of sport, did much to engage and nurture the sporting interest of boys of all capabilities. He also encouraged the pursuit of professional coaching, leading to the appointment of directors of cricket, rugby and football, and the recruitment of professional coaches for these and other sports, who in turn assumed responsibility for volunteer coaches. There was investment in improved drainage and more artificial pitches. In 2013 David Moss stepped down as master in charge of cricket after a remarkable 35 years.

Sporting choice was remarkable, as were the standards achieved, with countless trophies won at all age levels. In 2011, for instance, the water polo squad retained the national championship, the swimmers won the Sutton Trophy and were undefeated all season, the 1st XV rugby team won the U18 Lancashire Cup, the 1st XI soccer team won the Greater Manchester Cup and the chess team won the National Schools Championship. The MGS

Harriers achieved a string of successes in major events, including the Stonyhurst Invitational, Knole Run and the Coventry Cross-Country Relay. Under Rosie Morris, goalkeeper for the Great Britain women's water polo team, Craig Figes, the captain of the Great Britain men's water polo team, Steven Walsh, a former Great Britain squad member, and Simon Jones, the water polo squad proved immensely successful at every level. The strength of the squad was shown in 2011, when nine boys were selected for the Great Britain international squad. Similarly the chess team boasted six internationals, including one international grand master, Daniel Fernandez. Rowing, abandoned many years before because of pollution on the Irwell, was revived in 2008, based at the Agecroft Rowing Club. Lacrosse had been revived in 2004 and hockey underwent a renaissance. Cricketers toured the West Indies; rugby players toured Argentina and Chile; and footballers toured Portugal.

Individual sporting achievements were legion. In 2009 Oliver Lee rowed for Great Britain's junior men, winning two gold medals. In 2010 Christian Preece won the World U19 Duathlon Championship; Alex Haynes played for England Independent Schools FA U18s, captaining the side; Sam Hunter won a gold medal at the UK Independent Schools Judo Tournament; Charlie Kenyon won gold in the National Junior Open Fencing Tournament; and Matthew Parks won silver and Ben Caller bronze, swimming for Great Britain in the Youth Olympics. In 2013 Cameron Neild, an outstanding young rugby player, joined Sale Sharks immediately after leaving the school.

In 2013 Christopher Ray left MGS to become head of a British international school in the Middle East. It seemed appropriate as MGS approached its 500th anniversary that the governors should appoint an Old Mancunian as High Master. Martin Boulton had joined the sixth form on an assisted place in 1984. For him, MGS had been 'a transformational education', giving him among other things a love of European literature and a lifelong passion for mountaineering. 'My horizons were widened by being here. The school does hold a very special place for me.'[268] He followed his degree in mining engineering from Nottingham with a doctorate, but eventually decided to take up teaching, completing his post-graduate certificate of education at Manchester University. He had hoped to return to MGS to teach, but instead spent four years at Sherborne School, followed by 12 years at Westminster School, where he became Under Master.

Martin Boulton, High Master, with the school captain and school officers in the Paton Library in 2014; sixth form prizegiving in the memorial hall, 2011.

Martin Boulton's vision for MGS underlines the continuity that has served the school so well under a succession of High Masters. He is determined that boys coming to MGS should continue to benefit from a broad education, not just an academic one, that will help them to make the most of their potential in a globalised world.

Having attended MGS thanks to the Assisted Places Scheme, Boulton places a high priority on increasing bursary support. Martin Stephen's maxim of taking a boy and giving him a life he could otherwise never have dreamed of certainly applied to him. This ethos was one of the main reasons for his decision to return to MGS. In 2013 MGS will fund 220 bursaries, most of them covering full fees. This is a considerable achievement but the current system assists just one-sixth of all boys and every year lack of funds means as many as 30 boys who are offered places at the school have to turn them down. With more awards being made that covered full fees, it was important to carry on raising more money. Ultimately the school wishes to reach a point where all boys could be admitted on a so-called 'needs-blind' basis.

This is why MGS's 500th anniversary in 2015 is being marked by 'The Next 500 Appeal'. The school wants to raise a further £10 million 'to enable us to help more candidates and take us closer to our ultimate aim of admitting all deserving boys'.[269] In the longer term, MGS hopes to continue to increase funding for the support of means-tested bursaries. At current values and if every boy deserving of admission was to be assisted, about £100 million would be needed. The example in recent times of former pupils, former members of staff and others who simply admire the school's aims gives hope that one day through programmes of lifetime giving and legacies this may well be achieved. More than anything else this would help MGS to secure the ethos on which it was founded.

Hugh Oldham understood from personal experience the uplifting value of education. He believed his grammar school could be a place that would equip able boys from humble backgrounds to make their way in the wider world. Fundamentally this view remains the guiding tenet of the school 500 years later. Frederick Walker, who can be regarded as the founder of the modern school, believed in the fruits of marrying ability, self-motivation and hard work. Under him, it is worth repeating, 'a boy was made to act for himself, think for himself and read for himself'. So too are the words of his successor, Samuel Dill, that the purpose of the school

rested in 'preparing these boys to take their places as useful citizens of this great community'. For John King, like Hugh Oldham, MGS offered a ladder for able boys to move on and upwards, within Manchester, but also beyond it. For John Lewis Paton, perhaps the greatest of all High Masters, the school prepared boys to distinguish themselves through knowledge. All these views still hold true for the school today.

So, too, does the belief that as far as possible any able boy, regardless of his background, should be able to enjoy an MGS education. For most of its history the school has admitted fee-paying boys, and it can be argued that the school might not have survived without Walker's recognition that fee-payers were essential for its financial security. But ever since its foundation the school has striven to admit a proportion of boys free of charge or at a reduced fee. It is this in particular that has had such a formative effect on the enduring character of the school. The

diverse social composition of MGS has been a given for centuries.

In turn this social diversity created an ethos of tolerance remarked upon repeatedly by boys who found at MGS a refuge from prejudice and discrimination. It is a proud record that stretches from the first Jewish boys to enter the school in the early 19th century and the Anglo-Indian and Anglo-Chinese boys of the late 19th and early 20th century through the Belgian and Serbian refugees of the First World War and the German and Austrian boys fleeing persecution in the 1930s to the boys from Manchester's 21st-century Asian community. The register today reveals an eclectic mix of northern, Hindu, Muslim and Jewish names, from widely divergent backgrounds. Today, as previous generations have

Studying hard in the Paton Library; boys socialising at lunchtime in the refectory.

Lower school boys enjoying the sunshine.

influenced the policy of successive generations of governors towards fee levels. As Eric James said, 'all our limitations and economies are more than repaid by our complete accessibility'. This determination to remain accessible has more recently been demonstrated in the hugely successful campaigns to bolster the school's bursary funds.

Even in matters such as the curriculum and quality of teaching, MGS draws on its past. It is astonishing to think that MGS's reputation in classics, mathematics and science can be traced back several hundred years, and has been sustained ever since. So, too, can the school's record in sending boys to Oxford and Cambridge, and indeed to other universities as they were founded, establishing a remarkable achievement in sending for so long such a high proportion of senior boys into higher education. True, it can be argued that the system of sides and accelerated learning might have been reformed earlier, but given the school's results it was understandable that this was regarded as untouchable for so long.

MGS has always looked outward. It has always drawn pupils from a wide catchment area, part of the reason it has been semi-detached from the city from time to time. It has always sent many boys beyond the city boundaries, with MGS alumni making their mark in many different fields all over the world. It was Paton in particular, with his emphasis on 'each and all', who encouraged MGS boys to drink in the world around them; to dwell on the beauty of the world in all its forms, physical, cultural and emotional; to understand the inter relationship of different peoples worldwide; and so to appreciate the responsibility of taking what they had gained at MGS and applying it for the benefit of all those around them.

done in the past, these boys constantly learn from each other, tolerant and respectful of the diversity of their peers.

Yet MGS boys defy stereotypes. As the late Geoffrey Stone observed, MGS was a place for individuals. MGS boys do not conform. With their willingness to embrace the wide intellectual and cultural horizons offered by the school comes an antipathy towards compulsion. The pages of the school's history have been marked by riots, rebellion and rowdiness. MGS boys have an ambivalent attitude towards the school, treating it just as any other school yet proud of being part of such an historic institution with an outstanding reputation and defiant in its defence. This attitude is neatly summed up in the story of the MGS U15 soccer team playing Eton in the final of the independent schools football competition in 2009. As MGS moved closer to victory, the cry went up in the stands, 'We only cost ten grand! We only cost ten grand!'

Boys have always been MGS's first priority. It was in the 17th century that the school began giving financial assistance to help poorer boys pay their way through university. The relocation of the school was repeatedly postponed because of the anxiety that poor boys would be disadvantaged. The desire for the school to remain accessible to as diverse a range of boys as possible has

But all of this could never have been achieved without an ethos passed down from generation to generation of committed teachers. They have striven to bring out the potential of every individual boy, not only in the classroom, where so many boys have attested to the outstanding quality of so much teaching, but also beyond the classroom, running camps, leading treks, organising sport, drama, music and countless clubs and societies. For innumerable boys, many have been counsellors, informally and formally. They have not only taught, they have nurtured and developed their pupils; as one recent leaver put it, challenging the unchallenged boy.

In turn, such continuity has depended upon successive High Masters blessed with the skills to revitalise the teaching staff at frequent intervals. And each has built upon, and never demolished, the achievements of his predecessor, from the constant liberalisation of the curriculum to the development of pastoral

care, expecting only the highest standards from staff and pupils, and carrying an absolute belief in ensuring MGS will always find a place for able boys of every background.

MGS has relied for half a millennium on countless benefactors, from Hugh Oldham, Sarah, Duchess of Somerset, Edward Langworthy and Simon Marks, to the old boys of many different eras and the friends of the school past and present. In recent years, significant support for the Bursary Appeals has come from Old Mancunians Jon Aisbitt and Leon Howard among others. It is this generosity, spanning the centuries, that enabled the great John Lewis Paton to remind anyone who would listen that MGS 'had the proud distinction, among old foundations, of having kept nearer than any other to the intent and spirit of its Founder that it should primarily give to boys who had not much financial backing a chance of distinguishing themselves'.

Class of 2013 leavers gathering for their informal photograph outside the pavilion on their last day at MGS; stained-glass window in memorial hall bearing the school motto 'Sapere Aude' ('dare to be wise').

Sources and Bibliography

MGS has an excellent archive. I concentrated particularly on records covering the history of the school from the late 19th century onwards, supplemented by numerous secondary sources. Mumford's history is an assiduously researched work, and contains a wealth of fascinating detail, while he also published the only biography of the school's founder, Hugh Oldham. I feel sure that in disparate archives across the country there is still material to be found that would shed much more light on a man who left barely a trace of his rise to the political elite during a particularly volatile time in English history. I suspect, however, that it would be a hugely time-consuming project.

MGS Archives

This is a list of only the principal sources used from the archives.

Admissions Registers, 1888 onwards

Anon, *A Life in the Day of a Master at MGS*, c.1980s

Customs and Curricula, 1907

Dobson, Adrian, *The Manchester Grammar School Trekking Centenary*, 2004

Governors' Minutes 1849–2001

High Master's Reports to the Governors, 2004–13

Hodgson, R. D., *A Short History of the Manchester Grammar School*, 1905

Miscellaneous biographical material on High Masters

Miscellaneous material on curriculum and inspections

Miscellaneous material on the school history

Old Mancunians' Association, Annual Reports, 1912–

Old Mancunian newsletters, 1999 onwards

Register containing series of High Master's Reports, 1880–

School policies and plans

The Mancunian, 1966–

Ulula, 1873 onwards

National Archive, Kew

ED109/3036/ Report of full inspection of MGS by Board of Education on 17–21 Oct. 1910

ED109/3037/ Report of Inspection of MGS by Board of Education in Feb. 1920

ED109/3038/ Interim Inspection (Sixth Form Work) of MGS by Board of Education on 19–21 Nov. 1930

ED109/3039/ Full inspection report of MGS by Board of Education held on 11–14, 17–21 Oct. 1932

ED35/1342/ Miscellaneous papers relating to MGS 1871–1911 (includes a printed report of the Special Committee appointed by the governors to investigate masters' pensions and salaries c.1900)

ED35/1348/ Miscellaneous papers relating to MGS 1912–18 (includes an area report on Manchester Secondary Schools 1911–12, and details of a medical inspection in July 1914)

ED35/4947/ Miscellaneous papers relating to MGS 1921–35

ED35/4948/ Miscellaneous papers relating to MGS 1936–40 (includes papers relating to the evacuation of the School to Blackpool)

Books

Atherton, Mike, *Opening Up*, London, 2002

Bamford, Samuel, *The Autobiography of Samuel Bamford*, vol. 1: *Early Days...*, ed. W. H. Chaloner, London, 1967

Barker, Sir Ernest, *Father of the Man*, Leicester, 1948

Baxandall, Michael, *Episodes: A Memory Book*, London, 2010

Bentley, James, *Dare To Be Wise*, London, 1990

Birrell, Augustine, *Sir Frank Lockwood: A Biographical Sketch*, London, 1898

Briggs, Asa, *Victorian Cities*

Bruton, F. A., *The Story of Peterloo, Written for the Centenary*, Manchester, 1919

Carlisle, Nicolas, *A Concise Description of the Endowed Grammar Schools in England and Wales*, vol. 1, London, 1818

Clements, Keith, *Henry Lamb: The Artist and his Friends*, Bristol, 1985

Dumaresq de Carteret Bisson, F. S., *Our Schools and Colleges*, vol. 1: *Boys*, London, 1884

Eaton, Horace Ainsworth, *Thomas De Quincey: A Biography*, London, 1936

Graham, J. A., and B. A. Phythian, eds, *The Manchester Grammar School, 1515–1965*, Manchester, 1965

Hazell, Quinton, *The Life of an Entrepreneur*, Stroud, 1992

Hewitt, Martin, and Robert Poole, eds, *The Diaries of Samuel Bamford*, Stroud, 2000

Hobson, Harold, *What I Have Had: Chapters in Autobiography*, London, 1953

Hylton, Stuart, *A History of Manchester*, second edition, Andover, 2010

Jackson, Robert, *The Chief: The Biography of Gordon Hewart, Lord Chief Justice of England 1922–40*, London, 1959

Lee, Michael R., *Stood on the Shoulders of Giants*, Spennymoor, 2003

Lentin, Antony, *The Last Political Law Lord, Lord Sumner (1859–1934)*, Newcastle, 2008

McCulloch, Gary, 'Secondary Education', in *A Century of Education*, ed. Richard Aldrich, London, 2002

Mumford, Alfred A., *The Manchester Grammar School, 1515–1915: A Regional Study in the Advancement of Learning in Manchester since the Reformation*, London, 1919

——, *Hugh Oldham, 1452–1519*, London, 1936

Ridley, Rosamund, *Dear Friends, Liebe Freunde: International Friendship and the First World War*, Kentmere, 2010

Schurr, Peter H., *So That Was Life: A Biography of Sir Geoffrey Jefferson, Master of the Neurosciences and Man of Letters*, London, 1997

Smith, Revd Jeremiah Finch, *The Admission Register of the Manchester Grammar School*, Chetham Society, Manchester, 1866–74

Streat, Sir Raymond, *Lancashire and Whitehall: The Diary of Sir Raymond Streat, 1931–57*, ed. Marguerite Dupree, 2 vols, Manchester, 1987

Whatton, W. R., *History of the Foundations in Manchester*, vol. 3: *The History of Manchester Grammar School*, London, 1834

ENDNOTES

1   THE FOUNDER

1   Oldham's only biographer was Alfred A. Mumford, also historian of Manchester Grammar School, whose work *Hugh Oldham, 1452–1519*, was published by Faber & Faber in 1936. Many of the references in this chapter can be found in this book.

2   Mumford, *Hugh Oldham*, p. 21.

3   Mumford, *Hugh Oldham*, p. 23.

4   W. R. Whatton, *History of the Foundations in Manchester*, vol. 3: *The History of Manchester Grammar School*, London, 1834, p. 316.

5   Nicholas Orme, 'Oldham, Hugh (c.1450–1519)', in *Oxford Dictionary of National Biography*, Oxford, 2004 [http://www.oxforddnb.com/view/article/20685, accessed 23 April 2014].

6   Mumford, *Hugh Oldham*, p. 134.

7   Orme, 'Oldham, Hugh'.

8   Quoted in Orme, 'Oldham, Hugh'.

9   Alfred A. Mumford, *The Manchester Grammar School, 1515–1915: A Regional Study in the Advancement of Learning in Manchester since the Reformation*, London, 1919, p. 9.

10   James Bentley, *Dare To Be Wise*, London, 1990, p. 14.

2   THE EARLY SCHOOL, 1515–1808

11   Mumford, *Hugh Oldham*, p. 128.

12   Mumford, *Hugh Oldham*, p. 127.

13   See Mumford, *Manchester Grammar School*, Appendix 18.

14   Mumford, *Manchester Grammar School*, p. 34.

15   Whatton, *History*, p. 34.

16   Mumford, *Manchester Grammar School*, p. 93.

17   See Mumford, *Manchester Grammar School*, Appendix 18.

18   Mumford, *Manchester Grammar School*, p. 130.

19   See Mumford, *Manchester Grammar School*, Appendix 18.

20   Mumford, *Manchester Grammar School*, pp. 143–5.

21   Revd Jeremiah Finch Smith, ed., *The Admission Register of the Manchester Grammar School*, vols 1–3 (1730–1837), Chetham Society, Manchester, 1866–74.

22   *Register* (1730–75).

23   Mumford, *Manchester Grammar School*, p. 168.

24   Whatton, *History*.

25   J. A. Graham and B. A. Phythian, eds, *The Manchester Grammar School, 1515–1965*, Manchester, 1965, quoted on p. 27.

26   Graham and Phythian, *Manchester Grammar School*, quoted on p. 26.

27   Graham and Phythian, *Manchester Grammar School*, quoted on p. 25.

28   Mumford, *Manchester Grammar School*, quoted on p. 237.

29   Samuel Bamford, *The Autobiography of Samuel Bamford*, vol. 1: *Early Days…*, ed. W. H. Chaloner, London, 1967, pp. 82–3.

30   Whatton, *History*, pp. 8–9.

31   See Mumford, *Manchester Grammar School*, Appendix 17 and Appendix 18.

32   Horace Ainsworth Eaton, *Thomas De Quincey: A Biography*, London, 1936, quoted on p. 68.

33   Graham and Phythian, *Manchester Grammar School*, quoted on pp. 28–9.

34   *Ulula* (Manchester Grammar School magazine), 1980, quoted on p. 18.

3   STRUGGLE FOR REFORM, 1808–67

35   Mumford, *Manchester Grammar School*, quoted on p. 257.

36   Manchester's population rose from more than 70,000 in 1800 to 142,000 in 1831, with the 1820s seeing a 45 per cent increase (see Asa Briggs, *Victorian Cities*, pp. 88–9).

37   Stuart Hylton, *A History of Manchester*, second edition, Andover, 2010, quoted on p. 98.

38   F. A. Bruton, *The Story of Peterloo, Written for the Centenary*, Manchester, 1919.

39   *Ulula*, Nov. 1875, p. 88.

40   See Mumford, *Manchester Grammar School*, Appendix 17 and Appendix 18.

41   *Ulula*, May 1892, p. 83.

42   Carlisle, Nicholas, *A Concise Description of the Endowed Grammar Schools in England and Wales*, London, 1818, vol. 1, pp. 672–704.

43   Graham and Phythian, *Manchester Grammar School*, quoted on p. 39.

44   *Ulula*, July 1905, p. 112.

45   Graham and Phythian, *Manchester Grammar School*, quoted on p. 32.

46   *Ulula*, 1875–6, pp. 90–1.

47   Mumford, *Manchester Grammar School*, quoted on p. 270.

48   See *Ulula*, July 1892, June 1904, July 1904, Oct. 1904, July 1926.

49   *Ulula*, July 1892.

50   Governors' Minutes, 1849–66, 19 Oct. 1859.

51   Graham and Phythian, *Manchester Grammar School*, quoted on pp. 51–2.

52   Governors' Minutes, 1849–66, 8 Mar. 1860.

53   *Ulula*, July 1898, p. 116. The same writer recalled attending the distribution of prizes for the Oxford Locals by Gladstone at the Free Trade Hall in the same year, being 'much impressed by his clear musical utterance, and the beauty and gracefulness of his language'.

54   Governors' Minutes, 1849–66, 9 Oct. 1862.

55   Mumford, *Manchester Grammar School*, quoted on p. 340.

56   Governors' Minutes, 1849–66, 14 Jan. 1863.

57   Graham and Phythian, *Manchester Grammar School*, quoted on p. 67.

4   THE MODERN FOUNDATION, 1867–1903

58   C. L. Bounds, 'Beginnings of Science Education at MGS', *Ulula*, 1977.

59   Mumford, *Manchester Grammar School*, quoted on p. 355.

60   *Ulula*, Dec. 1876, p. 65.

61   *Ulula*, Feb. 1922, p. 16.

62   *Ulula*, July 1924.

63   *Ulula*, Mar. 1917, p. 43.

64   Antony Lentin, *The Last Political Law Lord: Lord Sumner (1859–1934)*, Newcastle, p. 16. Under Walker, scholarship winners were entitled to wear gowns.

65   *Ulula*, May 1881, pp. 141–2, and Feb. 1911.

66   MGS Archive, Folder – Biographies (Gs), F. W. Walker, obituary, 14 Dec. 1910.

67   MGS Archive, as above, letter dated 29 Mar. 1869.

68   *Ulula*, July 1875, p. 59.

69   Governors' Minutes, 14 Oct. 1868.

70   Governors' Minutes, 26 Oct. 1874. The criticism that the school's unique system of organisation led to specialisation too early and prevented boys from gaining an all-round academic education was commonly heard until the system was finally abolished in the early 1960s.

71   *Ulula*, Feb. 1922, p. 16.

72   Mumford, *Manchester Grammar School*, p. 351.

73   *Ulula*, July 1873, p. 31.

74   *Ulula*, Nov. 1873.

75   He took with him his secretary, Samuel Bewsher, who would found Colet Court, the prep school for St Paul's.

76   *Ulula*, Dec. 1876, p. 105.

77   *Ulula*, June 1888.

78   *Ulula*, Oct. 1878, p. 16.

79   *Ulula*, July 1878, p. 403, Oct. 1878, p. 16, and Oct. 1883, p. 16.

80   *Ulula*, June 1888, p. 11.

81   *Ulula*, Oct. 1885, p. 3.

82   *Ulula*, Oct. 1883, p. 15.

83   *Ulula*, Oct. 1881, p. 11.

84   *Ulula*, June 1888, p. 11.

85   *Ulula*, Oct. 1889, p. 150.

86   Sir Ernest Barker, *Father of the Man*, Leicester, 1948, p. 37.

87   *Ulula*, Oct. 1889, p. 150.

88   *Ulula*, Oct. 1894, p. 101.

89   *Ulula*, Oct. 1892, p. 138.

90   Mumford, *Manchester Grammar School*, quoted on pp. 407–9.

91   *Ulula*, Oct. 1894, p. 139.

92 National Archive, ED35/1342, Miscellaneous papers relating to MGS 1871–1911.

93 *Ulula*, Oct. 1898, p. 148.

94 *Ulula*, Oct. 1894, p. 139.

95 Governors' Minutes, 20 Sept. 1899, Inspection Report 25–27 June 1899.

96 Barker, *Father of the Man*, p. 49.

97 *Ulula*, Mar. 1901, p. 36.

5   WANDERBIRDS, 1903–14

98 *The Times*, 29 Apr. 1946.

99 MGS Archive, G2 – Box on J. L. Paton, 'The Man' by John Coatman, in *JLP: A Portrait of John Lewis Paton by his Friends*, Memorial University of Newfoundland, Paton College, n.d., pp. 18–24, and *Ulula*, 1998, p. 123.

100 *Ulula*, July 1946, p. 571.

101 *Ulula*, 1952, p. 26.

102 Peter H. Schurr, *So That Was Life: A Biography of Sir Geoffrey Jefferson, Master of the Neurosciences and Man of Letters*, London, 1997, and *Ulula*, 1955, p. 30; Sir Raymond Streat, *Lancashire and Whitehall: The Diary of Sir Raymond Streat*, vol. 2: *1939–57*, ed. Marguerite Dupree, Manchester, 1987, p. 129.

103 *Ulula*, Nov. 1905, pp. 187–8; Old Mancunians' Association (OMA) Annual Reports, 1914, p. 42; *Ulula*, Feb. 1914, p. 18.

104 *Ulula*, Feb. 1914, p. 18, Nov. 1905, p. 188, Oct. 1913, p. 172.

105 *Ulula*, Oct. 1903, p. 143.

106 *Ulula*, July 1913, p. 143; MGS Archive, G2 – Box on J L Paton, 'A Letter to a Boy on Leaving School' and 'A Letter to a Boy at School'.

107 Governors' Minutes, 1899–1913, 12 Oct. 1904, 12 Apr. 1905, 20 Sept. 1905, 17 Jan. 1906, 11 Mar. 1907 and 10 July 1907 (High Master's Report, 1907).

108 *Ulula*, 1933, pp. 22–6.

109 Gary McCulloch, 'Secondary Education', in *A Century of Education*, ed. Richard Aldrich, London, 2002, p. 22.

110 National Archives, ED109/3036, Report of full inspection of MGS by the Board of Education on 17–21 Oct. 1910.

111 National Archive, ED35/1348, Miscellaneous papers relating to MGS 1912–18, Area Schools Report on Manchester Secondary Schools 1911–12.

112 Governors' Minutes, 12 Apr. 1911, printed memorial from the staff dated 5 Apr. 1911.

113 Governors' Minutes, 13 July 1904, High Master's Report; *Ulula*, Oct. 1904, p. 178, and Nov. 1913, p. 199.

114 *Ulula*, Nov. 1948.

115 *Ulula*, Oct. 1911, p. 176.

116 R. D. Hodgson, *A Short History of the Manchester Grammar School*, 1905, p. 29.

117 Governors' Minutes, 11 July 1906, High Master's Report for 1906.

118 National Archive, ED35/1348, Miscellaneous MGS Papers 1912–18, Medical Inspection July 1914.

119 *Ulula*, Feb. 1910, p. 45.

120 OMA Annual Reports, 1958, p. 35.

121 Governors' Minutes, 22 July 1908.

122 Nine of them were boarders. The small boarding house finally closed in 1912.

123 *Ulula*, Mar. 1911.

124 OMA Annual Reports, 1967, p. 40.

125 Governors' Minutes, 16 Jan. 1907.

126 National Archives, ED109/3036, Report of full inspection of Manchester Grammar School by the Board of Education on 17–21 Oct. 1910; and *Ulula*, Oct. 1910, and Nov. 1910.

6   INTERRUPTIONS, 1914–31

127 OMA Annual Reports, 1914, p. 15.

128 OMA Annual Reports, 1956, p. 26.

129 Governors' Minutes, 11 July 1917, High Master's Report for 1917.

130 *Ulula*, June 1916, p. 121.

131 *Ulula*, May 1916, pp. 82–5.

132 *Ulula*, Feb. 1935, p. 321, July 1916, p. 144, Nov. 1916, p. 228.

133 *Ulula*, Mar. 1917, p. 38.

134 *Ulula*, June 1918, p. 61.

135 MGS Archive, G2 – Box on J. L. Paton, Letter, 28 June 1918.

136 MGS Archive, G2 – Box on J. L. Paton, Letter to an old boy, 19 Sept. 1918.

137 MGS Archive, G2 – Box on J. L. Paton, Letter, 19 Jan. 1919.

138 *Ulula*, Feb. 1919, p. 1.

139 National Archive, ED109/3037, Report of Inspection of Manchester Grammar School by the Board of Education for February 1920.

140 *Ulula*, Dec. 1921, p. 150, June 1921, p. 58.

141 Governors' Minutes, 13 July 1921, High Master's Report for 1921.

142 Inspection Report, 1920.

143 *Ulula*, Oct. 1923, p. 44.

144 *Ulula*, Autumn 1951, p. 64; and OMA Annual Reports, 1964.

145 National Archive, ED35/4947, Miscellaneous MGS Papers 1921–35.

146 Governors' Minutes, 15 Jan. 1924.

147 *Ulula*, Oct. 1924, p. 133.

148 Governors' Minutes, 10 Sept. 1924. The school certificate introduced after the First World War was the first universal national educational qualification.

149 *Ulula*, Summer 1974. Paton appears to have been the first High Master to have been commonly known as 'the Chief', and it was an appellation that was applied to all his successors up to and including Peter Mason.

150 MGS Archive, Folder – Biographies, G2, Douglas Miller, *Guardian* obituary, 19 May 1956.

151 *Ulula*, Feb. 1931, p. 6.

152 OMA Annual Reports, 1970, p. 17.

153 *Ulula*, Summer 1970, p. 45.

154 OMA Annual Reports, 1967, p. 37.

155 *Ulula*, July 1920, p. 87.

156 OMA Annual Reports, 1928, p. 46.

157 OMA Annual Reports, 1924, p. 43.

158 OMA Annual Reports, 1925, p. 48.

159 Richardson was also captain of school and won a place at Balliol, occasionally playing cricket for the university, but died at the early age of 21 in 1928.

160 National Archive, ED35/4947, Miscellaneous MGS Papers 1921–35.

161 *Ulula*, Mar. 1931, p. 45.

162 Streat, *Lancashire and Whitehall*, vol. 1: *1931–9*, Manchester, 1987, pp. 72–3.

163 *Ulula*, Autumn 1951, p. 64.

7   A DIFFICULT BEGINNING, 1931–45

164 Streat, *Lancashire and Whitehall*, vol. 1, p. 124; Governors' Minutes, 20 Oct. 1932; MGS Archive, Curriculum and Inspections, Inspection Report, 1932.

165 *Old Mancunian* newsletter, Sept. 2003; *Ulula*, 2000, p. 131.

166 Inspection Report, 1932.

167 Interview with Geoffrey Stone, 10 July 2013.

168 Interview with Sydney Dobson, 8 July 2013.

169 Interview with Sydney Dobson, 8 July 2013.

170 Interview with Geoffrey Stone, 10 July 2013.

171 Interview with Sydney Dobson, 8 July 2013.

172 Adrian Dobson, *The Manchester Grammar School Trekking Centenary*, 2004.

173 *Ulula*, July 1946, p. 575.

174 *Ulula*, 1985, p. 16.

175 *Ulula*, Dec. 1939, p. 101.

176 Governors' Minutes, 15 Sept. 1939.

177 National Archive, ED35/4948, Miscellaneous MGS Papers 1936–40.

178 OMA Annual Reports, 1939, pp. 15–16.

179 *Ulula*, 2000, p. 131.

180 Governors' Minutes, 8 Oct. 1940. In fact Dolores Graham was invited to stay by Miller's successor, finally leaving in 1955.

181 Governors' Minutes, 17 July 1945, High Master's Report for 1945.

8   DIRECT GRANT HEYDAY, 1945–64

182 Governors' Minutes, 16 July 1946, High Master's Report for 1946.

183 OMA Annual Reports, 1967, p. 41.

184 *Old Mancunian* newsletter, Sept. 2011.

185 OMA Annual Reports, 1953, p. 39.

186 *The Times*, 19 May 1992.

187 *Manchester Evening News and Chronicle*, 10 Mar. 1965.

188 *Ulula*, Apr. 1947, p. 614; OMA Annual Reports, 1950, p. 47.

189 OMA Annual Reports, 1952, p. 30.

190 *Ulula*, Autumn 1961, p. 12.

191   *Ulula*, 1992, p. 83.

192   Michael R. Lee, *Stood On The Shoulders Of Giants*, Spennymoor, 2003, p. 49; Interview with Ernest Fox, 10 July 2013; Alan Garner, 'Eric James: A Memoir', *Manchester Memoirs*, vol. 131, pp. 111–12.

193   *Daily Telegraph*, 18 May 1992.

194   *Ulula*, Autumn 1961, p. 12.

195   Governors' Minutes, 16 July 1946, High Master's Report for 1946.

196   Interview with Geoff Fox, 11 July 2013.

197   Graham and Phythian, *Manchester Grammar School*, p. 132.

198   Governors' Minutes, 1 Oct. 1951, Printed Copy of Inspection Report, 31 Jan.–9 Feb. 1951.

199   Baxandall, Michael, *Episodes: A Memory Book*, London, 2010, p. 49.

200   The school certificate and higher school certificate were replaced by O levels and A levels in 1951.

201   Governors' Minutes, 9 July 1957 and 7 July 1953.

202   Governors' Minutes, 1 Oct. 1951.

203   Governors' Minutes, 1 Oct. 1951.

204   Lee, *Stood On The Shoulders Of Giants*, p. 46.

205   *Ulula*, 1990, p. 18.

206   Interview with Michael Ainsworth, 20 June 2013.

207   Numbers grew from 65 in 1945 to 83 in 1961.

208   *Old Mancunian* newsletters, Sept. 2002.

209   Interview with John Horsfield, 10 Sept. 2013; *Dare To Be Wise*, p. 117.

210   Interview with Geoff Fox, 11 July 2013.

211   Governors' Minutes, 7 July 1953, High Master's Report for 1953.

212   Interview with Brian Taylor, 10 July 2013.

213   The ownership of the Grasmere camp site was transferred to the school in 1951, the previous trustees having been former pupils.

214   OMA Annual Reports, 1972, p. 17.

215   Governors' Minutes, 7 July 1953, High Master's Report for 1953.

216   Governors' Minutes, 10 Oct. 1961.

217   *Daily Telegraph* obituary, 24 Sept. 2009.

218   Interview with John Horsfield, 10 Sept. 2013.

219   OMA Annual Reports, 1962, p. 21 and p. 32.

220   OMA Annual Reports, 1965, p. 43.

221   OMA Annual Reports, 1964, p. 35 and p. 38.

9   Towards Independence, 1964–76

222   Graham and Phythian, *Manchester Grammar School*, pp. 86–7.

223   OMA Annual Reports, 1969; Governors' Minutes, 21 Apr. 1970.

224   Governors' Minutes, 7 July 1970.

225   *The Mancunian*, 16 Mar., 28 Sept. and 12 Oct. 1967; *Ulula*, Summer 1970, p. 62.

226   Interview with Jeremy Ward, 18 June 2013.

227   *Ulula*, Summer 1969, p. 16.

228   Governors' Minutes, 3 Oct. 1972.

229   *Ulula*, Summer 1969, p. 72.

230   *The Mancunian*, 16 Mar. 1967; interview with Ken Robbie, 10 Sept. 2013.

231   Interview with Ken Robbie, 10 Sept. 2013.

232   The A-level statistics may seem low by today's standards, but it is an almost impossible task to compare results achieved in examinations set at different standards over long periods of time.

233   Interview with Jeremy Ward, 18 June 2013.

234   *Ulula*, 2010, p. 11.

235   Interview with David Walton, 20 June 2013.

236   *Ulula*, Summer 1967, p. 6.

237   Interview with Ian Thorpe, 17 Sept. 2013.

238   Interview with Adrian Dobson; interview with Ian Thorpe, 17 Sept. 2013.

239   Governors' Minutes, 21 Jan. 1969.

240   Interview with Maurice Watkins, 18 June 2013.

241   Interview with Ken Robbie, 10 Sept. 2013.

242   Interviews with Jeremy Ward, 18 June 2013, and with John Shoard, 19 June 2013.

10   Challenging Times, 1976–94

243   *Ulula*, 1977; interview with Jeremy Ward, 18 June 2013.

244   Governors' Minutes, 18 Jan. 1977 and 20 Jan. 1976.

245   Interview with John Whitfield, 17 Sept. 2013.

246   MGS Archive, Folder, Biographies, G2, David Maland.

247   Interview with Sandip Jobanputra, 10 Sept. 2013.

248   MGS Archive, Box D4, School History, A Life in the Day of a Master at MGS, anon., n.d., *c*.1980.

249   Interview with Danny Downs, 11 July 2013; interview with Stuart Leeming, 17 June 2013.

250   Interview with Jeremy Ward, 18 June 2013.

251   By comparison, in 1996 the proportions were a 99 per cent pass rate for A level, 80 per cent A–B grades; and a 99 per cent pass rate for (GCSE), 76 per cent grade A*–A.

252   *Ulula*, 1991, p. 6.

253   Interview with Danny Downs, 11 July 2013.

254   *Ulula*, 1997.

255   *Ulula*, 1985, 1988 and 1991.

11   Celebrating 500 Years, 1997 Onwards

256   Interview with Martin Stephen, 28 June 2013.

257   Interview with Ian Thorpe, 17 Sept. 2013.

258   MGS Archive, Folder, Biographies, G2, Martin Stephen, draft for an article, 'Raising Standards', for *Parliamentary Monitor*, Feb. 2003.

259   *Ulula*, 1992, p. 11; MGS Archive, Folder G2, Biographies, Memoir of David Maland by Peter Laycock, n.d.; *Manchester Evening News*, 18 May 1984; *Ulula*, 1991, p. 6; Governors' Minutes, 29 Feb. 1996 and 18 Jan. 1977.

260   *Ulula*, 1998, p. 9.

261   *Old Mancunian* newsletters, Jan. 2000.

262   Interview with Martin Stephen, 28 June 2013.

263   Governors' Minutes, 12 Mar. 1998.

264   *Ulula*, 2004, p. 11.

265   MGS Archive, Box C4, School Policies and Plans.

266   Interview with Paul Thompson, 18 June 2013.

267   Interview with Gillian Batchelor, 19 June 2013.

268   Interview with Martin Boulton, 13 Aug. 2013.

269   'The Next 500 Appeal', Manchester Grammar School website, accessed April 2014: http://mgs.org/contact-us/48-mgs-global/landing-page-42357.

LIST OF SUBSCRIBERS

This book has been made possible through the generosity of the subscribers listed below.
The content and presentation of this list have been verified by the Development Office at MGS.

Ilan D. Aarons	1985–1992
William R. Abbotts	2008–
Sean M. Abbs	2014–(Staff)
Jonathan Abelson	1984–1991
Leo Abelson	2013–
Ali Abod	2010–
Hassan Abod	2004–2011
James Abu-Romia	1994–2001
E. John T. Acaster	1951–1952
Ernest L. Acaster	1919–1926
John N. Acaster	1924–1927
Julian Acratopulo	1982–1989
Michael Acratopulo	1980–1987
William F. Adam	2003–2010
David Adams	1959–1966
David H. Adams	1954–1961
Karl Adelman	2011–
Leo Adelman	2006–2011
Ausaid Adem	2012–
Suhaib Adem	2012–
Daniel O. Adeyoju	2009–
H. Gordon Adshead	1952–1959
Rishi Suraj Aggarwal	2003–2010; 2014– (Staff)
Hamza Ahmad	2013–
Mohsan Abas Ahmad	1992–1999
Qesser Khalil Ahmad	2008–
Ryaan Ahmed	2013–
Tenveer Ahmed	1992– (Staff)
Yusuf Ahmed	2013–
Zyaan Ahmed	2011–
Vijay Y. Ahuja	1992–2000
Peter Ainsworth	1945–1948
Iain Airth	2014– (Staff)
Jon Aisbitt	1968–1975
Adithya Ajay	2012–
Barry Akid	1945–1952
Saleem Al-Asady	2007–2014
Sarmed Al-Asady	2011–
Antony Alberti	1991–1998
George A. Albiston	1938–1942
Jeffrey P. Alderson	1945–1950
Ruth Aldred	2000–2012 (Staff)
Benjamin L. Alexander OBE	1936–1943
Edward M. C. Alexander	1977–1984
Eric Alexander	1942–1950
George R. Alexander	1966–1974
Gregory B. Alexander	2008–
Simon D. Alexander	1969–1976
Amar Ali	1990–1997
Maha D. Al-Khazragi	2014– (Staff)
J. Malcolm Allan	1946–1953
John Allan	1978–1985
Adam Allcock	2003–2010
Christopher Allen	1957–1964
David J. Allen	1960–1967
David W. Allen	1994–2001
Geoffrey Allen	1957–1964
Kenneth E. Allen	1939–1944
Michael Allen	1959–1965
Robert W. Allen	1939–1945
Jo Allinson	2008– (Staff)
Martin V. Allinson	1946–1952
Jim Allison	1966–1972
Martin Allweis	1958–1965
Muhammad Bilal Aly	2009–
Tam Amachree	2000–2007
Jayan Harsha Amandakone	2013–
Richard Ames	1981–1988
Ismaeel Rahil Amin	2008–
Akhil Anand	2007–2014
David C. H. Anderson	1999–2006
Louisa Anderson	2008– (Staff)
Richard A. I. Anderson	2011–2013
Donald Anderton	1936–1944
David Andrew	1952–1959
Philip Andrew	1954–1961
Eddie Ang	2011–
Elden Ang	2014–
Donald G. Annis	1944–1948
Michael J. Antrobus	1957–1964
Saif ur Rehman Anwar	2007–2014
Syme Ali Anwar	2005–2012
John P. Appleby	1943–1949
Matthew Appleby	2004–2011
Tom Appleby	2010–
Frank Appleyard	1952–1959
Alfred Archer	1955–1960
John H. G. Archer	1938–1943
William D. Armstrong	1996–2002
George Arnold	2011–
William Arnold	2010–
Adi Arora	2011–
Matthew Arrowsmith	2011–
Atheeshaan Arumuham	2002–2009
Vimoshan Arumuham	1994–2001
Arnold Ashbrook	1939–1944; 1951–1965 (Staff)
Dennis W. H. Ashton	1946–1953
Robert F. Ashton	1935–1940
Peter J. Ashurst	1944–1951
Noel H. Ashworth	1944–1951
Ben Ashworth Kwasnik	2008–
Robert Aspinall	1978–1980
Christopher Aston	2000–2005
Michael Atherden	2006–2013
Jonathan Atherton	1972–1979
Paul Atherton	1996–2003
Sir Michael Atiyah	1945–1947
David Atkins	1972–1979
Derek L. Atkins	1941–1946
Paul Atkins	1978–1985
Ben Atkinson	2007–2014
Robert Attree	1968–1975
Kate V. Atty	2014– (Staff)
Gerald Avison	1952–1959
Joanna K. Badrock	2013– (Staff)
Aria H. Baghai	2009–
David Baigel	1982–1989
Jonathan Baigel	1979–1986
Michael Baigel	1977–1984
Charles Bailey	1998–2005
Daniel Bailey	1999–2006
In memory of G. I. S. (Ian) Bailey	1927–1932
Kevin Bailey	1970–1976
Elliott J. Bains	2012–
Niall J. J. Bains	2011–
Donald W. Baird	1936–1942
Arthur de Chair Baker	1940–1947
Drew Baker	2011–
Steven Baker	1987–1994
Andrew D. Balcombe	1953–1959
George L. G. Baldwin	1948–1954
John R. Baldwin	1952–1959
Jake Ballin	2010–
Mark Ballin	1979–1985
Brian R. Ballinger	1948–1955
Richard Bannister	1945–1949
Frederic N. Barash	1949–1955
Peter J. Barber	1942–1949
Richard C. Barber	1974–1981
Simon J. Barber	1971–1978
Mark Barclay	2007–2014
Harry Bardsley	1982– (Staff)
John E. Bardsley	1955–1962
Ken Bardsley	1935–1940
Stuart Bardsley	1953–1959
David Barker	1987–1994
Duncan Barker	1983–1990
Oliver R. Barker	1989–1996
Andy Barlow	1994–2001
Peter A. Barlow	1961–1966 (Staff)
Ross Barnaby	1979–1986
Peter J. Barnard	1995–2002
N. Peter Barnes	1967–1974
Deborah R. Barnett	2014– (Staff)
Philip Barooah	1979–1984
Keith C. Barraclough	1950–1956
Ian Barrison	1961–1968
John H. Barrow	1959–1965
Philip Bartle	1963–1970
Adam Barton	2011–
Ian Barton	1982–1989
Russell Barton	2005–2012
Alex D. Bashich	2011–
Arthur Baskerville	1950–1957
Gillian Batchelor	1999– (Staff)
Luke Batchelor	1999–2001
Matthew Batchelor	1999–2006
Sam Batchelor	1999–2004
Mike Bateman	1960–1967
George L. Batham	2012–
James Bathurst	2011–
Michael Batson	1953–1960
Peter Batterley	1931–1938
Andrew Batty	1996–2003
Peter N. Baylis	1994– (Staff)
Ryan Beale	2008–
Calum Beardwood	2008–
Michael J. Beavis	1969–1976
Benjamin J. H. Bedell	2010–
Rory G. H. Bedell	2014–
Alex Bedwell	1999–2006
Louis Beer	2010–
Mark G. Beer OBE	1984–1990
Simon Beer	1991–1998
Tom Begg	2011–
Alex Bell	2008–
David G. Bell	1945–1952
George Bell	2014–
Ian S. Bell	1978–1985
John S. Bell	1938–1943
Malcolm T. Bell	1947–1953
Michael Bell	1977–1984
Ronald Bell	1955–1963
Philip Bellamy	1959–1965
Emily L. Bellieu	2006– (Staff)
Adrian Bennett	1987–1994
Benjamin H. Bennett	2004–2011
Ewan D. Bennett	2013–
Luke A. Bennett	1996–2003
Neil Bennett	1984–1991
Peter C. Bennett	1953–1959
Ian Benson	1963–1967
Stephen Benson	1959–1967
Chris Bentley	1993–2000
Tobias Berchtold	2007–2014
Geoffrey H. L. Berg	1966–1974
Adam A. Bernstein	2009–
James B. Berry	1939–1947
Noah Besbrode	2011–
Christopher R. Beswick	1946–1954
Chris Beswick	1961–1968
Anthony N. Bethell	1950–1957
Gareth Bevan	1989–1996
John T. Bever	1990–2000 (Staff)
Rishab Bhandari	2002–2008
Sahil Bhandari	1996–2003
Sadru Bhanji	1953–1960
Adam Bhatti	2012–
Benedict E. Bianchi	2008–
David Bickerstaffe	2003–2010
James Biggs	2007–2014
Herbert G. Billinge	1931–1937
Brian Billington	1964–1971
Tony Binns	1974–1981
Richard Birch	2008–
Jonny Bird	2011–
Nigel P. Bird	1966–1972
John Birkby	1961–1968
H. John B. Birks	1958–1963
Robert Birtwell	1967–1974
John K. Birtwistle	1947–1951
Colin Bishopp	1958–1965
Jonathan C. Bishton	1980–1987
David G. Bissell	1945–1953
John Bitton	1960–1967
Benjamin Black	1995–2002
Justin Blackburn	2013–
Eric Blackwell	1955–1961
Gary P. Blackwell	2006– (Staff)
Mark S. Blackwell	1977–1983
Derek P. Blain	1943–1947
Roger Blain	1970–1977
John Blair	2004– (Staff)
Peter Blake	1964–1970
Cathal J. Blakebrough	2013–
Finn P. Blakebrough	2012–
Brian Bland	1946–1952
Stephen Blank	1962–1969
Christopher Blick	1990–1997
Graham Bloor	1974–1981
Alex Blore	2012–
Christopher Blum	2010–
James Blum	2012–
Tom Boardley	1968–1975
Philip K. Boden	1965–1969 (Staff)
Walter Bodmer	1946–1953
Craig L. Bohrson	2008–2010
Marcus Bokkerink	1976–1982
Richard Bolchover	1971–1978
John Bolter	1938–1946
Matthew Bolton	2002–2009
Richard Bolton	2004–2011
Colin P. Bond	1953–1961
Freddie Booth	2009–
Henry Booth	2006–2014
Michael Booth	1969–1977
Peter Booth	1972–1979
Stephen Booth	1955–1960
John Borland	1950–1957
Thomas P. Borrows	1953–1960
Ernest Boughton	1946–1953
Alan Boulton	1951–1958
Martin Boulton	1984–1986; 2013– (High Master)
Chris Bounds	1972–1977 (Staff)
Francis W. Bowden	1954–1961
Laurie Bowden	2008–
Brian Bower	1945–1951
Malcolm Bower	1955–1960
Michael K. Bowker	1941–1948
Stephen Bowes	1971–1978
David E. Bowyer	1953–1960; 1968–1973 (Staff)
Derek Boxall	1942–1949
Ian Boyd	1944–1950
Stephen Boyd	1983–1990
John M. Boydell	1946–1953
Matthew Boyes	1989–1996
Gerard Boyle	1941–1949
John R. Bradburn	1954–1961
Vic Bradbury	1953–1960
Philip Bradfield	1969–1970 (Staff)
Felicity Bradley	2014– (Staff)
Harry Bradley	1942–1949
Paul Brady	1986–1990
Sebastian Brahma-Trumper	2011–
Nigel Brannan	1975–1982
Matthew Bream	2010–
Peter W. Brearley	1943–1950
Adrian Bridge	1952–1959
Peter H. Bridge	1949–1956
J. L. Keith Bridges	1952–1959
David J. Briscall	1951–1958
Mike Broadbent	1944–1950
Paul Broady	1961–1968
John Brocklebank	1943–1950
Ian Brocklehurst	1973–1980
Adrian Brodkin	1959–1966
Denis Brogan	1959–1966
George Bromley	2011–
Keith Bromley	1951–1959
Glen Brook	1963–1970
James R. Brookes	1952–1959
Andrew J. Brooks	2004–2011
Frank Brooks	1943–1950
Patrick J. Brooks	1938–1941
Andrew Brown	1948–1954
Andrew Brown	1988–1995

Benjamin Brown	2013–
Dennis Brown	1984– (Staff)
John Brown	1954–1962
Ken Brown	1976–1983
Leonard Brown	1952–1958
Nigel Brown	1976–1983
Danny Browne	2011–
Thomas Browne	2011–
George Browning	1958–1965
Michael Browning	1936–1939
Ben Brownson	2006–2013
Roger Brugge	1968–1975
Dennis Buchanan	1943–1950
John Buchanan	1944–1948
Chris Buckley	1993– (Staff)
David Buckley	1963–1970
George W. H. Buckley	2010–
Graham Buckley	1956–1963
Kate L. Buckley	2009– (Staff)
Ronald Buckley	1944–1948
Adrian Bull	1973–1980
Graeme E. Bullock	1956–1962
Simon J. Burch	1986– (Staff)
Christopher Burd	1947–1952
Frank Burd	1939–1943
Christopher A. Burin	1993–2000
Nigel Burin	1986– (Staff)
Richard T. Burin	1995–2002
John J. Burke	2011– (Staff)
John L. Burn	2000– (Staff)
Norman Burnell	1946–1953
Stuart Burnett	1994–2001
Aidan P. Burrows	2004– (Staff)
Joseph M. Burrows	2004–2006
Stewart P. Burrows	1987–1994
Keith S. Burton	1955–1962
Warwick Burton	1966–1973
Ian Busby	1962–1969
Simon Bush	2004–2011
Helen Butchart	1993– (Staff)
James Butchart	2007–2013
J. J. Bute	2007–2014
Adrian Butler-Manuel	1969–1976
Brian Butterworth	1952–1958
David Butterworth	1957–1964
Geoffrey Butterworth	1938–1940
Roger Butterworth	1960–1967
Oliver Buxton	1996–2003
Ian Byrne	1976–1982
Rodney P. Byrne	1953–1960
Simon Byrne	1985–1992
Ted Cadman	1962–1969
Simon P. Caldwell	1965–1972
Susan M. Callaghan	2010– (Staff)
Oliver Calmonson	2003–2010
Sam Calmonson	2006–2013
Hugh Campbell	1984–1991
James Campbell	2003–2010
Donald Candlin	1942–1950
John Cane	1945–1953
J. Graham Canham	1944–1950
Paul Cann	1982–1989
William Cann	2013–
Gerald Caplan	1944–1948
Jason P. Caplan	1986–1990
John Capper	1955–1958
Paul Capper	1987–1994
Alexander Carey	2011–
Robert M. Carey	2002– (Staff)
Samuel Carey	2013–
Thomas Carey	2011–
Ben Carlson	2007–2014
George D. T. Carmichael	1952–1959
Alison E. Carolan	2008– (Staff)
Reg Carr	1956–1964
Ron Carr	1944–1951
Oliver Carragher	2014–
Seamus Carragher	2014–
Leslie Carrick-Smith	1956–1963
Michael Carrier	1961–1968
In memory of Derek H. Carroll	1942–1949
David R. Carter	1948–1956
Eleanor E. Carter	2011– (Staff)
Nick Carter	1970–1977
Craig E. Cartwright	1993–2000
Oliver E. J. Celensu	2007–2014
Simon Chadowitz	1994–2001
Howard A. L. Chadwick	1973–1980
Michael Challenor	1946–1950
Joseph C. H. Chan	1998–2005
Kevin Chan	1989–1996
Raymond Chan	1988–1995
Matthew Chance	2003–2010
Stephen Chandler	1965–1972
Daniel Chapman	1984–1991
Richard Chapman	1987–1994
Donald Chare	1943–1951
John-Henry Charles	2005–2012
Anthony F. Charlesworth	1946–1952
Robert J. Charlton	1944–1951
David Chart	1983–1990
Aizaz A. Chaudhry	2013–
Ehtizaz Chaudhry	2008–
Irfan Chaudry	1984–1991
Harry Cheetham	2013–
John Cheetham	1947–1952
Adam M. Chekroud	2003–2010
Ameen N. Chekroud	2005–2013
Sammi R. Chekroud	2005–2012
Keith Chenhall	1949–1955
Andrew Chicken	1985–1992 (Staff)
Kiran Chitrapu	1984–1991
Rohan Chopra	2011–
Shamsul Choudhury	1989–1991
Martin P. Chow	1986–1993
Andrea Christian	1938–1946
Eric C. Cittanova	1991– (Staff)
Bernard J. Clare	1966–1973
Phil Clare	1978–1985
Graham P. Clark	1967–1974
Adam Clarke	2008–
Donald L. Clarke	1951–1959
Freddie Clarke	2012–
Geoffrey Clarke	1942–1949
Ian Clarke	1976–1982
Ian Clarke	1992–1999
John Clarke	1943–1946
Max Clarke	2008–
Theo Clarke	2005–2012
Jonny Clayson	2005–2012
Robert Clayson	2002–2009
Greg Clayton	2011– (Staff)
Richard Clayton	1990–1997
Richard Clegg	1986–1993
Adrian Clements	1978–1985
John Clemison	1962–1970
Jonny Cline	1987–1994
Bob Clitheroe	1949–1956
Alexander Cockerham	2007–2014
Elliot J. Coen	2003–2010
Lorraine Coen	2006– (Staff)
Mark Coffey	1995– (Staff)
Michael D. Coffey	1954–1961
Robert S. Coffey	1946–1951
Andrew Cohen	1988–1995
Geoffrey R. Cohen	1957–1964
Stephen H. Cohen	1985–1992
Jeremy Colbran	1958–1965
Hywel Coleman	1960–1967
Christopher J. Collier	1970–1974 (Staff)
Stuart Colligon	1981–1988
Robert M. Collinge	1942–1949
Dave Collins	1956–1964
Alan Colman	1960–1967
Jeremy Colman	1965–1972
Geoff Colton	1942–1949
Malcolm Combey	1949–1955
John C. Conacher	1952–1959
Allan J. Conchie	1953–1960
Ciaran Connolly	2010–
Peter C. H. Cook	1946–1951
William Cook	2003–2010
Peter A. Cooke	1945–1952
Nick Cookson	1992–1994
J. Allen Coombs	1949–1950
Leslie G. Coop	1955–1961
Michael G. Coop	2014– (Staff)
David A. Cooper	1983–1985
Kenneth J. Cooper	1952–1959
Steven Cooper	1991–1998
Samuel P. Cope	2002–2009
Zac Copeland-Greene	2012–
Laurence Copeland	1957–1964
Nigel Copeland	1945–1950
Lawrence M. Copitch	1966–1973
John Copley	1956–1963
Daniel Coppel	1984–1991
Michael Corbett	2010– (Staff)
David W. Cornforth	1971–1978
Luke A. Cornforth	2009–
David Costain	1959–1966
Charlie Cottam	1971–1978
Simon P. Cotterill	1970–1977
Robert A. P. Coupe	1946–1953
Steven Coupe	1990–1997
Keith Cousins	1946–1954
Richard Cowen	1984–1991
Edwin H. Cox	1951–1960
James Cox	2002–2009
John Coyle	1956–1963
Alastair Cranmer	2012–
Daniel D. Crawshaw	2010–
Sam Crawshaw	2008– (Staff)
Ian M. Creek	1980–1987
Sam Cressey	2009–
Mark Crewe-Read	2011– (Staff)
Theodore Crewe-Read	2011–2013
Michael Crick	1969–1976
Martin Crilly	1961–1968
Oliver Critchley	2012–
James Croft	1982–1989
John Crofts	1970–1977
Ron Crompton	1959–1966
Ian Cropley	1972–1979
William A. Crossley	1951–1958
Philip Crow	1961–1968
Nigel Crowther	1954–1960
Paul Crowther	1990–1997
Stephen Crowther	1978–2011 (Staff)
Alec Cruickshank	1936–1941
John Cruickshank	1945–1948
John Cruickshank	1971–1975
Ian Crutchley	1965–1972
David Cryne	1950–1958
J. P. Cryne	2005–2012
Garry Crystal	1989–1996
Joseph Cunningham	2013–
Robert Curl	1936–1939
Helen-Amy S. Curry	2006– (Staff)
Graham Curtis	1972–2010 (Staff)
Nicholas Curtis	2006–2011
Richard Curtis	2003–2010
Alan Dakeyne	1943–1950
Edward N. Dale	1946–1951
Richard Dale	1954–1961
Elisabeth R. Dalton	2000– (Staff)
John Dang	1991–1998
Muttaqee Dar	2010–
William Darling	2014–
Adam Darnley	2007–2014
Ian Dasiewicz	2001–2008
Shouvik Dass	1985–1992
Jonathan M. Daube	1960–1963 (Staff)
Len Davenport	1952–1959
Nigel W. Davenport	1979–1986
Donald M. Davidson	1939–1944
Euchael Davidson	1997–2004
Paul Davidson	1988–1995
Stephen Davidson	1983–1996 (Staff)
Alex Davies	2008–
Andrew R. Davies	2013– (Staff)
Gordon Davies	1983–1990
Howard J. Davies	1961–1968
John K. Davies	1948–1955
Martin H. Davies	1944–1952
Robert Davies	1965–1972
Simon Davies	2002–2009
Graham Dawber	1959–1965
Matthew Dawson	2009–
Robert Dawson	1977–1984
Thomas Dawson	2012–
Alan Dean	1960–1967
Michael Dearden	1954–1961
Graham Delves	1966–1973
Roger L. H. Dennis	1978–1994 (Staff)
Nicholas Denyer	1966–1973
Saurav Deshpande	2012–
Roger Devlin	1968–1975
David J. Dickinson	1968–1976
John Dickinson	1972–1979
Mathew Dixon	1985–1992
Chris Diggines	1961–1969
Jack Diggines	2004–2011
Jonathan Diggines	1964–1971
Colin Diggory	1976–1983 (Staff)
Charlie Ding	2005–2012
James Ding	2000–2007
Jonny Ding	2008–
Tom Ding	1998–2005
Edward Y. Dingley	2008–
Lancelot Disley	1949–1954
John A. Ditchfield	1947–1954
Michael Dittner	1960–1967
Jamie Dixon	2000–2007
Matt Dixon	2008–
Chris Dobbs	2010– (Staff)
Frederick M. Dobbs	2011–
Jo Dobbs	1995–
William F. Dobbs	2008–
Adrian Dobson	1962–1970; 1980– (Staff)
Sydney Dobson	1933–1939
Timothy Dobson	2002–2007
Andrew Dodd	1983–1990
Patrick Dodds	2003–2011
Alexander M. Doidge	2014–
Rodney Donaldson	1980–1995 (Staff)
Danny Done	1986–1993
Nana K. Donkor	2009–2010
James Donnelly	2008–
Richard Donner	1972–1979
Michael Doodson	1955–1962
Ryan J. Doodson	2005–2012
Adam Dooler	2012–
Josh Dooler	2008–
Peter K. Dooley	1965–1972
Thomas Dooley	2011–
Tom Dooley	1939–1945
Aidan Douglas	1983–1985
Julian Douglas	1987–1994
Ian Dowker	1983–1990
Graham Downing	1948–1953
Roger Doxey	1972–1979
Callum Doyle	2011–
Joe Doyle	2011–
Eric Drabble	1972–1979
Tariq Drabu	1976–1982
Tony Drake	1960–1967
Callum Drasdo	2009–
Tiernan Drasdo	2010–
John P. Drinkwater	2012–2014
Keith Drinkwater	1951–1957
Christopher E. Druce	1948–1955
Howard Druce	1966–1970
Oliver Druce	1991–1998
Raymond M. Drury	1948–1954
Naunidh Singh Dua	2010–
Anthony Duckett	1978–1984
Peter Duckworth	1948–1954
Colin J. Duff	1951–1958
Daniel Duffy	2007–2014
Simon J. Duffy	1985– (Staff)
Alexander G. Dunbar	1934–1939
Andrew J. Duncan	1970–1977
Philip Durden	1959–1965
Louis Duschenes	2011–
Marc Duschenes	1988–1993
Martin Dutton	1972–1978
David Dwek	2010–
Jake Dyble	2005–2012
Mark Dyble	1974–1981
Nigel Dyble	1981–1988
Richard Eagar	1970–1977
Tim Earl	1978–1984
Anthony Earlam	1949–1955
Jeffery H. Eastwood OBE	1938–1945
Michael Eastwood	1956–1963
Philip Ebert	1954–1961
Gordon B. Eccles	1943–1950
Joey Eccles	2005–2012
Holly L. Eckhardt	2009– (Staff)
Harrison D. Edmonds	2007–2014
Mason A. Edmonds	2010–
Peter Edward	1972–1978
Brian S. Edwards	1980– (Staff)
Bryan Edwards	1948–1955
Simon Edwards	1970–1977
W. A. (Tony) Edwards	1960–1967
Charles Eickhoff	1969–1976
Youssef El-Wahab	2010–
G. Mac Elder	1947–1954
Jeffrey Elder	1950–1958
Steve Elder	1955–1962
Matthew J. Elliott	1991–1998
John Ellis	1952–1958
David Ellwood	1966–1973
Peter Ellwood	1965–1972
Nathan Elly	2001–2006
Alec F. Elmer	1950–1957
Robert Elswood	1965–1972
Benjamin Elton	1991–1998

Daniel Elton	1994–2001	Timothy L. Frank	1977–1984	Jonathan A. Goldstone	1988–1995	Simon Hamilton	1993–2000
Chudi Emeagi	2005–2012	Harold Franks	1940–1947	L. Clement Goldstone	1960–1967	David W. Hamlyn	1936–1943
Philip Emmerson	2001–2008	Steve Fraser	1976–1983	Maurice J. Goldstone	1991–1998	Kiran J. Hampal	2006–2013
Harry Emson	1938–1945	Clive Freedman	1966–1974	Simon L. Goldstone	1985–1992	Alan Hampson	1951–1957
Harrison Engler	2010–	Paul Freeman	2008– (Staff)	Bob Gomersall	1977–1980 (Staff)	James Hampson	2007–2014
Jonathan Engler	1976–1982	Peter M. Freeman	1956–1963	Alan Goodacre	1963–1970	John Hampson	1962–1969
David Ensor	1971–1975	Charles Frieze	1950–1957	Andrew H. Goodchild	1975–1982	Neville Hampton	1952–1958
Gerald Epstein	1960–1967	Edward Frith	1976–1983	Martyn J. Goodger	1977–1981	Charles Hancock	2009–
Stephen Epstein	1964–1971	Roger Frost	1976–2009 (Staff)	Martin Goodier	1977–1983	Roger Hand	1973–2008 (Staff)
Andrew Etchells	1965–1972	Nicholas Fryman	2006–2013	Peter W. Goodliffe	1968–1975	Alex Handy	2001–2008
Enobong Bassey Etteh	1993–1998	Mark Fulford	1973–1979	Jon Goodman	1952–1959	Kenneth Hanmer	1949–1957
John A. H. Evans	1939–1944	Ernest W. Fuller	1947–1987 (Staff)	Zac Goodman	1995–2002	Benjamin Hanson	2011– (Staff)
Jonathan Evans	1976–1982	Matthew Fullerty	1988–1995	Rob Goodwin-Davey	1985–1992	Sir John Hanson	1950–1957
Jonny Evans	2009–	Steve Furber	1963–1970	Simon R. Goorney	2008–	Steve Hardicre	1990–1997
Michael Evans	Trustee	Alex Fynn	2011–	Daniel M. Gordon	2014–	Stephen Hardy	1965–1972
Neil Evans	1991–1998	Chris Fynn	2013–	Harry T. Gordon	2012–	David J. Hargadon	1970–1976
Peter Evans	1944–1950	Harry Fynn		P. Kenneth Gordon	1963–1969	David Hargreaves	1959–1966
Thomas Evenson	1953–1960	Mark B. Gabbay	1969–1976	Peter Gordon	1954–1959	John Hargreaves	1962–1969
Mark Facchini	2011– (Staff)	Nigel Gallier	1969–1975	Martin Gorin	1956–1964	Jonathan Hargreaves	2005– (Staff)
David Faddoul	2012–	Ed Galloway	2009–	Kenneth Gorman	1945–1952	Paul Hargreaves	1977–1983
Joseph Faddoul	2009–2011	Luke Game	2011–	Alan Gosschalk	1976–1982	William Hargreaves	2011–
Joseph J. Fagan	2011–	Edward Gardiner	1989–1996	Leonard Gossels	1974–1981	David P. Harlow	1942–1948
Bruce G. Fairbanks	1953–1959	Keith M. Gardiner	1944–1950	Arron Gould	2007–2014	Richard Harper	1955–1962
Peter Fallows	1954–1962	Chris Gardner	1989–1996	M. Dennis Gouldman	1946–1952	Alastair G. Harris	1972–1980
Michael J. Farnworth	1974–1978	Martin Gardner	1957–1963	Alex Gourlay	2007–	Andrew Harris	1992–1999
Omar Farooq	1989–1996	Peter Gardner	1967–1973	Elliot Gourlay	2013–	Charlie Harris	2008–
Peter Farquhar	1970–1983 (Staff)	Ross Garlick	2003–2010	Robert Gourley	2008–	Edward Harris	2008–
J. Alan Farquharson	1949–1956	Scott Garlick	2005–2012	Peter Gowling	1956–1963	Isaac Harris	2012–
Luke A. Farquharson	2011–	Alan Garner	1946–1953	John S. Gradel	1974–1981	Josh Harris	2011–
Richard J. Farquharson	1977–1983	James A. D. Garner	2005–2012	Leon Gradel	1972–1979	Richard Harris	2012–
Robert D. Farquharson	1980–1987	Jonathan J. D. Garner	2006–2013	Marcus H. Gradel	2009–	Sam Harris	2008–
Daniel Farr	2002– (Staff)	Thomas W. Garner	1950–1956	Robert Gradel	1979–1986	Thomas Harris	2010–
Ben Farrington	2012–	David Garnett	1968–1974	Andrew S. Graham	1986–1993	Daniel Harrison-Croft	2005–2012
Daniel Faulkner	1997–2004	Elizabeth Garnett	2013– (Staff)	Jack Graham	2010–	Oliver Harrison-Croft	2002–2009
David Faulkner	1947–1950	A. James Garretts	1968–1975	Jane Graham	2002– (Staff)	David J. W. Harrison	1948–1956
Richard J. O. Feingold	1995–2002	Damian Garrido	1980–1987	Susan Graham	2007– (Staff)	H. Ralph Harrison	1950–1956
Geoffrey V. Feldman	1931–1938	Simon Garrido	1981–1988	Tyrone A. Grainger	2014– (Staff)	George W. Harrison	2006– (Staff)
John Felton	1963–1970	Robert Garson	1987–1994	Thomas R. Grant	2004–2011	John Harrison	1944–1951
Ben S. Ferguson	2002–2009	Mark Gartside	1988–1995	Daniel M. Gray	2000–2005	Joshua Harrison	2012–
Daniel Fernandez	2011–13	Nick Gartside	1986–1993	Ian Graymore	1938–1942	Michael Harrison	1937–1943
Michael Fernandez	2010–	Timothy Gartside	1970–1976	David Green	1946–1952	Keith Hart	1954–1961
Simeon Fernandez	2011–	John Geary	1963–1970	Gerald B. Green	1946–1953	Neil Hart	1989–1996
Neville Fernley	1946–1952	John M. Geddes	1950–1956	Gordon Green	1948–1953	Malcolm Hartley	1949–1956
Malcolm W. Fidler	1951–1959	Ian E. Gee	1949–1954	Graham Green	1990–1997	Norman Hartley	1948–1952
Alan Fielden	1951–1956	John A. Gee	1935–1939	John A. Green	1960–1968	Stephen D. Hartley	1998–2005
Andrew J. Finn	1984–1991	Louis Gee	2008–	John R. Green	1948–1955	Louis Hartshorn	1999–2006
Bob Finch	1989–1996	Matthew Geiger	2007–2014	Nick Green	1984–1991	Chris Harvey	1957–1964
Brian Finch	1942–1950	Richard Geiger	2005–2012	Lawrence Greenberg	1958–1964	John Harvey	1952–1959
Geoffrey M. Fink	1942–1948	R. James Geldard	2013– (Staff)	Benjamin Greenfield	2004–2011	Frank J. Haslam	1945–1952
Simon Finn	1968–1975	Mark Geller	1988–1995	Jack H. Greenwood	2007–2014	Julius Haslam	2008–
Gareth Firth	1964–1971	Paul Gelling	1959–1966	Ann P. Greggs	2009– (Staff)	Justin Haslam	1977–1984
Grahame Fish	1955–1962	Tony Gelsthorpe	1971–1973	David Gregory	1972–1979	T. Jake Haslam	2009–
Colin Fisher	1949–1955	Louis B. Geng	2005–2008	Edmund Gregory	1979–1981	James Hassall	1983–1990
Daniel Fisher	1981–1988	Owen L. Geng	2013–	Geoffrey Gregory	1939–1946	Frank Hawkins	2008–
James Fisher	2011–	David Gent	1982–1989	Peter Gregory	1948–1953	Jonathan Hawkins	2000–2007
Jon Fistein	1982–1989	Malcolm George	1957–1964	Tom Gregory	2012–	Stephen Hawkins	1968–1974
Ronan Fitzgerald	2013–	James C. Gibb	1983– (Staff)	Robin Griffin	1953–1960; 1970–1997 (Staff)	Timothy Hawkins	2004–2011
Samuel Fitzsimmons	2011–	Charles Gibbon	1947–1954	Charles Griffiths	1938–1943	David A. Hawkswell	1948–1955
John A. Fixsen	1948–1951	Nick Gibbon	1974–1982	Chris Griffiths	1965–1972	Geoffrey Hawley	1956–1963
David Flacks	1965–1972	Anthony Gibbs	1961–1965 (Staff)	Ken Griffiths	1950–1957	George Hay	1949–1953
Richard Fleet	1965–1972	Peter J. E. Gibson	2003–2010	Tim Griffiths	1965–1972	Jack Hay	2009–
Ben Fleming	2011–	Andrew Giddy	1977–1983	Bob Grimshaw	1968–1973	Kenneth A. W. Hay	1961–1968
Thomas Fleming	2014–	Jonathan Gilbert	1999–2006	Rodney E. Grimshaw	1942–1949	Thomas G. Hayes-Powell	2008–
Antony Fletcher	1948–1955	Gordon Gilchrist	1956–1963	William Grimshaw	1933–1938	Jack Hayhurst	2013–
Ian Fletcher	1972–1978	Steve Giles	1961–1968	Michael W. Grove	2006–2011	Alex Haynes	2003–2010
John Fletcher	1966–1973	Mark J. Gilfillan	1974–1979	Roshan Gulati	2011–	Will Haynes	2009–
Matthew Fletcher	1983–1990	Adam Gill	2000–2007	Julius A. Guth	2003–2010	Ian J. Hazlehurst	1955–1962
Roger Fletcher	1955–1962	Oliver Gill	2002–2009	Mike Hack	1966–1973	Giles J. M. Heagerty	1993–2000; 2009– (Staff)
William C. Fletcher	2011–	Peter Gill	1954–1959	Eric Hadfield	1952–1960	Samuel Heath	2007–2014
Jonathan Fogerty	1984–1991	Waseem Gill	1972–1978	Rodney S. Hadwen	1952–1959	Kath Heathcote	2006– (Staff)
Chris Fogg	1988–1995	William Gill	1977–1985	James Haeney	1984–1991	Sean Heathcote	2003–2010
John Ford	1990–1997	Ishtiaq Gillan	1985–1992	Shalom Haffner	1981–1988	Chris Heaton	1951–1958
Neville F. Ford	1946–1952	Godfrey Gillett	1967–1974	Stephen Haffner	1975–1982	R. Ian Hedley	1953–1960
Daniel T. Forman	2011–	Pauline Gilmore	2001– (Staff)	John Haighton	2010–	Norman Heeley	1944–1951
Robin Forrest	1982–1989	Ben Gilmour	2009–	David O. Haines	1952–1958	Kathryn Hellier	2007– (Staff)
Adam Forshaw	2008–	Suzanne Gilmour	2013– (Staff)	Matthew Haji-Michael	2008–	Alexander J. Hemingway	1992–1999
Josh Forshaw	2009–	Joseph Glass	1962–1969	Ritvik S. Halder	2012–	Christopher J. Hemmings	1998–2005
Fiona Forsyth	1990– (Staff)	Oliver P. Glass	2011– (Staff)	David I. Hall	1979–1986	Martin A. Hemmings	1992–1999
Gordon Forsyth	1940–1948	Lionel K. J. Glassey	1956–1963	Geoffrey Hall	1958–1965	Matthew J. Hemmings	1995–2002
John Foster	1951–1957	Ian Gledhill	1957–1964	Jonathan Hall	1979–1985	Robert F. Hemmings	1936–1943
Steven Foster	1988– (Staff)	Thomas Glennie	2011– (Staff)	Jonathan Hall	2003–2008	Stephen Hempling	1956–1962
William C. Foulkes-Brooks	2012–	Bob Glitheroe	1949–1956	Richard Hall	1972–1973	Robert A. Hempstock	1954–1961
Ernest Fox	1943–1951	Samuel Goddard	2009–	Richard A. Hall	2013–	Rory Hemsted	2007–2014
Geoff Fox	1949–1956; 1961–1969 (Staff)	Malcolm Goff	1949–1955	Roger Hall	1954–1962	Anna V. Hemsworth	2008– (Staff)
Mike Fox	1953–1960	Sim Goldblum	1958–1966	William D. Hall	1950–1957	Ethan Hennessy	2011–
Simon Foy	1979–1986	Alex Golding	2009–	In memory of W. T. (Tim) Hall	1941–1946	Ravi J. Hensman	2014– (Staff)
In memory of Michael Frame	1977–1984	Oliver Golding	2009–	Gerald Halon	1963–1970	Ashley R. Hern	2003– (Staff)
David E. Francis	2005– (Staff)	Michael Goldman	1940–1947	Garry Hambleton	1951–1958	Max Herrmann	2013–
Nicholas D. Francis	2007–2009	A. Barrie Goldstone	1970–1978	Linda Hamilton	2008– (Staff)	Peter Hesham	1943–1949
Peter I. Frank	1947–1951	Anthony K. Goldstone	1954–1962	Nicholas Hamilton	1995–2002	Liam P. J. Hesketh	2007–2014

Mark Hesketh	1986– (Staff)
Tracey Hesketh	1996– (Staff)
Andrew Hesp	1985–1992
Roger Hesp	1961–1968
Simmone M. Hewett	2012– (Staff)
Jack Hewitt	2007–2014
Richard Hewitt	1975–1982
Sam Hewitt	2000–2007
Stephen Heywood	1977–1985
Roger M. Heyes	1947–1953
Robert F. Heys	1940–1946
Robert Higginbottom	1949–1955
Pam J. Higgins	2006– (Staff)
Richard Higgins	1978–1984
Keith W. Higham	1942–1945
Alexander Hill	2007–2014
Jonathan R. Hill	1995–2002
Oliver Hill	2013–
Robert D. Hill	1940–1950
Tobias Hill	2010–
Paul Hilton	1961–1968
Richard A. Hinchliffe	1979–1985
Stephen A. Hinchliffe	1981–1988
Stewart J. Hinchliffe	1984–1991
Tom A. Hinchliffe	1992– (Governor)
David Hind	1948–1955
Robert J. Hinds	1950–1955
Ishaan Hinduja	2013–
Samuel D. Hinton	2013–
Mesh Hira	1983–1990
J. Timothy Hirst	2000–2007
Christopher H. S. (Kit) Hitchcock	1942–1949
Brian P. L. Hitchen	1944–1950
George Hobson	1953–1960
George W. M. Hobson	2006–2013
John Hobson	1961–1964
Oliver Hobson	2013–
Samuel Hobson	2014–
Sam J. Hodari	2009–
Jonathan Hodes	1980–1987
Robert Hodgkinson	1970–1977
Richard J. Hodgkiss	1964–1971
Alan Hodson	1946–1953
David Hoffman	1983–1990
Oliver Hoggart	2013–
Derek Hohne	1937–1942
Peter Hohne	1935–1940
Graham Holden	1955–1962
James E. Holden	1997–2004
Peter Holden	1938–1945
John Holding	1938–1945
Michael J. Holland	1961–1968
Michael R. Hollingdale	1957–1964
Henrik Holm	2011–
Delwyn Holroyd	1981–1987
Andrew S. Holt	1978–1984
Ken Holt	1957–1964
Peter J. Holt	2007– (Staff)
Russell L. Holt	1952–1959
Ross Hook	2008–
Carl Hope	1969–1975
Keir Hopley	1973–1979
Joshua Horan	2011–
Ben Hornby	1986–1993
Dan Hornby	1982–1989
Gregory Horne	1963–1969
Herbert R. Horsfall	1942–1948
John P. Horsfall	1940–1947
John Horsfield	1947–1954; 1961–1966 (Staff)
Vivienne Horsfield	2007– (Staff)
William Horsfield	2011–
Marcus Horwich	2004–2011
Malcolm Hoskinson	1947–1954
Steven Hough	1991–1998
Leon Howard	1953–1961
Alexander Howarth	2008–
Alan Howe	1938–1944
David Howe	1951–1959
Kenneth Howe	1944–1950
George R. Howling	2014–
James R. Howling	1981–1988
Tom Howling	1983–1990
Harry Hudson	2010–
Max Hudson	2007–2012
Adam Hughes	1986–1993
Alex Hughes	2006–2013
Anthony R. Hughes	1946–1952
Edward Hughes	2009–
Geoff Hughes	1967–1974
Hilary Hughes	1987– (Staff)
Martin Hughes	1946–1953
Michael Hughes	1958–1965
Derek O. Hull	1935–1940
Richard Hull	1989–1996
Anders Hulme	1998–2005
James Hulme	1988–1995
Keith Humphreys	1945–1952
Nicola Humphreys	2012– (Staff)
Ray Humphreys	1971–1977
Gregory Hunstone	1954–1962
Richard M. S. Hunt	1981–1988
Simon J. Hunt	2003– (Staff)
Andy Hunter	2001– (Staff)
Louis J. Hunter	2012–
Sam Hunter	2006–2013
Keith Hurst	1963–1970
Steven Hurst	1961–1968
James B. Hutchinson	1994–2001
Peter Hutchinson	1991–1998
David G. Hutton	1971–2003
Daniel Hyman	2004–2011
Franklyn Hyman	1988–1995
James C. M. Hyslop	1943–1952
Farrel Igielman	1979–1986
Agni Ilango	2009–
Oliver M. Iliffe	2011–
Martin Illingworth	1967–1975
Jacob Inerfield	2004–2011
R. Graham Inskip	1942–1948
Gordon Isles	1952–1960
Takao Ito	2011–
Christopher Izod	1991–1998
Timothy Izod	1989–1996
Aline Jacinto	2008– (Staff)
Godfrey Jackson	1974–2006 (Staff)
Julian Jackson	2008–
Matthew Jackson	1995–2001
Nicholas Jackson	1996–2003
Oliver Jackson	1999–2006
Peter Jackson	1999–2006
Phillip Jackson	2004–2010
Stewart Jackson	1948–1955
Nick Jacott	1966–1973
Isaac (Yitz) Jaffe	1944–1948
Joseph Jaffe	2011–
Victor Jaffe	1964–1971
Wayne Jaffe	1973–1979
Ian W. Jagger	1954–1961
Rohan Jain	2011–
Taresh Jairath	1994–2000
Ceri James	1979–1984
Ethan O. N. James	2003–2011
Gavin James	1996–2003
Luke A. Q. James	1999–2006
Susan C. James	2001– (Staff)
Terri C. James	2007– (Staff)
Craig Jamieson	2009–
John A. Jamieson	1933–1940
Shahzad Jamil	2009–
Christopher M. Jarrett	1996–2003; 2012– (Staff)
Jibril Javed	2013–
David Jefferson	1952–1959
Ethan Jenkins	2010–
Thomas Jenkins	1995–2002
Paul S. Jenkinson	1979–1986
David C. Jennings	1962–1996 (Staff)
Peter Jennings	1949–1956
Neil Jepson	1947–1953
Tom Jervis	2004–2011
Piers B. D. Jess	1999–2006
David Jeys	1988– (Staff)
William J. W. Jeys	2010–
Sandip Jobanputra	1984–1991
James Jobling	2008–
Oliver Jobling	2006–2013
Andrew Johnson	1957–1964
Andrew Johnson	1982–1989
Haeden Z. Johnson	2013–
Thomas P. Johnson	1947–1953
Fergus Johnston	2011–
Gordon Johnston	1948–1956
Phillip F. Johnston	1946–1954
Alan Jones	1944–1951
Alan Jones	1961–1966
Chris Jones	1984–1991
David R. T. Jones	1980–1987
Helen L. Jones	2008– (Staff)
James Jones	1998–2005
Jim Jones	1961–1967
Michael Jones	1957–1964
Neil A. Jones	1946–1951
Peter R. Jones	1965–1973
Robert Jones	2012–
Robert A. Jones	1973–1980
Roger Jones	1955–1961
Sally Jones	2005–2010
Simon Jones	1988–1995; 2004– (Staff)
Stephen Jones	1982–1989
Thomas Jones	1947–1951
W. Russell Jones	1943–1949
John Jordan	1950–1956
In memory of Howard Joseph	1970–1977
Philip Joseph	1966–1973
Rohan N. Joseph	2010–
Steven F. Joseph	1967–1973
Aleksandar Jovanovic	2011–
Hamza Ali Jowiya	2004–2011
Alan M. Judkins	2000–2007
Kenneth Kaiser	1961–1968
Michael Kaiser	1954–1961
Stephen Kaiser	1959–1965
Michael Kalra	2008–
Muntaka Kamal	2011–
Peter J. Kaminski	1964–1970
Arjun Kapoor	2011–
Harish Kapoor	2012–
Shonal Kapoor	2011–
Shaurya Kashyap	2013–
Andrew Kaufman	1980–1986
Geoffrey H. Kay	1954–1961
Nigel Keddie	1949–1953
Sinan Kelenchy	2007–2014
Daniel Kelly	1979–1996 (Staff)
Leo Kelly	2010–
Mark Kelly	2004–2011
Rick Kelly	1983– (Staff)
Robin Kelly	1966–1972
Oriana L. Kelly Saltaleggio	2014– (Staff)
Jonathan A. C. Kemsley	2001–2008
Harold W. Kelner	1945–1951
Nigel Kendall	1975–1982
Melvin Kenyon	1968–1975
Michael Kenyon	1967–1974
Geza Kerecsenyi	2013–
Oliver T. Kerr	1999–2006
Tom Kerr	1949–1956
Dominic Kerrison	2009–
George Kerrison	2012–
Jonathan Kershaw	1971–1978
Michael Kershaw	1943–1951
Rodin Khalilazar	2014–
Abdul-Rahman Khan	2010–
Abdullah Khan	2007–2014
Atif Khan	1983–1990
Irfan Z. Khan	2003– (Staff)
Jacob Khan	2008–2013
Lewis Khan	2011–
Umar M. Khan	2004–2011
Wakkas Khan	1991–1998
Amit Khanna	1990–1998
Vinay Kumar Khosla	1982–1989
Damien Kiefer	1983–1990
Kenneth S. Kiernan	1943–1950
Robert Kilgour	2009–
Emma Kilheeney	2010– (Staff)
Maurice Kindler	1964–1971
Oliver Kingsley	2008–
Calum Kirkby	2010–2013
Andrew Kirkman	1983–1990
Daniel Klin	2009–
Joseph Z. Klin	2007–2014
Ben Kneale	1975–1982
Rachel A. Kneale	2010– (Staff)
Saul F. Knights	2011–2014
Chris Knott	1969–1976
Peter J. Knowles	1944–1947
Jake Knox	2008–
Ismet Serfatih Kocak	2010–
Akhil Kochhar	2014–
Christopher Kolbeck	2008–
Adam Kousgaard	2005–2012
Iryna Kovtunenko	2014– (Staff)
Anthony Kravitz	1955–1962
Ethan Krell	2008–
Martin Kukla	1971–1977
Reuben Kumar	2012–
Louis Kypriadis	2011–
Daniel O. Lacey	2012– (Staff)
Andrew Lacy	2008–
David Lacy	2006–2013
Shondipon Laha	1984–1991
Kai Conway Lai	2012–
Keith F. Lainton	1951–1958
William Laird	2010–
Ru Lan	2007– (Staff)
Alastair Land	1982–1989
Nicholas Lander	1963–1970
Andrew Larah	1986–1991
Julian Larah	1994–2001
Simon Larah	1985–1990
Nigel Lashbrook	1984–1992 (Staff)
David Last	1951–1958
Samuel Y. K. Lau	2009–2014
Mike Launer	1958–1964
Patrick Lavallin	2001–2008
Gabriel Lavan	2013–
Danny Lawrence	1973–1980 (Staff)
Peter Laycock	1967–2004 (Staff)
Eric Layland	1942–1949
Huw T. Layzell Smith	2007–2014
Rowland A. Layzell Smith	2004–2011
Leo Layzell	2013–
Daniel J. Lea	2008–
James Leach	2005–2012
Michael J. Leach	1947–1954
Will Leach	2008–
Harry Leaitherland	2012–
James G. Leathley	1966– (Staff)
Mark J. Leathley	1997–1999
Russell A. Leaver	1931–1938
Alan Lee	1958–1965
Joshua Lee	2006–2013
Laurie Lee	2013–
M. David Lee	1947–1954
Roger Lee	1960–1966
Wai On Lee	2008–
John Leech	1982–1989
Richard Leech	1978–1984
Brian Lees	1957–1964
Elizabeth J. Lees	2014– (Staff)
John J. Lees	1997–2004
Oliver Lees	2005–2012
Peter Lees	1952–1958
Thomas A. Lees	2008–
Robert Leese	1975–1982
Claude Lefort	1964–1965 (Staff)
Roger Legge	1958–1965
Jonathan L. Leggett	2013– (Staff)
Brandon Leigh	1982–1989
Christine Leigh	1994– (Staff)
Keith Leigh	1958–1965
Matthew Leigh	1994–2001
Anthony Lemon	1956–1964
Jack L. Leonard	1943–1949
David Lever	2009–
Jack B. Levy	1997–2004
Jonathan Levy	1963–1970
Raymond I. Levy	1972–1978
Harry F. Lewis-Mitchell	2008–
Adam Lewis	2005–2012
David Lewis	2013–
Noah Lewis	2013–
Robert C. Lewis	1997–2004
Sam Lewis	2003–2010
Ben Leyland	1991–1998
Oliver Leyland	1994–2001
Gordon Limb	1943–1949
Clive Lindemann	1963–1970
James Lindsay	2002–2009
Thomas Lindsay	2003–2010
Aidan Lines	1966–1974
Jeremy Lingard	1969–1975
Allan Lingley	1958–1966
Neville Lister	1956–1963
Paul Lister	1975–1982
Roger Lister	1950–1957
Stephen W. Lister	1967–1975
Richard (Brian) Little	1974–1980
Stephen Little	1986–1993
John Littlewood	1962–1968
Walter K. Livesey	1952–1959
Callum Livingston	2013–
Oliver W. Llewellyn Smith	2014– (Staff)
Matthew I. H. Lloyd	1999–2006
Timothy D. M. Lloyd	2003–2010
Meredith Lloyd-Evans	1960–1967
Annabelle Lloyd Hughes	2009– (Staff)
Andrew Lock	1958–1960
Daniel Logue	2000–2007
Emma Loh	2008– (Staff)

Name	Dates	Name	Dates	Name	Dates	Name	Dates
Adam C. M. Longden	2008–	Robbie McKendrick	2008–	Oliver Murphy	2014–	Christian M. A. Owen	2011–
Thomas Longshaw	1976–1982	Geoffrey I. McLeish	1958–1965	Sebastian Murphy	2011–	Mark Owen	1975–1981
Dennis A. Longstaff	1946–1954	Frances McNamara	2000– (Staff)	Tom Murphy	1996–2003	John Oxley	2001–2008
Richard Longworth	1966–1973	Bruce R. McNicholl	1999–2006	Gregory F. Murray	1981–1988	Daniel Pack	2014–
Basil Lord	1949–1954 (Staff)	Graham I. McNicholl	1996–2003	Christopher C. Musgrave	1993–2000	John Packer	1957–1964
Patrick Lord	1985–1992	Graeme J. McSherry	2014– (Staff)	Alan Mushing	1975–1982	Robert Packwood	1949–1957
Nicola A. Loughlin	2001– (Staff)	Callum McWalter	2008–	Daniel Musson	1961–1968	Wilfred Page	2012–
Ronan Loughney	2000–2007	Barry Meakin	1959–1966	John H. Mutch	1944–1952	Brian Palmer	1943–1950
David Low	1962–1969	Nigel Meir	1968–1975	Olly E. Mwaniki	2009–	Sammy Palmer	2012–
Michal A. Lowe	2005– (Staff)	Caroline A. Mellor	2005– (Staff)	Kenneth W. Mycock	1964–1970	Maharsh Pandya	2010–
Thomas Lowe	1989–1996	Derek Mellor	1953–1961	Mike Myerson	1962–1970	Nikul Pandya	2008–2010
Douglas Lowey	1941–1947	Hugh Mellor	1952–1956	Bryan R. Nagle	1937–1943	Jason S. Panjeta	2014–
Ian Lowrey	1978–1985	Jack W. Mellor	2010–	Thomas J. Napier	2012–	Ares Papangelou	1977–1983
Dougie Loynes	2006–2013	Peter J. Mellor	1992– (Staff)	Zaf Naqui	1984–1991	Stephen Pardoe	1959–1961
Phil Loynes	1970–1977	Vicente F. Orts Mercadillo	2006–2013	Tom Nash	2004–2011	Julian T. Parker-Martinez	2010–12
Michael E. Lucas	1951–1958	Michael J. Meredith	1959–1965	David V. Naughton	2014– (Staff)	Charles B. Parker	2011–
Sunny Y. M. Lum	1986–1993	Lucy E. Merlo	2006– (Staff)	Abdullah Ali Naveed	2011–	Richard B. Parker	2008–
Marc Lundwall	2012–2014	Luke Merrill	2010–	Guy Naylor	1995–2002	Jonathan Parkin	1966–1974
Howard Lyons	1962–1969	Charles Merry	2006–2013	John B. Naylor	1947–1953	David Parris	1976–1983
David C. Lysons	1950–1957	James Merry	2003–2011	Monty Naylor	2013–	Richard J. Parris	1978–1984
Akhlaq A. Maan	2005–2012	Alberto Meschi	2007–2014	Roger Naylor	1986–1993	Derek Parry	1945–1953
Keith MacDonald	1972–1978	Peter Metcalfe	1947–1951	Ron Naylor	1949–1956	Ken Parry	1951–1958
Samuel J. Machin	1960–1966	Bernhard Mevenkamp	1964–1965 (Staff)	Keith Neal	1976–1999 (Staff)	Tom Parry	2008–
In memory of Bob Mackay	1982–2000 (Staff)	Karen S. Michael	2010– (Staff)	Peter Neal	1983–1990	John A. Partington	1946–1952
Donald MacRae	1957–1964	Christopher Millard	1970–1977	Robert Neal	1988–1995	Kishan Patel	2010–
James Madeley	1996–2003	Elliot Miller	2009–	George Needham	1956–1963	Alexander Patt	2010–
Harry Magnall	2000–	Gavin Miller	1978–1985	Joseph Needoff	1934–1940	Sam Pattison	2008–
Ezekiel Maguire	2008–	Lawrence Miller	1958–1964	Cameron C. Neild	2006–2014	Tim J. Pattison	1992– (Staff)
Fergal Maguire	2010–	Vincent Miller	1946–1952	Solomon L. Neild	2010–	Ivan Paul	2008–
Finn Maguire	2008–	Roger G. Millman	1964–1966	Tracy C. Neild	2008– (Staff)	Sarah J. Paulson	2005– (Staff)
Myles Maguire	2012–	Edward Milloy	1959–1966	Will Neill	2011–	Robert Paver	2008–
Patrick Maitland	2011–	Alan R. Mills	1945–1950	Bruce R. Nelson	1978–1984	Sherwin Paykazadi	2008–
Anudarshi Majumdar	2011–	Alexander Mills	2004–2011	Adrian Newby	1976–1982	Roger W. Payne	1953–1959
David Maland	1978–1985 (High Master)	Don Mills	1943–1951	Alan Newcombe	1968–1975	David C. A. Pearce	1999–2006
Akeel Malik	2006–1913	Matthew Mills	2007–2014	Adam Newman	1998–2005	Dominic S. Pearce	2004–2012
Imran Malik	2011–	Robert J. B. Mills	1995–2002	Malc Newsome	1986–1993	Gisela K. Pearce	2007– (Staff)
Rohan Malik	2003–2010	Debora Minguito-Pantoja	2010– (Staff)	Clive Newton	1961–1966	Vikram I. Pearce	2011–
Derek Mangnall	1938–1943	Rahan Adil Mirza	2007–2014	Daniel R. Newton	1993–2000	Alexander C. Pearson	2012–
Jim Mangnall	1993– (Staff)	Carl Mitchell	1987–1994	Ian Newton	1969–1973	David Pearson	1960–1967
Edward D. Manson	1992–1999	Grant Mitchell	1985–1992	Rory Newton	2010–	Frank Pearson	1943–1950
Ian W. Manson	1942–1950	Ian Mitchell	1965–1972	William J. Newton	1991–1998	Simon Pearson	1978–1984
Jonathan L. Manson	1958–1965	Ian Mitchell	1960–1968	David Ng	2012–	John S. Peet	1946–1951
Benjamin Manton	2012–	Philip Mitchell	1965–1972	Nathan Ng	2013–	Colin J. Pemberton	1951–1957
Daniel Manton	2010–	Rupert Mitchell	2010–	David M. Nicholas	1959–1967	Marcus I. Pemberton	1999–2006
Jacob Manton	2009–	Andrew Moakes	2010–	David M. Nichols	1966–1972	Anthony Penfold	1963–1971
Hugo Marfani	2014–	Mischa N. C. Mockett	1986–1993	Matthew J. Nichols	2011– (Staff)	David Pennycuick	1951–1958
Dan Margolis	2007–2014	Frederick J. Moffat	1945–1952	Anthony J. Nield	1953–1960	Ben Peppi	2002–2009
Harry Margolis	2009–	John Moffat	1961–1968	G. Stanley Nield	1949–1956	Lindsay Perks OBE	1943–1949
Jack Margolis	2006–2013	Ravi Mohindra	2006–2013	Oliver J. Nield	2007–2014	Sam Perry	2011–
Simon Margolis	1973–1980	Rohan Mohindra	2008–	Jonathan L. Niman	1972–1980	Colin H. Petch	1944–1951
Finlay Markham	2007–2014	Daniel R. Molyneux	1998–2005	Stuart Niman	1974–1981	Elliot Peters	2008–
David Marks QC	1957–1965	Stephen R. Molyneux	2009– (Staff)	David Noble	2006– (staff)	Robert Peters	1968–1974
Thomas Marland	2010–	William J. Molyneux	2004–2011	Robert Noble	1962–1969	Michael Peterson	1971–1978
Rachel E. Marshall	2012– (Staff)	Myles Monaghan	2013–	Derek Norman	1949–1955	Andreas C. Petrou	1997–2004
John Marsland	1983–1988	Richard Monk	1970–1977	Richard Noronha	2011–	Dan Phillips	1990–1997
Rachel E. Marshall	2012– (Staff)	Christopher J. Moody	1963–1970	Allen Norris	1958–1965	Brian A. Philpott	1933–1937
Simon D. Marsland	1979–1981	Jay Moore	2014–	In memory of Geoffrey S. Norris	1937–1942	Robert Pickles	1966–1974
Alexander Martin	2008–	Darragh Moran	1996–2003	Toby Norris	1949–1954	Graham B. Pickup	1974–1979
Peter Martin	1976–1983	James Moran	2007–2014	David Norwood	1940–1945	Alan C. Pickwick	1975–2013 (Staff)
Tim Mascall	1971–1978	Jonathan Moran	1995–2002	Kofi Nuamah	2011–	Ian Pidgeon	1953–1959
Charlie Maslen	2009–	Barry Morgan	1965–1972	David G. Nuttall	1962–1969	Anne and John Piercy	
Gavin Mason	1955–1961	Cathryn Morgan	2011– (Staff)	J. R. L. (Bob) Nuttall	1937–1944	J. Stewart Platts	1946–1951
Rupert N. Massey	1997–2004; 2008– (Staff)	David Morris	1994–2001	Peter R. Nuttall	1940–1945	Tom Plaut	2013–
Zac Matlow	2014–	Geoffrey Morris	1944–1951	Femi Nylander	2006–2013	Joseph Plumb	2008–
Andrew Matthews	1998–2005	Geraint J. Morris	2002– (Staff)	Sola Nylander	2007–2014	Jim Pollard	1967–1974
Charles Matthews	1940–1946	Philip Morris	2004–2011	Pyaesone Nyunt	2012–	John Pollard	1936–1943
David Matthews	1999–2006	Stephen Morris	1986–1993	Christopher O'Brien	1962–1969	Charles Pollick	1960–1967
Edward Matthews	1997–2004	Jeff Morrison	1967–1973	Rhys O'Brien	2012–	Andrew Pollock	1969–1976
Neil Matthews	1987– (Staff)	John Morrison	2003–2009	Steve O'Brien	1979–1985	Robert J. C. Polya	2012–
Richard Matthews	1995–2002	Patrick Morrison	2007–2014	James O'Hara	2014–	Oliver Pooler	2010–
Andrew Mauchan	1955–1962	Thomas Morrison	1997–2004	Daniel R. O'Toole	1999–2006	Jonathan W. Y. Poon	2013–
Julian Maurer	1984–1999	Helen Mortimer	2008– (Staff)	David Oakes	1957–1965	Samuel J. Porter-Frakes	2011–
Roger May	1962–1968	Neville Mortimer	1950–1955	Daniel Ogden	1975–1982	John A. Porter	1953–1960
Stephen May	1967–1974	Nicholas Morton	1969–1972	Harold Ogden	1943–1948	Thomas Porter	2010–
George P. Maycock	1949–1955	Richard Morton	1986–1993	Keith Ogden	1952–1959	Dave Postlethwaite	1973–1980
Jonathan R. G. Mayes	2003–2010	Kelly Moses	1978–1984	Peter Ogden	1957–1964	David P. Potter	1954–1962
Ken Mayhew	1958–1965	David Moss	1977– (Staff)	Richard A. Ogden	1962–1969	Matthew Pountain	1982–1989
Mohsin Mazhari	1987–1994	John R. Moss	1931–1938	Simon Ogle	1981–1988	Robert Povey	2005–2012
Connor B. McAlister	2012– (Staff)	Richard E. Moss	1953–1960	Isaac Okeregha	2014–	Roy Povey	1963–1970
Stuart McCandlish	1979–1986	James Muckle	1948–1955	Joseph Okeregha	2014–	Sam Povey	2008–
D. Garth McCormick	2013– (Staff)	Alexander K. Muir	1972–1979	Iain R. Oldcorn	1953–1961	W. Peter Povey	1946–1953
Matthew McCormick	2012–	Sanjay Mulchand	1987–1994	Geoff Oldham	1953–1959	Johann Power	2011–
Roger McCormick	1962–1969	Roderick Muller	1972–1974 (Staff)	Peter M. B. Oldham	1955–1963	Mark F. Power	1987–1994
Murdoch McCrum	2012–	John P. Mumford	1944–1951	Rodney Oliver	1957–1965	Ruaidhri Power	2010–
Lawrence McDonald	1984–1991	Nick Munday	1979–2009 (Staff)	David Ordman	1980–1987	Ian F. Poyser	1949–1956
John M. McDonnell	1960–1967	Asim Munshi	2010–	Peter Orgill	1968–1974	Charlie Pozniak	2008–
Cameron McEwan	2010–	Kenneth G. Murdie	1944–1950	Simon J. Orth	2013– (Staff)	Fiona Pozniak	2008– (Staff)
Joe McEwan	2012–	John A. Murdoch	1954–1961	Donald Oswald	1942–1946	Tomek Pozniak	2009–
Ian McFarland	1954–1961	Ben Murphy	1995–2002	Max W. B. J. Otway	2013–	Eric Pratt	1960–1967
John McIlwain	1958–1965	Derek Murphy	1947–1952	Alexander Owen	2013–	William Pratt	1965–1969
Hugh McIntyre	1976–1983	Lisa J. Murphy	1998– (Staff)	Chris Owen	1986–2008 (Staff)	Rahul Premrajh	2011–

Ian Prendergast	1954–1961
Nicholas Prest	1964–1970
Anthony Preston	1966–1973
David J. Preston	2005– (Staff)
Edward Preston	1996–2003
Martin Preston	1994–2001
Neil Prestwich	1948–1956
Tim Prestwich	1962–1968
Duncan Price	1970–1977
Malcolm Price	1968–1975
Geoffrey B. Priest	1947–1955
In memory of Maurice B. Priestley	1944–1951
Tom Priestner	2006–2013
Jamie Primrose	2013–
Roger Pritchard	1950–1958
Joseph Prudham	2014–
Matthew Prudham	2012–
Lionel S. Pullan	1948–1955
Jim Putz	1943–1948
William B. Pye	2011– (Staff)
Ahmad Ali Qasim	2011–2013
Shahbaz Qasim	2008–2010
Andrew Quick	1987–1994
Edward Quince	2013–2014
Alex Race	2007–2014
Christian Race	2010–
Robert Race	1973–1979
David Raff	1970–1977
Arthur Raffle	2010–
Tim Raffle	1973–1981
Satish Raghavan	1996–1998
Yashpreet Raj	2011–
Rehan Mohammad Raja	2013–
Harry Rangeley	2013–
Tejas Rao	2012–
Louis Rapaport	1943–1949
John Ratcliffe	1964–1971
Richard G. Ratcliffe	1965–1971
William J. J. Ratcliffe	1948–1954
David Ravenscroft	1948–1955
Raj Rawal	2008–
Angus Rawson	2014–
Michael Ray	1945–1953
Simon Rea	1982–1989
Alexander Read	2009–2014
Alexander T. Read	2005–2012
Howard Read	1968–1975; 2011– (Staff)
John Reddish	1961–1968
Anthony Redford	1948–1954
David Redhouse	1978–1984
Angus B. Reed	2008–
Shona C. Reed	2009– (Staff)
Andrew Reekie	1947–1954
William C. Rees	1966–1971 (Staff)
Daniel Reeves	1919–1924
Michael J. Reeves	1983–1985
Jack C. Reilly	2008– (Staff)
Iain Renfrew	1992–1999
Neil Renfrew	1989–1996
Michael Rennie	2002–2009
Andrew Renton	1974–1981
Mark Renton	1971–1978
Phil Reuben	1970–1977
Anthony M. Revington	1952–1957
Frank G. Rhodes	1946–1954
Ali Riaz	2011–
Thomas Rice	1978–1984
Charles H. Rich	1998–2005
Andrew Richards	1960–1965
John Richards	1969–1975
George Richardson	1946–1954
Keith Richardson	1982–1989
Kenneth Richardson	1940–1947
Peter Richardson	1971–1978
Lucas Richman	2012–
Robert Richman	1957–1965
Sam Richmond	2008–
Thomas Richmond	2002–2009
Richard Riddell	1964–1971
Adam F. W. Rigby	2006–2013
Kenneth Rigby	1936–1940
John Riley	1944–1950
David Ritchie	1959–1966
Andrew Ritchings	1993–2000
Len Rix	1977–2005 (Staff)
Kenneth M. Robbie	1964–1971
Fay C. Roberts	2008– (Staff)
Gareth Roberts	1973–1980
Harrison Roberts	2012–
Mark Roberts	1990–1997
Peter Robertson	1946–1949
Michael Robins	1944–1947
Alex Robinson	1951–1958; 1964–1972 (Staff)
Andrew Robinson	1957–1964
Avi Robinson	1991–1998
In memory of Edward L. Robinson	1917–1919
Gordon Robinson	1960–1967
In memory of John R. Robinson	1922–1924
Judy Robinson	1999– (Staff)
Lewis Robinson	2008–
Michael Robinson	1956–1963
Richard Robinson	1962–1969
Tom Robinson	2013–
Michael Roche	1944–1948
William Rochford	2012–
Matthew J. Roe	2011– (Staff)
Christopher M. Rogers	1976–1982
Jonathan Roland	2002–2009
Simon (Joey) Roland	1962–1968
Hugh Rolfe	1943–1947
Joseph Rooney	2012–
Laura L. Rooney	2013– (Staff)
William Rooney	2008–
David H. Roscoe	1951–1958
Glyn O. Roscoe	1943–1950
Daniel Rose	2012–
Gary Rose	1968–1975
James Rose	1989–1996
Paul Rose	1959–1967
In memory of Sidney Rose	1929–1935
Max E. Roseman	2008–
Robert B. Rosenberg	1988–1995
Harry Rosenblum	1966–1972
Dan Rosenfield	1988–1995
John Rosenfield	1961–1969
Herbert Rosengarten	1951–1959
Daniel P. Rosenthal	1990–1997
Marc J. Ross	1988–1995
Neil M. Ross	1991–1998
David Rothwell	1969–1975
Andrew N. Round	1949–1956
In memory of Ivor J. Rowe	1943–1949
In memory of John Rowe	1921–1924
John J. Rowe	1945–1954
Tony S. Rowe	1972–1979
Daniel Rowland	2013–
David Rowland	2004–2011
Thomas Rowland	1996–2003
J. P. Rowley	2010–
Chris Royle	1979–1985
Joseph A. Royle	2012–
Erik Rudzitis	1965–1972
Swithun Rumble	2008–
Alex Rutherford	2011–
Connor Rutherford	2010–
Chris Ryan	1976–1983
Harvey Sagar	1958–1966
David J. Sagi	1951–1959
Peter Sampson	1949–1957
Mark Samuels	1982–1989
Sefton Samuels	1942–1947
Tim Samuels	1986–1993
Oliver P. Sandall	2011–
Bryan M. Sandford CBE	1945–1951
Michael Sandiford	1951–1958
Rodney M. Sandler	1946–1952
Derek Sands	1951–1958
Tony Sareen	1951–1957
Nicholas D. Saremi	2012–
Michael H. J. Sargent	1945–1953
Eric Saunders	1938–1940
John Saunders	1945–1952
Lee Saunders	1985–1992
Mark Savile	2002–2009
Neil B. Saville	1950–1957
Richard Saxon CBE	1953–1960
Michael Scaife	1945–1953
Henry Scanlon	2009–
Stephen Schaefer	1958–1965
David Schofield	1975–1982
Peter Schofield	1945–1951
Walter Schwarz	1940–1948
Philip Schwarzmayr	2010–
Nicholas Sciama	2011–
Ned Scott	1964–1971
Roger Scotts	1974–1981
Max Seagger	2012–
Donald A. Seanor	1945–1954
Aaron M. Searle	2004–2011
David A. Searle	2003–2010
Paul Sedgwick	1960–1967
Paul Seed	1959–1966
Ezra H. Seeley	2007–2014
Jacob B. Seeley	2004–2011
Ralph Seeley	1958–1964
Paul Seidman	1978–1985
Daniel Seligman	2003–2010
David Seligman	2001–2008
Christopher Sellars	1984–1991
David Selouk	1992–1999
Joshua Selouk	1996–2003
Samuel Senior	2014–
John Sennett	1963–1977 (Staff)
Paul Sennett	1973–1977
John Severn	1971–1977
David Sewart	1955–1962
Reuben Seymour	2011–
Bryan R. Shacklady	1990–1997
Rohan Sood	2008–
Adam A. Shakir	2009–
Hashim Sharif	1998–2005
Rachel L. Sharkey	2008– (Staff)
Roy Sharma	1965–1972
Ian Sharp	1975–1981
Graeme D. M. Sharpe	1976–1984
Nicholas J. Sharples	2003– (staff)
Ben Sharrock	2013–
David Shasha	1967–1974
Arthur Shaw	1947–1952
Barry Shaw	1964–1969
David Shaw MBE	1972–1979
David Shaw	1996–2003
Jeremy Shaw	1985–1992
Judith R. Shaw	1994– (Staff)
In memory of Lester Shaw	1979–2007 (Staff)
Mark Shaw	1997–2004
Oliver M. Shaw	2012–
Pat Shaw	
Alexander Sheard	2009–
Benjamin A. Shearer	2014–
Ricardo Sheena	2007–2014
Amin A. Sheikh	2004–2011
Andrew Sheldon	1990–1997
Thomas L. Sheldon	2012–
Peter Shelswell	1961–1968
Alan Shenton	1940–1945
Colin J. Shenton	1980–1987
Joseph Shenton	2013–
Celia Shephard	2014– (Staff)
Ben Shepherd	2010–
Colin Shepherd	1957–1963
Danielle Shepherd	2012– (Staff)
David Sherburn	1956–1963
In memory of Vincent Sherburn	1934–1940
Emily M. Shercliff	2014– (Staff)
Raphael Sheridan	2002–2009
Xavier Sheridan	2005–2012
Jackie Sherratt	2007– (Staff)
Adam Sherwood	2012–
Neville P. Shevloff	1939–1942
Daniel Shields	1982–1989
Jon Shields	1959–1966
Robert Shields	1956–1964
Veronique Shingler	2011– (Staff)
John Shippen	1955–1962
John H. Shoard	1970– (Staff)
Victor M. Shorrocks	1943–1951
Daniel P. Short	1981–1987
Jacob Shovlin	2012–
Andrew Showman	1991–1998
In memory of Alexander Shragah	1921–1927
In memory of Sam Shragah	1916–1923
Jonathan Shrager	1994–2001
Tom Sibley	2000–2007
Richard B. Siddall	1959–1966
Avi Silver	1990–1997
Natan Silver	1995–2002
David Silverman	1948–1954
Brian Simister	1959–1966
Andrew Simmons	1998–2005
Chris Simms	1961–1966
Gavin Simms	1981–1987
Michael C. Simms	1953–1960
Michael Simon	1980–1987
Mike Simon	2010– (Staff)
Clifford R. Simpkin	1951–1958; 1965–1971 (Staff)
David A. Simpson	1989–1996
Graham R. Simpson	1951–1957
Ian H. Simpson	1958–1965
Jonathan Simpson	1976–1983
Joseph Simpson	2013–
Michael C. Simpson	1995–2002
Nick Simpson	1979–1985
Paul A. Simpson	1988–1995
Richard W. Simpson	1977– (Staff)
Trevor J. Simpson	1959–1966
Frederick Sinclair-Brown	1972–1978
Charlie Sinderson	2011–
Ayush Vijay Singh	2012–2014
N. Roy Singham	1965–1966
Barrie Singleton	1961–1989
Martin Sixsmith	1966–1972
Fraser Skirrow	1975–1982
Graham K. Slack	1948–1955
George Slade	2008–
Harry Slade	2006–2013
Joel Slater	2011–
Adam C. Smart	1997–2004
Adam D. Smart	1986–1993
David Smart	1957–1964
James Smart	2013–
Otto Smart	2010– (Staff)
Eric Smedley	1950–1956
Martin J. Smedley	2009– (Staff)
Adam Smith	2011–
Adam M. Smith	2000– (Staff)
Alistair P. Smith	1969–1977
Andrew Smith	1994– (Staff)
Daniel P. Smith	2010– (Staff)
David Smith	1976–1982
Glyn Smith	1964–1971
Huw Smith	1976–1982
Ivor J. Smith	1942–1950
Jack Smith	2010–
Keith J. G. Smith	1960–1967
Neil D. Smith	2002– (Staff)
Peter F. Smith	1961–1968
Richard J. W. Smith	1976–1982
Sol D. H. Smith	2011–
Vernon Smith	1951–1958
Zach Smyth	2013–
Jacob J. E. Snelson	2007–2014
Neil Snowise	1966–1974
Abhinav Sobti	2011–
Tom Solomon	1977–1983
Edward Somerville	1952–1959
Mark South	1970–1976
John A. Spechko	1958–1964
Ludmila Speed	1992– (Staff)
Michael Spellman	2009–
Eddie Spence	2008–
Will Spence	2003–2010
Geoffrey Spiby	1949–1955
Zyllan P. Spilsbury	2000–2007
Sean P. Spratling	2005– (Staff)
Andrew Springett	1971–1978
David Stafford	1947–1955
Anthony Standing	1955–1962
James R. Standing	1990–1992
David Stanford	1989–1996
Iain Stansfield	1979–1986
John Stansfield	1950–1956
Edward Staples	2011–
Cameron Stark	1989–1996
Milan Starkie	2008–
Penelope R. Staufenberg	1987–1994 (Staff)
Joe Stavisky	1979–1986
Andreas M. Stavrinou	2013–
Walter R. Stead	1949–1956
Jordan M. Steel	2005–2012
Graham A. Steele	1945–1951
Martin Stephen	1994–2004 (High Master)
Ralph Stevens	1953–1960
Fergus S. Stevenson	2014–
Michael Stevenson	1991–1998
Henry J. Stevinson	2009–
Malcolm Stewart	1950–1957
Cameron F. Stewart-Syme	2008–
Charles M. Stewart-Syme	2008–
Iain T. C. Stewart	1972–1978
Neil Stinson	1981–1988
Anthony Stock	1953–1957
Samuel Stockman	2008–
Luke C. Stockton	2008–
Matt Stoker	1989–1996
Jeremy Stolberg	1972–1979
Joshua Stolberg	1999–2006
In memory of Ellis George Stonehewer	1913–1917
In memory of Samuel Stonehewer	1911–1913
Jonathan Stones	2001–2008
William Stones	1967–1974
John A. Storer	1974–1980
Clive Stott	1950–1957
David Stott	1960–1967

Reuben J. Stott	2013–
Daniel J. Stout	1998–2005
Theodore T. Strang	2010–
David H. Stratton	1955–1962
Michael G. Strother	2003– (Staff)
Paul Stuart	1996–2003
Luke Stubbs	1989–1996
Adrian Sullivan	1994–2001
James Sullivan-McHale	2010–
David Sumbler	1958–1966
David Summersgill	1962–1969
Brian Sutcliffe	1946–1954
Alex Sutherland	1984–1991
Richard A. Sutherland	2008–2010
John Sutton	1958–1965
Paul Sutton	1985–1992
Peter Swales	1959–1966
Chris Sweetman	1976–1983
Alexander Swift	2000–2007
Stuart Swift	1952–1959
Steve Swindells	2003– (Staff)
Toby Swindells	2011–
Seyed M. M. (Saied) Tahaghoghi	1985–1987
John T. Tame	1950–1955
Kaan Tamer	2008–
Samir Tariq	2011–
Richard Tasker	2002–2009
Rodney Tate	1945–1952
In memory of Edward Tawil	1919–1923
Muhammad Yusuf Tayara	2012–2014
Adam M. Taylor	1996–2003
Alex E. Taylor	1987–1994
Alexander N. Taylor	2007–2014
Anthony G. Taylor	1949–1955
Barry S. Taylor	1965–1971 (Staff)
Bethany S. Taylor	2013– (Staff)
Brian Taylor	1945–1950
Dan M. Taylor	2006– (Staff)
David Taylor	1958–1965
Ian Taylor	1956–1963
Mike Taylor	1980–1987
Neil P. Taylor	1982–1989
Nicholas Taylor	1986–1993
Simon Taylor	1977–1983
Stella Taylor	2006– (Staff)
Stephen M. Taylor	1978–1984
Trevor C. Taylor	1955–1962
Kenneth Teare	1947–1954
Jan-Christof Telford	1979–1986
Ian Tempest	1969–1977
Paul Tempest	1947–1954
Philip Tepper	1959–1966
Arnold Thackray	1949–1957
Bill Thatcher	1982–1989
Alexander Theodossiadis	2005–2012
Sebastian Theodossiadis	2007–
Lucy Thewles	2012– (Staff)
John J. Thewlis	1965–1973
Peter F. Thewlis	1969–1976
Christopher W. Thom	2005–2012
James Thom	1999–2006
Patrick Thom	1988– (Staff)
Ben A. O. Thomas	2011–
Fiona J. Thomas	2008– (Staff)
Graham Thomas	1960–1967
Huw A. Thomas	1993–2000
Luke O. G. Thomas	2007–2014
Nicholas Thomas	1996–2003
Nicholas D. Thomas	1992–1999
Steven P. Thomas	1972–1999
David Thompson	1956–1963
Guy E. V. Thompson	1973–1980
Harry Thompson	2005–2012
Ian Thompson	1963–1970
Paul A. Thompson	1989– (Staff)
Peter J. Thompson	1968–1974
Peter M. V. Thompson	1969–1977
Frank W. Thomson	1936–1943
Jonathan Thomson	1978–1984
Christopher J. Thornber	2005–2012
Eileen M. Thornber	2005– (Staff)
Philip J. R. Thornton	1958–1965
David Thorpe	1981–1988
Hugh Thorpe	1990–1997
Ian Thorpe	1962–1969; 1977– (Staff)
David Tickle	1975–1981
Peter Tiffin	1974–1980
Nathan Tildesley	2013–
Richard Tilsley	1969–1971
Peter Tiltman	1992–1999
William Tindall	2012–
Garreth M. Tinker	2010– (Staff)
Katie J. Tinslay	2012– (Staff)
Colin Tipping	1955–1962
Roy Tipping	1954–1961
Robert M. Titterington	1969–1976
Michael Tobias	1952–1958
Mark Tobin	1987–1994
Reis Tobolski	2008–2013
Christopher J. Tolley	1983–1990
Geoffrey P. Tolley	1987–1994
John P. Tolley	1953–1960
Matthew J. Tollitt	2013– (Staff)
Peter Tomkinson	1948–1953
Stephen Tomlinson	1964–1970
Christopher Toole	1972–1979
William Torevell	2011–
Derek Torrington	1945–1950
Barry Townsend	2006– (Staff)
Neil Townsend	1959–1966
Anthony S. Trafford	1947–1952
Andrew Travis	1960–1967
Graham P. Trevitt	1985–1992
Allan Truman	2008–
Bernard Tsui	2012–
John N. Tucker	2004– (Staff)
Jim Tully	1979–1986
Jack Tunney	2006–2013
Adrian Turner	1992–1999
Jonathan Turner	1988–1995
Josh Underhill	2007–2014
Richard Underwood	1944–1949
Andrew P. Unwin	1973–1979
Mark Upton	2006–2013
Adam Usden	2000–2007
Warren Usden	1971–1978
David Usher	1951–1959
Thomas Vallely	2009–
Cedric Van Duffel	2010–2013
Karl Vanters	1967–1974
Benjamin Varnam	2013–
Clair Vaughan	2013– (Staff)
Spencer Vell	2009–
Lucas Veltkamp	2013–
Ashwin Venkataraman	1997–2004
John Venning	1973–1977 (Staff)
Ian Verber	1962–1968
Daniel L. Virr	2014– (Staff)
Michael Wacks	1989–1996
In memory of Philip J. Wade	1994–2001
Martin Wadsworth	1963–1970
Rick Wagstaffe	1979–1985
Nigel Wait	1956–1963
Adam F. G. Waite	1984–1991
Andrew J. Walkden	1997–2004
David Walker CMG CVO	1951–1958
David Walker	1964–1966
Graham Walker	1958–1965
Michael J. Walker	1957–1964
Philip M. Wall	1945–1952
Hayley J. Wallen	2013– (Staff)
Alan Wallington	1970–1977
Brian Wallis	1966–1973
Christopher C. Wallis	1941–1946
Geoffrey J. Wallwork	1954–1959
Philip Wallwork	1956–1964
Adrian T. Walmsley	1951–1959
Mark A. Walmsley	2007– (Staff)
Gary Walsh	1991–1998
Stephen R. Walsh	2011– (Staff)
Brenton M. Walshaw	1974–1981
Antony Walters	1971–1978
David S. Walton	1967–1974
John R. Walton	1971–1978
Matthew Walton	2012–
Charles Wander	1965–1970
Andrew Wang	2011–
James Wang	2011–
Michael Wansborough	1954–1960
Alex Ward	2008–
Dario Ward	2009–
Jeremy Ward	1974–1997 (Staff)
Joseph S. J. Ward	2003–2010
Julie Ward	2010– (Staff)
William H. Ward	2006–2013
Zoey L. Ward	2011– (Staff)
Jim Wardle	1949–1953
Philip J. Wardle	1956–1962
Anthony J. Waring	1949–1956
Nigel Warrack	1988– (Staff)
Thomas C. Warrack	2002–2009
Matthew Warren	2011–
Nathan Warren	2009–
John Warrington	1962–1969
Rodney G. Wasey	1940–1942
John W. Waters	2008–
Joshua Waters	1997–2004
Matthew Waterson	2012–
The Watkin Family	2010–
James Watkins	2006–2013
Maurice Watkins CBE	1952–1960
Peter Watkins	1993–2000
Tim Watkins	2000–2007
David S. Watson	1987–1994
Peter Watson	1944–1952
Arthur P. Watterson	1938–1943
Xenon Watts	2008–
Andrew Waxman	1976–1982
David Waymont	1970–1976
Peter R. Webb	1966–1973
Roger J. Webb	1953–1960
Thomas G. Webb	1946–1952
Frank Webster	1958–1965
Jonathan Webster	1996–2003
Peter Webster	1979–1985
Simon Weinberg	1994–2001
George Weir	2012–
Daniel Weisberg	1996–2003
Matthew Weller	1984–1991
Nigel P. Wells	1976–1982
Colin F. Wells	1943–1946
George K. Wells	1941–1946
James E. Welsby	1943–1950
Jessica M. Welsh	2013– (Staff)
Alan West	1948–1955
Brian Westhead	1967–1973
Dean O. Whaley	2013–
Neil Wharmby	1969–1976
David J. G. Wheeldon	1976–1977
John D. Wheeldon	2000–2007
Patrick J. Wheeldon	2002–2009
Nik Wheeler	1988–1995
Ollie Wheeler	2009–
Paul Wheeler	1992– (staff)
Tom Whiston	2008–
Chris Whitaker	1958–1966
Iain S. Whitaker	1987–1994
Michael J. Whitaker	1989–1996
Jack Whitby	2005–2012
Jonathan Whitby	2003–2010
Aaron N. White	2011–
Alasdair J. White	2011–
Joe W. F. White	2011–
Philip J. White	1974–1979
Sam H. G. A. White	2007–2014
James Whitehead	2002–2009
Richard Whitehead	1988–1995
Steven Whitehead	1990–1998
Suki J. Whitehouse	2014– (Staff)
David Whiteley	1956–1963; 1992–2002 (Staff)
In memory of Martin D. Whitesmith	2000–2007
John Whitfield	1976–1983
David Whitney	1995–2002
Jane A. Whittell	2004– (Staff)
Peter Whitworth	1943–1948
Anna C. Wicking	2005– (Staff)
Robin Wilcockson	1953–1960
David A. Wild	2007–2009
Lee Wild	1984–1991
Philip A. Wild	1970–1975
Thomas E. Wild	1999–2006
Melanie Wilde	2002– (Staff)
David T. Wilkinson	1950–1957
Richard P. Wilkinson	1938–1945
Richard Wilkinson	1932–1939
Andrew Wilks	2002–2009
Benjamin J. R. Willert	2011–
Andrew Williams	2006–2013
Ben Williams	1990–1997
Bradley G. Williams	2011–
Christopher Williams	1947–1954
Colin Williams	1964–1971
Gareth Williams	1988–1995
Matthew Williams	2013–
Michael Williams	1963–1966 (Staff)
Nancy M. Williams	2010– (Staff)
Nicholas G. Williams	1999– (Staff)
Oliver J. Williams	2003–2010
Philip T. Williams	2003–2010
Rachel G. Williams	1996– (Staff)
Robert O. Williams	1998–2005
Simon C. Williams	1975–1982
Stephen Williams	1966–1973
Stephen J. Williams	1961–1968
James Williamson	1993–2000
Malcolm J. Williamson	1961–1968
Toby Willis	2008–
John Willson	1972–2007 (Staff)
Brian J. Wilson	1949–1954
David L. Wilson	2014– (Staff)
Douglas Wilson	1949–1955
Eugene Wilson	2002– (Staff)
Jamie Wilson	2011–
John H. Wilson	1954–1961
John H. Wilson	1940–1947
Nigel Wilson	1965–1972
Roan Wilson	2010–
Zack Wilson	1985–1992
Matthew Winstanley	2005–2012
Chris Wiseman	1946–1954
Ian Wiseman	1950–1956
Peter Wiseman	1950–1957
Richard (Dickie) A. Wiseman	1948–1953
John Withington	1958–1965
Ken Woffenden	1966–1973
Danny Wolfson	1964–1971
John O. Wolstenholme	1931–1937
Peter H. G. Wolstenholme	1945–1953
Michael Wong	1980–1984
Stephen Wontner	1975–1982
Alex J. M. Wood	1998–2005
Andrew T. Wood	1995–2002
Brian J. Wood	1953–1959
David E. Wood	1992–1999
Michael Wood	1956–1963
Peter Wood	1953–1960
Richard Wood	1972–1978
Stephen K. Wood	1946–1952
W. Malcolm Wood	1947–1952
Phil Woodruff	1954–1962
Oliver Woods	1995–2002
Thomas Woodthorpe	2012–
Alex Woodward	2011–
Daniel Woodward	2013–
Sam Woodward	2010–
Brian Woolley	1965–1972
Dennis Woolley	1952–1959
Chris Worthington	1958–1965
David Wrench	1943–1948
Barney Wright	2011–
David A. Wright	1974–1981
Ian W. Wright	1945–1952
John L. Wright	1949–1955
Julie Wright	2008– (Staff)
Michael Wright	1973–1980
Michael J. Wright	1982–1989
Robert G. Wright	1931–1937
James Wroe	1994–2001
Andrew Wychrij	2001–2008
Daniel Wychrij	2007–2014
Iain Wyder	1945–1952
David Wylde	1971–1976 (Staff)
Ian Wylie	1949–1956
Angus Yardley	2011–
Michael Yates	1952–1960
Michael G. Yates	1989–1996
Richard Yeomans	1950–1957
Alexander Yeramian	1997–2004
Hagop Yeramian	1963–1969
Kent Yip	1998–2005
Adrian Yonace	1954–1961
John Young	1968–1975
James Younger	1977–1983
Janet T. Yuen	2008– (Staff)
Michael J. Yule	2004–2011
Emile Yusupoff	2004–2011
Joel Yusupoff	2008–
Andrew J. Zafar	2011–
Cameron J. Zafar	2008–
Nathan J. Zaman	2012–
Felix Zambelli	2010–
David Zemmel	1989–1996
Enda Zhang	2007–2014
Limeng Zhu	2010–
Peter Zimmermann	1959–1967

INDEX

Locations for illustrations are entered in *italics*.

PICTURE ACKNOWLEDGEMENTS

MGS and TMI Publishers would like to thank Chris Bull, George Ramsay and Sefton Samuels for their images as well as the individuals and organisations listed below for allowing us to use material. The bulk of the photographs in the book comes from the school archive. While every effort has been made to trace copyright holders, if you find that you have been inadvertently overlooked please contact TMI.

p12 Burlison & Grylls (stained-glass makers) / Peter Moore; p13L Classic Image / Alamy; p13R, p27 both, National Portrait Gallery, London p39L, p41; p14, p25T Mary Evans Picture Library / Alamy; p19 Leiden University Library; p20 Harris Museum and Art Gallery, Preston, Lancashire, UK / Bridgeman Images; p21R Russell Hart / Alamy; p22L Victoria and Albert Museum, London; pp22–3 Tate, London 2014; p24 John Bennett; p26, pp44–5, p46 Manchester Libraries, Information and Archives, Manchester City; p28L Historical & Special Collections, Harvard Law School Library; p28R Ralph Williamson; p31 Budby; pp32–3 The University of Manchester; p36 The Art Archive / Eileen Tweedy; p38 National Trust / Donald Bovill and Susan McCormack; p40T Royal Collection Trust © Her Majesty Queen Elizabeth II, 2014 / Bridgeman Images; p42R Ashmolean Museum, Oxford; p48R City of Salford Museums and Art Gallery; p51T Ken Walsh / Bridgeman Images; p54T Paul Thompson Images / Alamy; p54B Queen's University, Belfast; p83L E. Hulton and Co. (From the *Daily Sketch*, which was absorbed into *The Daily Mail*); p104T Allied Newspapers Limited; p110T *Manchester Guardian;* p110R Greater Manchester Police ; p117 *The Illustrated London News/* Mary Evans, p121B Picture Post/Getty Images; p133L *Daily Express Manchester;* p134 Associated Newspapers Limited (DMG Media)